Liberating
Our Dignity,
Saving
Our
Souls

Liberating Our Dignity, *Saving Our Souls*

LEE H. BUTLER JR.

CHALICE
PRESS

ST. LOUIS, MISSOURI

Bible quotations, unless otherwise noted, are from the *New Revised Standard Version Bible,* copyright 1989, Division of Christian Education of the National Council of the Churches of Christ in the United States of America. Used by permission. All rights reserved.

Those quotations marked RSV are from the *Revised Standard Version* of the Bible, copyright 1952, [2nd edition, 1971] by the Division of Christian Education of the National Council of the Churches of Christ in the United States of America. Used by permission. All rights reserved.

Scripture quotations marked (NIV) are taken from the HOLY BIBLE, NEW INTERNATIONAL VERSION®. NIV®. Copyright © 1973, 1978, 1984 by International Bible Society. Used by permission of Zondervan Publishing House. All rights reserved.

Cover art: Getty Images
Cover and interior design: Elizabeth Wright

Visit Chalice Press on the World Wide Web at
www.chalicepress.com

10 9 8 7 6 5 4 3 2 1   06   07   08   09

Library of Congress Cataloging–in–Publication Data

Butler, Lee H., 1959-
  Liberating our dignity, saving our souls / Lee H. Butler, Jr.
    p. cm.
  Includes bibliographical references.
  (pbk. : alk. paper)
    ISBN 10: 0-827221-36-3
    ISBN 13: 978-0-827221-36-9
  1. African Americans–Religion. 2. Black theology. 3. African Americans–Race identity. 4. African Americans–Ethnic identity. 5. African Americans–Gender identity. I. Title.
  BR563.N4B89 2005
  305.896'073–dc22   2004030144

Printed in the United States of America

Contents

For my daughter
Adia Mary Robinson Butler
God's Gift

Preface

This book is an attempt to answer the question, Who are we as African Americans? As I consider the pain and suffering Blacks in America are experiencing, the end to our suffering must take into account the person we see when we look in the mirror. Confronting the person in the mirror is the starting point for transforming our sorrow, yet the mirror is often the last place we will look as we long for a new way of being. The mirror is not only a reasonable starting point, it is the most appropriate starting point for our reclamation. Even God requires that we begin our healing journey by confronting ourselves and confessing. Attempting to answer the question, Who are we? is one way we participate in the works of salvation. The Egyptian directive, "Know thyself," is, therefore, more than just a kindly adage. Self-knowledge is the first possibility for new life.

My central questions emerge from my observations and assessment of what I consider to be the primary challenges to the identity and integrity of African Americans. By the conclusion of this discussion, I hope that the benefits of answering the question, Who are we as African Americans? will be evident. Ultimately, I will present a framework for understanding our identity formation that will be a contribution to our liberation activities and participate in our salvation. The new framework for interpreting the process of how we come to know ourselves will be an important step toward resolving the crises of identity and integrity within the African American community. To be sure, discussing an identity crisis—or an *integrity* crisis—is not necessarily a bad thing. A crisis can mean that possibilities previously unavailable are now close at hand. So to identify the African American community as a community in crisis could mean that we are on the verge of something new as a people.

Identity Is the Focus

Guiding this inquiry is a concern for how the forces of race, gender, and spirituality impact the formation of an African American identity. My inquiry presupposes African American identity formation to be a distinctive process within American life. The fact is, identity formation is a distinctive process for any and all ethnic and cultural groups. I assume that beyond one's identification with a homeland are formative experiences unique to every cultural identity. I am, however, focusing specifically upon persons of African decent. The forces of racism, color-consciousness, sexism, genderism, and American religiosity have manipulated the formative experiences for persons of African descent. Manipulation by such forces has perverted self-esteem, challenged social stability, and threatened existential security. The crisis of identity necessitates liberating activities that are charged with salvific potentialities that extend to the very core of our being.

To explore identity is to explore the existential questions of how one locates herself or himself within the context of community and culture. To come to the clearest, most appropriate conceptualization of an identity, it is imperative to reflect on history. The real challenge to such a reflection is that it must be done without interpreting and clinging to historical traditions that extinguish one's own voice. In other words, it is important to accommodate the old to the new. Sometimes, we can be so intent on embracing the past that we ignore the revelations and new opportunities that come to us in the present. The most valuable way of lunging into the future is to build on a foundational past using the circumstantial mortar and stones of the present. We must learn from the past and walk into the future with the benefit of knowing and appreciating where we have come from.

Guiding Questions

My basic question, Who are we as African Americans? prompts a variety of other questions:

1. What does it mean to be an African in America?
2. Why is it important, or even necessary, to prefix the "African" to the "American?"
3. What are the influences that have shaped and continue to shape the African American identity?
4. What are the best resources for exploring African American psychic functions as separate and distinct from a majority of the American population?

All these questions are being addressed in one way or another by a variety of disciplinary communities. The various disciplines consider the formative forces to be a matrix of issues such as racism, issues of color, locus of control, social stability, sexual domination, and existential security. While these forces do not constitute an exhaustive list, all have been instrumental in the shaping of the African American's particular world view. Furthermore, the answers to these questions may vary depending upon one's disciplinary orientation.

Methodology

I am using an interdisciplinary approach for interpreting phenomena. My theological orientation is African American liberation theology, and my psychological orientation is African American pastoral psychology. Black and womanist theologies guide my hermeneutics, and Black (African) psychology directs my diagnostics, although I also resource psychodynamic psychology.[1] The psychodynamic psychology tradition consists of several psychological approaches for understanding human processes. This tradition emphasizes the influence of unconscious processes on daily living and decision making. All the traditions resourced by my interdisciplinary approach make historical, cultural, anthropological, sociological, and religious considerations. Although

I am assessing African American identity formation from this interdisciplinary perspective, the specific disciplines I will employ are theology, psychology, and Africentricity.

I have reflected on both individual and communal experiences for the purpose of discerning the multiple levels of influence that impact our decisions and direct our relational lives. This approach assumes more than one causal relationship between condition and outcome. Indeed, several influences are always negotiated. The preeminent influences of any given moment will vary according to experience and legacy. I distinguish experience and legacy this way: experience has to do with the individual's personal history, while legacy has to do with the individual's coping skills acquired through earlier family learnings and traditions.

An Early Challenge

One of the early challenges of this project was finding the appropriate disciplinary language to test and express my observations and intuitions. I felt it very important to be able to communicate my reflections in a way that crosses boundaries and allows everyone an equal opportunity to engage the issues. Initially, my own development as a pastoral theologian seemed inadequate for the task. Because my considerations involved conscious and unconscious processes, biological and genetic promptings, symbolic language and behavior, and familial influences, I was more inclined to rely on the thoughts of others more than on my own theoretical reflections. Accepting the challenge, however, resulted in my becoming a more thorough pastoral theologian. From my wrestling and reflections, I have identified a series of issues that I believe have had the greatest influence upon African American identity. This text is, perhaps, the first text to present a psychological framework for understanding African American identity formation from the field of African American pastoral psychology.

Contextualization

Central to this discussion is the idea of context. Theological disciplines acknowledge context through the process of contextualization. Contextualization[2] is the active voice of the "observed" rather than the observer's interpretive voice. Instead of imposing a view or theory on the lives of others, the process of contextualization allows the context to declare itself in relation to some other. The practice of universalizing makes things fit, but contextualization speaks out about the way things do not fit. Furthermore, contextualization is, to a large extent, a phenomenological methodology[3] because it says that one's experience is valid, that it is acceptable to have differing perceptions of a particular context. In fact, phenomenology[4] is implicit in the contextual approach. Phenomenology as a philosophical discipline acknowledges the uniqueness of individuals without devaluing the collective experiences of humanity. It is not overt individualism, rather it allows for individual expression and diversity among the collective. This means that the manner in which I experience the world is not necessarily the same nor different from the experiences of others, but I am entitled to my perspective as I attempt to understand and describe my environment.

The controlling feature that keeps contextualization from being simple introspection is that the phenomenological description is placed within the context of historical facts, normative social behavior, or some other principle that locates the researcher in a relevant time-space relationship. Without this controlling principle, reliability is immediately brought into question. Because my approach to the African American community is interdisciplinary and not strictly psychological, a phenomenological methodology is indispensable.

While researching, one must be conscientious not to interpret too swiftly what is observed; rather it is important to note the nuances of community accommodation. The difference is subtle, but if I approach a text as critic and interpreter, my attitude and results will be different than if I approach a text with the hope of being informed and transformed by the encounter.

Social Location

The psychological approach to context must make the same considerations. Psychological disciplines acknowledge context through considerations of "social location." Within psychology, it is understood that theory and theoretical considerations are informed by social location. When human scientists critique a setting, their methodological orientation sometimes shades their analysis, making them less conscious of the multicultural issues and influences within the setting. Human likenesses, as well as the differences, need to be distinguished. Thus, the contextualization of theoretical perspectives through a recognition of social location contribute to theoretical explorations.

Theologically, life is described in terms of what God has done and will do based on an understanding of who God is and who we are in relation to God. Psychologically, life is described in terms of the mediating influences that have shaped us into what we have become based on the potentials of what we could become and what we ought to be. In both disciplines, life is interpreted according to a particular set of standards that tend to be deemed valid according to one's values and lived experience. In other words, many considerations that are thought to be purely intellectual actually have emotional origins—our expositions, whether theological or psychological, are essentially personal; that is, phenomenological.

Africentricity

Africentricity has to do with the interpretation of data being African-centered. Although the original term was *Afro*centricity, most proponents have begun to identify the approach as *Afri*centricity. The transition of the term is not unlike the re-identification process of Black Americans. We no longer self-identify as Afro-Americans—the main rationale being we are not "Afrocans" from the continent of "Afroca." We now self-identify as African Americans, persons of African descent from the continent of Africa. Consequently, Africentricity has become the preferred term for identifying African-centered thinking. I will only use the term "Afrocentricity" when it appears within a direct quote.

"Afrocentricity means placing African ideals at the center of any analysis that involves African culture and behavior."[5] Molefi Asante, who popularized the "Afrocentric idea," says that "Afrocentricity is not a matter of color but of perspective, that is, orientation to facts."[6] But the inference is that I, as an African American, bring resources for studying and interpreting data that a non–African-American may not. Africentricity, as an interpretive perspective, is consistent with, although not the same as, African and African American epistemology. Introspection and intuition are important ways of African and African American knowing.[7] The phenomenological reflections presented in this study show that the theoretical articulation of my experience with the African American community is a valid perspective. Although I may depart from more widely accepted methodologies to employ more indigenous methodologies, my departure may be meritorious because the experience I share may not have been the experience of the other theorists. This is why Africentricity is an important concept for this book.

In recent years, J. Deotis Roberts has reflected on the efficacy of Africentricity for Christian ministry. Drawing on his readings of Africentricity and his personal conversations with Asante, he states that "africentricity is a dynamic intellectual theory, not a system of thought but a philosophical and theoretical perspective."[8] Roberts further identifies the approach as "accept[ing] the multiplicity of cultural centers and therefore do[es] not negate Eurocentrism except where Eurocentrism promotes itself as universal."[9] For the purposes of this book, it is also important to recognize that "africentricity has a psychological dimension. For example, psychological misorientation or disorientation may characterize our attitudes as African people when we consider ourselves to be European or believe that it is impossible to be simultaneously African and human. An African centeredness can be helpful toward self-pride and people affirmation."[10]

Although the Africentric approach to history is important, it is not without its limitations. Because I am presenting an African American theory of identity formation from an interdisciplinary approach that emphasizes theology and psychology, it is important to consider African retentions. Asante, in his book *The Afrocentric Idea*, notes, "African-American culture and history represents developments in African culture and history, inseparable from place and time. Analysis of African-American culture that is not based on Afrocentric premises is bound to lead to incorrect conclusions."[11] Therefore, from Asante's standpoint, Africentricity as an interpretive principle is indispensable to my topic. Yet, according to Roberts, Africentricity, for Asante, "is a substitute for any religion or ideology."[12] As a confessing African American Christian, the religious and psychological perspectives that I bring relegate Africentricity to a supporting rather than a leading role. It is an interpretive perspective that informs my analysis, not the central methodology that guides my analysis.

An Identity Inventory

During my research phase, I developed an inventory to access perceptions on race, sex/gender, religion, and identity. The presupposition that guided the development of the questions was that people have been conditioned to function under racist and sexist assumptions regarding national ethos—that is, we assume and act in accordance with national ideologies resulting in oppression without recognizing their exclusionary (that is, their racist, sexist, classist) origins. Each question is intended to probe the response to the previous question, thereby leading the respondent into self-critical reflection. I utilized the inventory in group settings with persons who were most often affiliated with the Christian Church and had an interest in diversity issues.

Because the questionnaire was not intended to be a quantitative instrument, there are problems implicit in its organization, most notably its biased design. The questions have not been organized categorically, but they have been organized for the inventory to serve as a teaching tool to stimulate reflection and conversation. It has been administered to Blacks, Whites, Asians, and Latinos from a variety of ethnic backgrounds. The responses and reactions to the questions of the inventory suggest that the inventory is both valid and reliable for exposing exclusionary attitudes in spite of its biased overtone.

Chapter Organization

This text has five basic thematic categories, with each focusing on a different aspect of identity. The first thematic category addresses identity formation. In chapter 1, I reflect upon race and gender as significant formational forces. Our identity as American is never separate from our African heritage. Furthermore, the same oppressive forces that promoted the racialization of our citizenship have also emphasized our gender separation, and, thereby, have influenced our self-understanding as African American men and women. Chapter 2 explores our origins as African Americans. Because identity always forms the question, "Who am I?" it is especially important that this question be explored. African American life has not been constructed around the principles of individualism, unlike much of America. As a result, the identity question has been restructured to ask, "Who are *we*?" Our history of being racially oppressed has always sought to define *what* we are rather than helping us to declare *who* we are.

The second thematic category addresses the issue of racial identity. Chapter 3 discusses the oppression of racism. The development of race became one of the most devastating influences upon our being. Race is a construct, that primarily denotes color, that has been developed as a criterion for determining sociopolitical and economic status and communal relationships. Chapter 4 examines color prejudice and the impact of colorism as a psycho-historical reality maintained by religiosity. "Psychohistory can be divided into two main branches, that of psycho-biography, dealing with the study of individuals, and group psycho-history, dealing with the psychological characteristics or formative experiences of groups."[13] As I indicated earlier, my focus will be upon the formative experiences of African Americans as a group rather than on individual narratives. Joel Kovel notes that psycho-history "is an approach involving a concept of culture as a system of shared meaning, an organized structure of symbols, made by (human beings) in order to define their world and regulate their mutual relations."[14] My psycho-historical critique of race and color prejudice as religious phenomena stresses the formative influence of culture upon the racial identity of African Americans.

My approach to culture has to do with the collective practices and social institutions of a people. It comprises the traditions, norms, taboos, rituals, and cultic practices that influence and are influenced by one's identity. Hence, a cultural identity, from a psycho-historical approach, has to do with the past and with past experiences that affect present responses and the processes that negotiate internal and external promptings. One's cultural identity creates the social context and a perspectival reality. Furthermore, reflecting on a cultural identity using psycho-history, which is a modality for accessing the psychic legacy, can reveal what has been inherited through conscious and unconscious messages—messages that are often generations old.

The third thematic category addresses the issues of gender identity. Chapter 5 discusses the impact of genderism and its related oppressions of sexism, heterosexism, and homophobia. This fierce combination of oppressive forces powerfully influences our understanding of social order. This combination of forces also purports to be essential to the maintenance of society and social relations. The formative impact of the racialization of sexism, heterosexism, and homophobia has frequently blinded African Americans to the unhealthy attitudes we project upon one another. We psychically defend ourselves through masking and forcing others to wear the masks of roles based upon socialized hierarchical rules of conduct. Gender identity begins at birth and continues to exert influence until we die. It plays a leading role in our spiritual formation and declares the nature of our relationship with God.

The fourth thematic category considers religious identity. Chapter 6 presents a conceptual understanding of the psychodynamics of African American religiosity. I will reflect on the dynamic forces that provoke psychological changes. I give significant weight to unconscious motivations as a defining source for social interactions and human expression. Since African (Black) psychology is an important resource for my reflections, it is important to note the fact that African (Black) psychology has its foundations in philosophy and religion. One of its expressions is dedicated to a search for understanding of the human soul, human relationships, and human suffering by maintaining a focus on spirituality. The human condition cannot be examined without acknowledging the profound religiosity and ritualistic nature of humanity. The focus of this chapter declares the importance of African American religious experiences to African American identity formation. Chapter 7 considers the issues of African American religion and spirituality within the context of survival. African American spirituality was an inexhaustible resource for the adjustment and survival of the early Africans to the hostile environment of the colonial and antebellum periods. Furthermore, I consider spirituality to be a cultural trait central to contemporary African American identity. This approach articulates an opinion that considers the trappings of denominationalism and pietism (both have oppressive histories in the context of the United States of America) as having distorted the African Americans' earliest senses of spirituality and as having thus launched us headlong into identity and integrity crises.[15]

The final thematic category addresses the issues of identity liberation. While my approach in many ways follows the pastoral psychology method, it is not a typical pastoral psychology. Chapter 8 reflects on the meaning of liberation for African Americans. Through the phenomenological process of contextualization, Black theology developed as the theological voice for the liberating activities taking place within the African American community. In an emerging field, Black theologians moved beyond German theology to articulate Black religion and faith. Womanists then moved beyond the Black theological and feminist critiques to articulate a perspective more representative of a Black woman's experience. This perspective emphasizes liberation from race, sex, and class oppression. The African (Black) psychologists established their ground of being based on the premise that Western constructions of psychology denied the life of the spirit and the human dignity of persons of African descent. Their work emphasizes self-understanding and collective identity for the purpose of liberation. African American pastoral theologians, who coordinate the work of Black and womanist theologians and Black psychologists, speak to the breath of life that is the African American community. Chapter 9 is a synthesis of African and African American cultural history and development, African and African American religious history, Black and womanist theologies and ethics, and African and African American psychologies of childhood and adulthood in education and society into a framework for understanding African American conscious and unconscious psychic processes.

This work establishes a psychological framework for understanding African American identity formation. I stress history, spirituality, psychic security, and social influences[16] to encourage the restoration of our souls by presenting a new paradigm for renegotiating our identity and integrity crises.

Acknowledgments

This book represents a major turning point in my life as a thinker. The earliest draft of this text was in the form of my dissertation completed in 1994. Although this work represents a complete revision of my dissertation, I must thank my dissertation committee, chaired by Arthur Pressley, for walking with me in the early stages of my thoughts. Dr. Pressley continues to be an important mentor and friend. He helped to provide the African American pastoral psychology ground for me to stand on. Other members of the committee–Dorothy Austin, H. Dean Trulear, and Marcia Riggs–continue the journey with me in very creative ways.

I thank Delores Williams and Marcia Riggs–the mother and sister of my womanist concerns–for helping me to expand my theological and ethical considerations of African American life. Dr. Riggs continues to be an important voice for helping me to be responsible in my efforts to develop a liberating praxis for the entire community. The words of all my womanist sisters are of vital importance now that I have the responsibility of walking with a daughter who is a womanist-in-training, a title given her by Cheryl Kirk-Duggan. I also thank my colleague and sister, JoAnne Terrell, who has always been present to remind me that my gifts are blessing lives and my writing speaks to power.

Very special thanks go to Carroll Watkins Ali, who insisted that I send this manuscript to Jon Berquist and Chalice Press. Without her marching orders, this project probably would have remained on the shelf of ideas never shared. I appreciate Jon Berquist for inspiring confidence by his affirmation of my work. This book has not been published under his editorial leadership, but it was given new life by his editorial guidance. The various transitions at Chalice Press resulted in my working with Trent Butler to bring this work to publication. Many thanks go to Trent for helping me to articulate my hope. Special thanks also go to Randall Bailey, who not only helped to "keep my feet to the fire" in the final days of revision, but who also encouraged me to keep faith with the hermeneutical traditions of African Americans. Na'im Akbar is, without a doubt, my most consistent and valuable psychological conversation partner. His support of my work encourages me to never surrender the goal of liberating Africans in America. The list of colleagues and friends who have supported this project with a variety of gifts of encouragement are too numerous to mention one by one. For everyone who inspired me and supported this project, thank you.

Finally, the deepest thanks go to my wife and daughter, Mary and Adia, who excused me from family-time outings to support the completion of this book. A neighbor once shared a Nigerian proverb that says, a wife is like a blanket covering the weaknesses and faults of her husband. Through the thin, the lean, the bad times, and the doubts, Mary has been my blanket, allowing the world to see only my strength and valor. Adia, special gift that she is, has been a constant reminder of the joy that comes with living life to the fullest.

1

The Significance
of Race and Gender to
African American Identity

[God] has told you, O mortal, what is good;
and what does the LORD require of you
but to do justice, and to love kindness,
and to walk humbly with your God?

MICAH 6:8

Identity Vignettes

I am an African American man. That is the most succinct statement I can make to declare who and what I am while simultaneously making a statement of where I come from. Yet because of the long history of how I came to be able to identify myself in such a way, that very simple statement has many implicit layers of racial, sexual, and engendered meaning. I would like to begin by sharing a few vignettes from my life to help identify the context for my reflections.

My self-concept and identity were formed in the context of "integration." As an elementary-school-age child during the middle to late 1960s, I was bused out of my all-Black urban community into an all-White suburban community. Believing myself to be "a child that happened to be negro," I never quite understood some of the treatment I received. Although I never thought myself to be inferior to White classmates, a clear sense of difference prevailed between us. That sense of difference expressed itself when I, as a child, asked my mother, "Why do colored people like to drive old cars?" I

1

don't have a clear memory of what prompted the observation. What is clear is my observation of the lived differences of Blacks and Whites.

Christianity has been the only religion I have ever practiced. I have been a Baptist within the Black Church tradition my entire life. I revered the Black preacher, but I prayed to an Aryan Jesus. All my Divine images were of a White male God whose Son was blonde-haired and blue-eyed. All my angels were White. Every biblical character I could think of was also White, beginning with the Moses of America, Charlton Heston. Also during the middle to late 1960s, I remember an African representation of Jesus on the cover of an issue of *Ebony* magazine. Totally shocked by such an image, I exclaimed to my mother, "*They* have gone too far now!" Clearly up to that point the only religious images I had ever seen where European. There could conceivably be one exception. In most Black households, one would typically find pictures of John F. Kennedy, Martin Luther King Jr., and the Aryan Jesus fixed together on a home altar.

I entered college in 1977, approximately the same time the U. S. Supreme Court was deliberating over the Allan Bakke case. *Alan Bakke vs. University of California at Davis* was the case in which Bakke sued the school for denying him admittance into their medical school. He argued that less qualified applicants were given preferential treatment and admitted into the program. This was the case that established the term "reverse discrimination." Because of the Bakke case, the "buzz words" of the times were *quota* and *minority,* which always translated as "inferior."

The college I chose was a "little ivy" university located in an isolated, all-White residential community in northern central Pennsylvania. Being at a predominantly White school was not a new experience; however, being in a place where I did not have a significant African American community support network was traumatic. I was in a White intellectual community, studying White sources, being "exposed" to and taught the value of European and European American culture. As a religion major, I read Paul Tillich, H. Richard and Reinhold Niebuhr, Mary Daly, Rosemary Reuther, Jacques Maritain, and Martin Buber. Without a doubt, I was being exposed to intellectual giants. However, I never became acquainted with other giants such as James Cone, J. Deotis Roberts, C. Eric Lincoln, E. Franklin Frazier, Charles Copher, or Charles Long. I read the work of Mary Daly long before I ever heard mention of any African American woman religious scholar or theologian. Consequently, I graduated with a mind well-trained in Eurocentric ideology and intellectualization. Did I forget that I was a Black man? Never! Nothing in the United States of America would allow that to happen. But what it meant *to be* a Black man was not well defined.

I remember the first time I heard a woman preacher at the church of my youth. I can remember listening to her proclamation from the pulpit and noticing that this congregation, a congregation usually very responsive, was sitting quietly. I recall her message as being quite homiletically sound, but she was identified as a speaker rather than a preacher. When I shared my observation with my mother, she very plainly stated that the silence was because the proclamation came from a woman. Had she been a man preaching the same message, the response would have been different.

These vignettes not only illustrate race, sex, religion, and culture, they are also illustrative of the presence of race, sex, and gender issues that are also religious issues. Religion is regularly understood as the system people have developed to bring order to a chaotic world. Within religion, rituals are developed to control the conditions that exert power and control over human existence. This process frequently results in the identification of human features that are easily distinguishable and, therefore, are targeted for extreme control. Race, sex, and gender are the most prominent targets of religious zeal. This also means that race, sex, and gender are active players in the experience of forming an identity. Subsequently, my life experiences have taught me a great deal about what it means to be African American. Through the previously identified experiences, and many other frustrating and painful experiences, I have come to a clearer sense of self. I understand myself to have been formed into a spiritual being by the constructed categories and issues of race, sex, gender, and religion as experienced within African American culture.

What Is Identity?

Identity is a consistent sense of self discerned through relationships, whereby the character traits contained within every individual are expressed with constancy. An identity is only discernible through relationships, with the first and most fundamental series of relationships being the family. A person begins to experience himself or herself through the nurture received at home. Seeking to discern the answer to the question "Who am I?" is shaped within the context of a family that simultaneously states, "This is who we are, and this is who you are to us."

Identity and Relationships

As a person matures and ventures into the larger world, the identity takes on new dimensions with more depth and range of expression. When an individual encounters another like herself or himself in the expanding world of relationships, the individual recognizes and acknowledges one who is like oneself–an identification. Yet because a person will not have an identification with everyone he or she meets, the individual rejects those with whom no connection is felt. Identifications expand and form groups that constitute collectives. Those who are rejected, however, also have the opportunity to form separate groups. And they do, resulting in group identities standing in sharp contrast to one another. Due to the fact that the identity forms as a result of relationships, a person's identity functions on an individual and collective level simultaneously. The maintenance of these identities often leads to conflict between the differing groups.

It is vitally important to remember the two levels of self-concept and expression: the individual and the collective. Because identity develops in the context of relationship, identity formation is a psychological process that is simultaneously intra-psychic (individual) and inter-psychic (collective). Identity has to do with what one feels on the inside, as well as how one feels as one relates to others. Identity is the expression of one's self-understanding and offers a context for sharing one's life experiences. Identity is the organizing principle that coordinates all that we are into one consistent sense of "self." A clear sense of self means that individuals do not understand themselves to be one *type* of person in one setting and a different person in other settings, never having a consistent self-under-standing. Rather, the person with a clear sense of identity always has a unifying self-concept that regulates the identity. Given the variety of contexts in which every individual must function, the self-concept maintains the consistency of the identity.

Identity and Crisis

One of the ways we come to grasp the idea of self-concept is through situations of crisis. Most psychodynamic psychology theories have been constructed around the presence of crises in a person's life. The fundamental idea is that a person grows and matures through a series of crises and their resolution. Without these crisis experiences, we remain stagnant and lose the dynamism of life. A variety of experiences qualify as crises–such as death, trauma, change, finances, marriage, divorce, or social upheaval. During times of crisis, people's defense mechanisms are often greatly reduced; therefore, a crisis is a time of increased vulnerability. However, because the defenses are lowered, crisis is also a time of heightened possibility. This dynamic interplay contributes to the formative process by both fostering and redefining identity.

A child's first day of school, for example, often represents a significant crisis in the child's life. Many children are venturing out for the first time into a completely foreign context on that first day of school. The familiar and the comforting are typically nonexistent, and so vulnerability increases. But this also means the child must seek out new relationships and learn new ways of being within this very new environment. Crises allow us to experience our strengths and our growing edges. Unfortunately, crises can also reveal our deepest fears and promote our most cruel behaviors in an effort to seek our own safety. Crises become for every person the formative experiences that determine self-concept and identity.

Identity and Role

A term often confused with identity is "role." Role has to do with *what* one does–that is, social responsibility–rather than *who* one is. Although one might say that one's personality comes through in *what* one does, the role one fulfills does not reflect the fullness of one's personality. Likewise, identity is not entirely the role one fulfills. One's role within a given context is really a supporting character of the identity within the dynamic relationship between identity and role. Identity actually assists in integrating the variety of roles that we all play in our various relationships. When a person has a consistent sense of self, a different person will not be experienced with the fulfillment of every new role. A person will be the same recognizable person no matter where that person is and regardless of the social responsibility of the context.

The confusion that many people have about the dynamic relationship between identity and role is the source of many relational tensions. When crisis is added to the confusion, a great many misunderstandings are ascribed and attributed to race, sex, and gender roles. Specific social responsibilities have been ascribed to race, sex, and gender that, in turn, resulted in racial, sexual, and gender identity confusion. Working through the dynamics of an identity crisis is, therefore, more significant than simply changing contexts or jobs. One must be formed and reformed at the very core of one's being for the fullness of identity to be expressed and not be simply reduced to a changing role. Changing one's role through promotion or demotion should not be the defining feature for declaring one's identity. One's self-understanding and self-worth needs to be larger than what one does.

Discerning Identity

Identity is the sum total of one's life experiences. It answers the question "Who am I?" or in the case of a collective/communal identity, the question, "Who are we?" But identity is more than being able to say, "I am _____ from _____." An identity creates the occasion to state one's location within the context of a family, an extended family, and a community with a unique legacy and heritage of experience. These locations serve as resources for looking back and identifying the relationships and events that shape one's present understanding. They also serve as resources for moving forward by directing one's future possibilities. When tracing an individual life, reviewing a family history is often an important activity. Likewise, when tracing a community's life, reviewing the history of that community is critical to understanding the community. Consequently, an important resource for the exploration of identity is history. This study, therefore, gives considerable attention to historical information of all types, e.g., testimony, oral narratives, documentation on specific time periods, and the documented retelling of contextual events.

Discerning the African American Identity

The starting point for beginning to understand the contemporary African American is an African past that is coordinated with an American past. The proper casting of our context is essential for a clear presentation of an African American identity. We must not be confused by the fact that Africa was not regarded as a homeland with a respected history as the continent of Europe was. Culturally, Africa and Africans were considered soulless objects for plunder. "We must begin with Africa, the motherland of the Black Diaspora, from that the sea captains of Europe and America took, in the course of four centuries, unnumbered tons of gold, uncounted shiploads of ivory, and millions upon millions of black men and women. To the plunderers, Africa was the "Gold Coast," the "Ivory Coast," the "Slave Coast." But it was never a community of people deserving Christian recognition and concern."[1]

The coordination of our past with our present will offer a future of wonderful possibilities. Many would suggest that the spirit of America was more benevolent than the shapers of America. But we should not be caught up in the illusion that we were present in the heart of the American idea as beneficiary participants. Africans were never thought to be equal partners in the development of the nation. The faith and egocentrism of the founders would not give room to the full humanity of Africans as colaborers.[2] Consequently, the relational dynamics made us outcasts as colonists began to assert their American identity:

> With few exceptions, [Catholic] European and [Catholic] European-American Christians believed that they were justified in conquering American Indians and enslaving Africans to spread the religions and cultures of Europe, that they assumed were superior to those of other peoples. Church and state officials issued orders to colonists in America to arrange for the religious instruction of slaves...Protestant Europeans, like Catholics, claimed that the potential conversion of slaves to Christianity justified the enslavement of Africans. But British Americans resisted religious instruction of their slaves because they suspected that it was illegal under British law to hold a fellow Christian in bondage. If this were true, baptizing a slave would in effect free him, contrary to the slaveowner's economic interest. Colonial legislators solved the problem by passing decrees that baptism had no effect upon the status of the baptized in regard to slavery or freedom. Despite the legislation, British American slaveholders remained suspicious of teaching Christianity to slaves because they believed that becoming Christian would raise the slave's self-esteem, persuade them that they were equal to whites, and encourage them to become rebellious. Religious assemblies might present slaves with the opportunity to organize resistance, and teaching slaves to read the Bible would have the dangerous effect of making them literate. British-American Protestants also feared that including Africans

in the fellowship of Christian community would blur the cultural and social distinctions that an effective system of slavery required.[3]

The critical ideologies that I believe are at the core of a discussion of African American identity are race, sex, gender, religion, and spirituality. Within the context of the United States of America, race, gender, spirituality, and religion are intimately connected to one another. Exploring the origins of racial or gender ideology and spiritual expressions without reviewing the impact of religion on our understandings is difficult. In fact, the maintenance of racial systems often has the character and emotionality of a religious system. As a result, race and color issues are often religious issues. Likewise, sex and gender ideologies are most often negotiated by spirituality while being maintained by the social-political-religious systems that created them. Therefore, identity, being greatly influenced by race and gender ideologies, can be understood as being directed by religiosity and spirituality. Furthermore, race, sex, gender, spirituality, and religion are all components of the container of culture.

Race, Sex, Gender, and the American Idea

This country has produced a culture founded on the social ideas of liberty and justice, while all social interactions were being governed by survival needs. Everyone who landed on these shores had to negotiate with the challenges of a new land and survival. The stated mediating principle for living the social ideas of liberty and justice was equality, even as it was recognized that all who came did not come equally. There was still a promoted ideology that this was the land of promise and opportunity. That guiding hope, however, did not include the Africans who came to America. For reason of race, color, sex, gender and creed, Africans were denied the expression of an identity supported by the American ideas of liberty, justice, and equality before God and others.

> The Protestants ignored Rome and bowed instead to an incipient racism that, ere long, would develop a ponderous psychology of justification that would burden both church and society in the West for generations. The Englishman considered *himself* first, above all. And when he contemplated his own perfection, he saw the alleged heathenism of the Africans as but one aspect of a gener-alized disparity. They were beings apart. They were not merely black; they were black *and* heathen. It was all a matter of the black man's depraved condition. Since he was not an Englishman, his importance and his place in the Englishman's scheme of things was predetermined. From such a perspective the Anglo-Saxon could scarcely be expected to develop a warm appreciation of the

African's humanity, his naive religion, or his capacity to benefit from Christian instruction.[4]

The American Identity and Developmental Understandings

Reflecting on the foundations of the nation developmentally, the dynamics of the earlier stages of human life are experienced by the "newborn" nation. America in its infancy experienced crises just like every newborn does. A newborn understands himself or herself to be the center of the universe and demands all of her or his needs to be met, no matter how challenging the requests become. The newborn nation ignored what others had to say about how to best follow the guidelines of the Christian faith and declared its own rules of faith and order. In fact, the newborn nation experienced the guidelines as an imposition and as oppressive. From this relationship the new nation sought to be free; however, in seeking its own freedom, it denied freedom to others based upon race, sex, gender, religion, and ethnicity. The new rules the new nation established did not begin from the faith statement, "There is neither English nor African, slave nor free, male nor female." The new nation made no such identification as it sought to answer the question, "Who are we?"

Anyone with children knows that children have a way of defining and redefining life. As one psychotherapist says, children have a way of giving out job descriptions to everyone in the system. The young nation was no different. The goals of the "America idea" caused the dynamic features of a young America to clash. The rhetoric of equality quickly resulted in the establishment of dividing lines that declared some to be more valuable than others. The lines that were drawn divided people according to race, sex, gender, and class identities. Drawing the lines and maintaining the lines became an integral component of American culture. American culture has been radically influenced by racism, so much so that even the sexism we experience is racialized genderism. And all of this has been interpreted and articulated through our religious imagination. The ideas of liberty and justice were promoted and empowered by a religious idealism that made becoming an American a sacred task.

Becoming African American

For African American culture to be truly "American," it has to express the founding ideas of America. Liberty, justice, survival, and equality are all important expressions of the African American identity, just as each one is vital to what it means to be American. African American culture, first and foremost, is a resistance culture dynamically constructed around the thematic ideas of freedom and justice. Central to what it means to be an American is the principle that declares individual dignity and privilege–by virtue of our humanity–as being the soil that nurtures the American soul. To that extent, America's darker children are as American as any other child of the nation. In fact, freedom and justice have always been high on the agenda of African Americans for as long as we have been transplanted and planted on these shores. Although we have had differing ideas regarding how we ought to go about securing our freedom and what constitutes justice, we have always agreed on the principles of freedom and justice. The most significant strides in our quest for freedom and justice were always orchestrated and marshaled by African American spirituality and religiosity. The African American community has always understood that those whom the Spirit makes free are free indeed. This belief has meant that no one in this life has ever had the power or the right to bind us. This understanding did not only refer to spiritual freedom but also included physical freedom.

The development and evolution of an African American identity has been a stance against the denigrating dividing lines that have been so important to the American experience. African American culture—so deeply rooted in the traditions of "slave religion" and African traditional religions—combined the liberation narratives of the Hebrew Bible, the liberating work of Jesus as prophet and divinity, and a spirituality of hope and creativity as our way of surviving the horrors of our American experience in order to know liberty and justice in this life. I will give considerable attention to these ideas in chapters 6, 7, and 8.

2

Who Are African Americans?

The African slave was uprooted from his land, his territory, and brought forcibly several thousand miles away to another land completely alien to his spirit and his gods. All ties that gave him a sense of belonging, of counting, of being a person nourished by a community of persons were abruptly severed, lacerated, torn asunder. Bodies that were emotionally bleeding hulks were set down in the new world of the Americas. Initially he had no standing, even of that of outsider. In terms of his access to the sources of nourishment for community, initially he had none. No, not even the status of a human being.

HOWARD THURMAN

During my teenage years, a neighborhood friend and I regularly debated. The issues and topics were far-reaching, but they always related to Black life. On one occasion, we debated about the language used to describe our relationships to the church. Without fully understanding why, I was adamantly opposed to the individualistic language he used to talk about church membership. As the debate went on, his point continued to be made using the language of "my church." My counterpoint to his position was to use the language of "the church where I am a member."

Placing this debate in the context of an identity discussion, the "my church" position addresses the question "Who am I?" while "the church where I am a member" addresses the question "Who are we?" In many ways, I have continued this debate with others over the years. A dynamic tension, with marked distinctions, exists between the development of individualism and the individual within the community. This chapter focuses the debate by considering the larger issue of who we are as African Americans.

The Historical Context of African American Identity Formation

From the moment Black folks landed on these North American shores in 1526, the struggle to declare our sense of being has been a very significant life engagement for us. Like death-defying acrobats, we confronted dehumanizing, life-denying forces in our efforts to declare a self that was affirmed by the bonds of love. The forces of race, sex, and gender maliciously directed against us were transformed into a power for our survival. Instead of becoming inconsistent and fragmented as a result of the various demeaning roles and tasks we had to fulfill, our clear sense of identity helped us to maintain our stability and integrity as relational beings. As I discussed earlier, the issues of identity tend to be addressed by answering the question, "Who am I?" Although I believe it is important that we continue to be attentive to the identity question—as we have in the past—today we have far more important ways to ask the question. Because of our orientation to life and relationships, the identity question to be asked is: "Who are we as *African* Americans?"

Africa, Our Motherland

African America is a unique cultural experience because of the combination of our distant African past and our more recent American past. It is extremely important that all reflections on the question of "Who are we?" include our African heritage. Almost every ethnic group in America qualifies its American identity by identifying a country of origin. Because America comprises people who have immigrated here from all over the world, each ethnic group maintains an identity connection with its "motherland." Therefore, it is vitally important that a construction of African American history and spirituality begins with Africa.

If the Black American identity grounds its sense of origin in America alone, our sole identity connection is "slave." Grounding our identity in America results in a false identity that we truly must be liberated from if we are to be restored to peoplehood. We do not consciously identify ourselves as "Slave Americans," and yet many Black folks, consciously and unconsciously, live by the historical interpretation of Black being chattel and "slave for life." This identification, "slave for life," is a fundamental factor influencing our "shame-based" understanding of Black life. When we want to see ourselves as equal to other Americans with a sense of historical pride, yet base our identity on slave as our origin, we have based our identity on a depraved identity. When we exclude Africa from our sense of beginnings, "African American" consciously and unconsciously becomes a synonym for the powerless, hopeless, helpless, degraded Black body in America. It is a human responsibility to seek and struggle for freedom. It is, therefore, our responsibility to work out our souls' salvation by seeking to liberate ourselves from the depraved identity of "Slave American."

Slave or Enslaved

We were not slaves when we landed on these shores, but became *enslaved* Africans who had a story to tell. Understanding ourselves as Africans in the face of American slavery changes our identity orientation and our interpretations of history. Throughout human history, all peoples have experienced some form of slavery. But how many of those peoples still have slavery as an identity so closely associated with their being? Even in America, the indenture system was a slave system that included Europeans. Yet Africans are the only group in America identified and frequently self-identified as slaves. Slavery was our circumstance, not the essence of our being. We will take a major step toward freedom when we liberate ourselves to say that we are Africans who were *en*slaved, rather than slaves who left Africa.

The distinction between slave and enslaved is an important distinction as we seek to express ourselves as citizens of these United States of America. We are taught the virtues of citizenship and make choices to conform to the principles of the nation. But we also need to recognize the lessons that the nation teaches its resident Africans. The nation teaches us to "know our place"–that is, on the banks of mainstream America and not navigating the currents like all other Americans. To make the point in terms of critical pedagogy, we are "trained" to be slaves by the forces of racism, sexism, classism, and heterosexism. This means we have not been encouraged to know ourselves. We have only been encouraged to blindly follow, without any thought to where the destructive oppressive force is leading. What we need is to be "educated" into knowing who we are and where we have come from. Armed with self-knowledge, we can chart the plan for our freedom and make straight the paths of justice. If we deny our African heritage, we revive the image of America as the "melting pot" and doom ourselves to identity confusion. The denial of our African heritage will result in a "Black Anglo Saxon Protestant (BASP)" identity, which is another way of saying "Slave American." I will say more about this construction of the self in chapter 3.

As I have already stated, focusing on identity through the question, "Who am I?" is, however, an individualistic way of attending to identity. Although all African Americans at some point will explore their identity by asking, "Who am I?" that question is not the best question. Because the African self is not grounded in individualism, we should always reshape the question to be, "Who are *we*?" In fact, I believe something essential in our being will reshape the question for us. Our communal sense of being has been an essential force for declaring who we are in the world and how we relate to one another.

Self-identifying as African American

One very important answer to the question, "Who are we?" is the statement, "We are African Americans." Given this answer, one might ask,

"What does that mean? Who are African Americans, really?" "African American" is the most recent self-deterministic identification for persons of African descent in America. To self-identify as African American is to claim more than just a racial identification. The essence of this particular identification is to claim a historical and a cultural past along with declaring a nationalistic understanding of what it means to be an American. For me to self-identify as African American means that I acknowledge myself as a person of African descent with American citizenship. This identification acknowledges differences. To declare oneself to be African American acknowledges a life experience and cultural history that differs from the most prominent features of American cultural life that European architects have constructed. We have had a different set of formative influences that have shaped and continue to shape the collective known as "African American." The differences, however, tend to reflect experience more than some stereotypical characterization defined by race.

The greatest challenge to our identity struggle in America has been the maintenance of our humanity. Everything within this context pushed us to know ourselves as nonhuman, and sought to destroy our lives. Some people might argue that American slavery was not a genocidal system, meaning the system did not seek our mass destruction. The argument might emphasize that the system needed to keep us alive for the system to work. But to do every evil thing imaginable to control another, to deny the dignity of another, to imprison and defile the soul of another, is far from being life-giving.

Life is meant to be lived out in relationship, in family. The current agenda to protect marriage and family is not a new phenomenon. It is as old as time itself. We, however, have been pushed to separate ourselves from one another, to live individually and isolated from each other. Had this separation been totally successful by making individualism normative for our being, it would have fractured the self and made us crazy. To be crazy means the pains of life are more powerful than the passion for life. But we were able to be resistant and maintain our sanity because our identity was informed and nurtured by African spirituality. African spirituality is an integrative process that maintains that there is no separation between blood and nonblood relations, public and private life, physical and spirit world, church and community. We answer the question, "Who are we?" by declaring our humanity. A human identity says a great deal about what it means to be alive by defining all of one's relationships, including one's relationship with God. Declaring our humanity means that we have direct contact with God and a responsibility to and for one another. In chapter 7, I will give attention to African spirituality as a resource for our resistance and survival.

Africa Is the Origin

Accurately answering the question of identity is as much a matter of context as it is of information. If one misunderstands the context for negotiating the question of identity, the answers to the question will misrepresent the true nature of one's being. Context is vitally important to any reflection. The absence of context as a feature of one's reflection will result in statements based upon stereotypes and personal opinions rather than informed considerations. When identity formation includes context, the question reveals itself to be a question of origins. Seeking clarity on who one is always produces questions of where one comes from. Countless illustrations could be offered to make the point, but within every human being is a desire to know concretely where we have come from as individuals and as family. Consequently, if one maintains the context for understanding African Americans to be the U.S. context alone, then the answers to the question have a greater probability for misrepresenting who we are than if the context includes continental Africa.

For the most insightful understanding of who African Americans are, we must reflect on our general impressions of African culture. Wherever people of African descent live, African culture is present as a living history. Through oral transmissions and ritualistic retentions, African views on the nature of relationships are revealed as a way of life. The various cultural traditions from across the African continent have been blended and affirmed as a living African testimony among all Africans of the diaspora.

Growing up, I was taught many things about the shaping of reality and about the people who shape it. What I did not know was the extent to which my meaning making had been tainted by introjected racism. I learned this only as I began to respond to the call to return to the headwaters of my being, my African soul. Therefore, looking to Africa as a rich cultural heritage initially required a radical adjustment in my thinking. Before I could find truth within myself, Africa needed to be liberated within me.

Like many others, my initial look at Africa conjured a variety of images. Many of those images presented Africa as irreligious, uncivilized, magical, superstitious, cannibalistic, naked, and infantile. Because of Africa's legacy as the "Dark Continent," people have assumed that Africa has had no influence on the history of the world, nor impact on the development of Western culture. This erroneous legacy totally removes Africa from the center of any discussion of human equality. As a result, the conjured legacy depicts everything African as savage, primitive, and debased. Liberating Africa from its erroneous legacy allowed the symbols and creative strength to speak to me in new ways. The initial work of liberating Africa within my consciousness did not require a pilgrimage to the motherland. The liberating journey actually began as an inward journey. My journey resulted in the expression of a true historical memory. It was a great awakening. New questions were asked as images and symbols began to speak in new ways. This inward journey encouraged me to end my acceptance of the negative projections and introjections of Africa and ultimately allowed for a more accurate interpretation of African history and culture and of my experiences.

I was able to move in the direction of becoming who *I* ought to be because I could more accurately see who *we* have been.

African American Culture

African American culture has developed in the crucible of pain and struggle. As colonials sought to establish an identity that was separate and distinct from their British overseers, a formative process was put in place. Although identity is always worked out in the context of relationship, it is not always necessary for the rejection of others to be an integral part of the process. Unfortunately, rejection has been an important part of how we Americans have come to know ourselves as Americans. Look, for instance, at the old metaphor of "melting pot" as the process for becoming an American. The metaphor reflects a process of blending into one. And yet, with the melting also comes the separation of elements. The biblical image of the melting pot speaks of the gold being separated from the dross.

The American melting pot emphasized blending even as it forced separation. The forces of rejection fueled the heat beneath that pot and brought about the melting. One was forced to reject vital attributes of one's culture of origin. If one chose to resist those forces, then one would suffer the consequences of being rejected by American society. This was the experience for many groups that came to America, especially those who came through Ellis Island. Many new immigrants received their first lesson in the melting separations by having their names changed to become American. Nevertheless, African Americans face a more devastating and unfortunate truth. Even if we submit to the forces, rejection is so embedded in the process that even our compliance is rejected. While Europeans could melt by changing their names and language, thereby blending in, Africans always have stood out because of our physical characteristics.

Being forced to stay outside the mainstream has been one of African American culture's formative experiences. We must, however, consider other influences beyond the forces of rejection. Another more powerful and positive influence has been our religiosity. African traditional religions and our religious interactions in America have helped to mediate our courage and construct a world of hope for a better tomorrow. During my travels through Ghana, West Africa, and the Republic of South Africa, I was amazed by the extent to which we Africans in America still resemble the cultures of our continental roots. African spirituality and the cultures of West Africa have blended with our American experience to become African American culture. African retention can be clearly seen in the activities of African American Christianity and the religious rituals of everyday African American life. I will reflect more extensively on these concerns in chapter 6.

The separating heat of the melting pot has encouraged many to think that African American culture sits somewhere on the fringes of American culture. Our social location on the outside of the mainstream has caused many of us to simply want to declare ourselves as American. We do not desire to be on the banks. We want to be flowing in the middle of the mainstream as full participating citizens. Many of us, though we are persons of African descent, have known no land other than this land. We have pledged allegiance to no country other than this country. We have fought and died for no flag other than this flag. Because we desire so deeply to be accepted as human citizens of the United States, many of these persons would be insulted if they were identified as Africans.

African American Culture Seen as Popular Culture

Society regularly associates African American culture with popular culture, which is most often defined as the expressive and widely accepted (that is, the popular) cultural forms that are part of dynamic social exchange. Transmitted through film, radio, and television, popular culture tends to be directed toward young people and youth culture. This general understanding of popular culture seems to describe the unbiased and passive expressions of popular opinions related to what it means to live in society.

The Transmission of Pop Culture

The suggestion of an unbiased definition regards the media of transmission as presenting the popular reality to the masses without influencing the views of culture. Thought of as a presentation of "the real," popular culture is, in some ways, considered the evidence of a society's vibrant cultural exchange. This view of popular culture hides a significant shortcoming. To define popular culture as an agreed upon expression of reality without any indication of the destructive ethos contained within that definition avoids the potential devastation of persons wrought by the media of transmission.

While I can appreciate the most common definition of popular culture, I have an alternative view of popular culture as an expression of life. I understand culture to be the complex system that results from human social collectivity. Culture develops through social interaction, and it both creates and sustains group cohesion. Influenced by the human need for security and consistency, culture is a cluster of human expressions that include religion, values, traditions, rituals, and language.

Mass Culture vs. Pop Culture

Culture is geographically constructed and given meaning by its participants. Within any particular cultural context, differing degrees of adherence to the culture will be present. The different levels of adherence to a culture within a given context tend to be described with "majority-minority" language. Another way of talking about the different levels of adherence is with the terms *dominant culture* and *subculture*, as well as *mass culture* and *popular culture*. In my usage of the terms, mass culture and popular culture are synonymous with what society commonly identifies as dominant culture and subculture, respectively. Viewing culture as a dynamic and developmental system, I would prefer not to use the term subculture. I consider America to have a dominant culture that has deep traditional roots while acknowledging a separate contemporary cultural experience.

A peculiar relational dynamic exists between mass culture and popular culture. Although mass culture stands in contrasting position to popular culture, popular culture can become a part of mass culture. This induction results in popular culture's change. The moment mass culture absorbs popular culture, it ceases to be popular culture. Interestingly enough, this absorption does not necessarily make mass culture evolve into more than it was. Because of the ways in which systems maintain themselves, mass culture rarely seeks to be changed by popular culture. To better understand this point, consider mass culture's relationship to popular culture by considering America's recent popular culture history. Many of our popular cultures have been associated with, yet not limited to, a particular musical expression. These various musical styles identified as popular culture are always influenced by an attitude of rebellion. From rock 'n' roll's rebels to hippies, disco, punk, Black revolutionary culture, grunge, and hip-hop, each popular cultural expression stood against mass culture with an ideology of nonconformity and rebellion. This history reveals popular culture as always existing in opposition to a set of traditional mass cultural values.

As I listen to people talk about popular culture, they often employ the language of classism to describe the values and desires of the group. As an example of the ebb and flow, while popular culture regularly stares in the face of traditional mass culture, one can be a part of the underclass, ascribe to upper-class values, and still self-identify as a part of popular culture. From a different vantage point, mass culture can see the economic viability of popular culture and invest in its growth potential in exploitative ways, while never absorbing the new cultural expressions into the mainstream.

Pop Culture as Complicit or Nonconformist

Popular culture can be complicit and live according to the defining influences of mass culture, or it can be nonconformist. For instance, who defined "Generation X"? Those who were on the inside and self-identified as Gen-X, or those who were on the outside from a more traditional cultural perspective? Although many Gen-Xers did not agree with the description, most did not deny the label. Popular culture can resist the traditions of the masses by giving itself a name, value, and significance. Think about classical music, which many regard as a mark of high culture. Defying ideals that claim classical music always to be musical scores written by composers from Europe, a popular culture rooted in resistance names its own reality and defines what is classical for itself.

Like culture in general, popular culture tends to be seen as a well-developed system. My position on the development and maintenance of popular culture is that popular culture emerges from mass culture through relational discord. Although popular culture stands outside mass or dominant cultural norms, an ebb and flow occurs between mass cultural values and popular cultural values. Each effects and influences the vital features of the other.

Popular culture can also be a proactive force rather than simply a reactive force. Race and ethnicity, which also carry class connotations, participate in defining or being defined as popular culture. Identifying race or ethnicity as popular culture is different from identifying the culture of popularity. Neither racial nor ethnic differences are widely accepted by mass culture. This lack of acceptance results in racial and ethnic vitality becoming popular culture that creatively resists mass culture's domination. As an example, Chicago is one of the most segregated cities in America. Each named community has its own racial and ethnic flavor. Would anyone ever think or attempt to melt the diverse communities into one blended Chicago? The separate communities would never allow such a change. Consequently, popular culture can also be understood as the countercultural voice of rebellion, as the collective cry of the group resisting the power structure of mass culture. This is the context for my understanding African American culture as a popular culture; that is, African American culture is a resistance culture.

More than Popular Stereotypes

As a social phenomenon, popular culture expresses our societal dividing lines. Declaring who is socially inside and outside, popular culture exposes the currents and trends of the times. Popular culture is not simply the transmission of what everyone enjoys within the culture. If one looks beyond the entertainment factors of the transmission of popular culture, the expressions of "who" and "what" are acceptable or objectionable within society can be clearly observed. For instance, politically correct language is often the negotiated result of popular culture's ebb and flow with mass culture. Popular community icons tend to represent the characteristics and status of that specific community within mass culture.

Hence, generations of African Americans have been portrayed in film and television as developmentally immature mammies, maids, and "steppin' fetchits" exclusively as a way of reinforcing the idea that Blacks are the inferior, permanent slaves of America. These popular images were not created by African Americans, nor did they represent who we are. If popular culture is only understood as the expression of widely accepted cultural forms, such as media-projected stereotypes, the manipulative impact of its transmission is lost. When ostracism produces popular culture, it is a tool for communicating who and what is culturally most valuable.

As a case in point, American mass culture has declared the nuclear family to be the primary system for saving the nation. To ensure this understanding, the media denigrates extended family systems. The use of popular transmission destroys extended family systems and reinforces America's individualistic nuclear family system. This has not always been the case; *The Waltons* did have a good run on television, but in our contemporary setting, most media project the nuclear family as the preferred system.

African American families are prime examples of media denigration. African Americans value the extended family system, but African Americans have been portrayed as violent due to a perversion of the extended family. We have become the popular culture icons who signify and symbolize family dysfunction, domestic violence, and criminality within our society. The media readily represent African American households as matriarchal, replete with single mothers, absentee fathers, and drug-addicted children. When the extended family system is destroyed, the resources of African American culture also are destroyed.[2]

Pop Culture as an Oppressive Force

Viewing popular culture from the underside or backside of the experience, we observe an oppressive force. Wreaking havoc on the human dignity of targeted groups, popular culture is sometimes becomes society's strategic resource for maintaining the predetermined distance between those who are entitled to life, liberty, and happiness, and those who are said to be entitled to *pursuing* life, liberty, and happiness. I know our language stresses the "pursuit of happiness," but entitlement is the critical determinant.

Mass high culture, as the authoritative voice of social power, declares who is entitled to power. Popular culture, then, as the exercising voice of social power, declares who will be given the privilege of access to power. From this perspective, popular culture does not result from a groundswell of popular opinion without there first being an injected high culture (upper class) idea originating above ground. Popular culture, disseminating high culture's position on entitlement, maintains the social standards and structures for identifying who is in and out. White supremacy is not simply the cry of an illiterate, uneducated, poverty-stricken population, as is often portrayed. It is a top-to-bottom ideology that has caused one group to feel that other groups have been given more privileges.

Closer to where I live…within popular culture as transmitted by media, I am a dangerous "thing." I am seen as the dark-skinned, violent criminal who raises anxiety wherever I go. No matter how I cover this dark skin–in casual, business, or formal wear–the anxious response is the same. As I walk through Hyde Park, people cannot see my Ph.D. on my face. A white guy can walk by a white woman on the streets and stir no reaction. If I walk by that same woman a few steps after that white guy, she gets nervous and clutches her purse. If I am walking across campus behind someone, it cannot be because I just happen to be walking in the same direction. I am walking behind because I am following, waiting for the right moment to strike. I am not seen as a shopper but a shoplifter. If I have material wealth, it must be the result of illegal activity rather than hard work or a family inheritance. This construction of popular culture presents me as "the one to fear."

*A personal story…funny, ironic, and true…*It was my day off. Banking was on my list of things "to do." I needed to make several deposits and cash a check. I went to the teller. Handling each transaction separately, I gave her the deposits for my checking account. After that, I gave her my deposits for my savings account. The two deposits were not incredibly large, but they were significantly larger than the third transaction. I handed her a $25 check to be cashed. With a very pleasant smile, she looked at me and asked, "Do you have an account with us?" Shocked out of my mind, I replied, "I just deposited to two!" Whipping her head back to her monitor, mouth open in amazement, she responded, "Is that YOU?" Making a quick recovery, she asked, "How would you like that?" Still in shock, I answered, "CASH!" In this teller's mind, money management and Black folks did not go together. In my experience, popular transmissions of culture support her mentality.

How We Came to Be Who We Are

African Americans have a strong and long tradition of resisting the oppressive forces that have sought to destroy our lives. The leading resources for resisting have been our spirituality and faith in God. Clearly, answering the question, "Who are we?" happens within the context of relationships. But the question of identity also has religious dimensions. We, African Americans, have answered the question through reflecting on our relationship with God. In our efforts to develop a consistent sense of self rooted in human dignity, we developed a highly sophisticated theological anthropology. The God-human dynamic, as experienced in African traditional religion, has been the primary source for maintaining our self-understanding as human beings. When the world told us we were less than human, we experienced in our being that we were fully human and loved by God.

The prominence of the rejecting forces in America has meant that the theodical question (that is, how can we experience so much evil and suffering in the presence of a good and loving God?) has guided our outlook. We have been keenly aware of the presence of evil in the world and its impact on our living circumstances. Our experience of suffering and our knowledge of God have been critical resources for coming to know ourselves as human beings. We have always understood ourselves to be an "Immanuel people," fully knowing that God is with us regardless of our circumstances. This has been our primary source for resisting the life-denying forces we constantly confront. The heat we have experienced has helped us to know who we are.

3

Race, Racism, and the African American

We hold these truths to be self-evident, that all men are created equal, that they are endowed by their Creator with certain unalienable rights, that among these are life, liberty, and the pursuit of happiness.

THOMAS JEFFERSON

I have a clear memory of both sets of paternal great-grandparents. I remember the weathered texture of their skin. I can also remember their facial expressions as they gazed at life. Those eyes, which looked at me with great gentleness and compassion, saw many cruelties in life. They knew the horrors of slavery from the days of their youth, having parents who had been enslaved or relating to people who had been enslaved. They certainly knew the problems of Reconstruction and the lynchings that were so frequent for generations. My memory of these foreparents has given me direct contact to a memory that extends back into the antebellum period of America. They carried the burden of this nation's racial atrocities in their being. They were Africans born free in the Caribbean, free Native Americans, and the children of emancipated Africans in the United States. Their lives have been imprinted on my being as a living legacy of who we are.

I do not know a great deal about my genealogy, but I know enough to say several non-African groups are part of my family tree. I know my family tree has several tribes of Native Americans, European Jews, and other European branches. When I, however, am seen face-to-face, my non-African heritage is not what people see. No one ever looks at me and says, "My, you look Jewish!" Nor do people look at me and comment, "I can see you have some Native American features. What tribe are you from?" No, people see the African and treat me accordingly. The presence of the African is what defines my relationship to America.

The Soil That Nurtured Racial Identity

The most popular historical date for identifying the start of slavery in North America is 1619, the year commonly identified when the first Africans arrived in the colonies as indentured servants. That year, however, represents the time the *English* arrived on these shores with enslaved Africans. But enslaved Africans actually arrived in North America nearly a whole century earlier. In 1526, Spanish conquistador and explorer Lucas Vázquez de Ayllón established a colony on what is today St. Helena Island, one of the sea islands off the southern coast of South Carolina. By identifying St. Helena Island as slavery's place of genesis in North America, from its inception to its end with the Thirteenth Amendment to the U.S. Constitution American slavery had a 339-year history.

Founding Principles

Although African enslavement in America began with the Iberian Catholics, the history of our enslavement is largely an English story beginning in the thirteen English colonies. Writers have tended to describe slavery in America as a southern phenomenon, but slavery and its racial ideologies were as much a part of the Puritan culture as they were that of the southern planters.[1] The establishment of the new nation necessitated a new identity that shifted from "royal subject/subject of the crown" with England as their sovereign, to "citizen" of the democratic society of the United States of America. Taking on a new identity is never an easy task and is always fraught with the challenge to identify the defining features and characteristics of the being. This means that some will be described as insiders, and some others will be described as outsiders.

Concerned with the meaning of community as America struggled with civil rights and "Black Power," Howard Thurman explored the dynamics of identity. Keenly aware of the shifting ground that is characteristic of crisis, he wrote a meditation entitled "The Search in Identity." He reflected on America's challenge to be open to identify all of its residents as citizens while remaining keenly aware of America's difficult history of relating to those declared to be outside the American ethos. He wrote:

> Whenever citizens are denied the freedom of access to the resources that make for a sense of belonging, a sense of being totally dealt with, the environment closes in around them, resulting in the schizophrenic dilemma of being inside and outside at one and the same time. Or worse still, they are subject to the acute trauma of not knowing at any given moment whether they are outsiders or insiders.[2]

America's Schizophrenic Producing Context

Historically, mass culture understands the opening words of the Declaration of Independence to represent the essence of the United States of America. Referenced as a statement of who we are and what we hold sacred as Americans, the Declaration declares equality and human rights to be American principles. The patriotic creed and identity of the citizens of these United States of America has its foundation grounded in the activities of revolution. All of our nationalistic expressions hold revolution and independence to be the core of the American identity and culture. Even our national anthem comes to a grand definitive crescendo with the words, "the land of the free and the home of the brave."

A Land of Opportunity?

For many, the United States of America has been traditionally and historically understood as the *new* promised land "flowing with milk and honey." Another prominent ideal is that this is a land of opportunity where dreams can come true. The popular experience, however, is that the "self-evident truth" that "all *men* are created equal" was a very specific reference made to a particular class, sex, and race of people rather than a universal hope of humanity. This fact becomes especially clear as one reviews how the unequal realities of persons living within this society have influenced the American consciousness.

Although we would like to think that we are a classless society, the stratifications of "haves and have nots" are as clear as they have ever been. The "unalienable rights of life, liberty, and the pursuit of happiness" were not necessarily intended for men and women alike, neither then nor now. Hence, the pervasive ideological images of United States citizenship—most notably democracy, prosperity, and dignity symbolized by "Lady Liberty"– are not experienced as having been "endowed by the Creator" in an equitable fashion.

The United States of America is an immigrant nation, and the pledge of "freedom and justice for all" is a luxury granted to only a few. Even the indigenous people of this nation have not always experienced the full range of privileges afforded most citizens of this nation. The colonists claimed rights that superseded the rights of others. The "pursuit for happiness" was understood to be an individualistic priority list to be fulfilled at one's own expense through the "Protestant work ethic" and at the expense of others within a capitalistic economy supported by the enslavement of Africans. This "pursuit of happiness," guided by religion and culture, both promotes and resists oppression. It has prompted, interpreted, and perpetuated the "American Dream."

American Dream Interpreted Again

While it might appear that yet another exploration of the efficacy of the American Dream is a waste of time, it is essential that we continue to evaluate the American Dream. The Dream remains very much alive as a guiding image and ethos of the American way of life. Every presidential election year, the national conventions never fail to make prominent the importance of strategizing the fulfillment of the promises of the American Dream. In his book, *Martin, Malcolm, and America,* James Cone reflected on America and the American Dream through the lives of Martin Luther King Jr. and Malcolm X (El Hajj Malik El Shabbazz). It remains imperative that we all continue to reflect on the question: Has the "American Dream" become an inescapable nightmare of unattainable images? As someone whose family history includes the dehumanization of antebellum slavery, the dislocation of life and land in exchange for a faraway reservation in the name of Manifest Destiny, and genocide in both my African and Native American bloodlines, reinterpreting the American Dream is essential.[3]

The "American Dream" has meant terror and despair for many who have experienced its influence. Americans are encouraged to dream in this, the land of dreamers and promise. The Dream projects equal opportunity, equal justice, and equal rights. But for generations of my family, the Dream has been a movement toward separate and unequal. Limitations have been placed upon freedom and dignity in the name of promoting harmony. When one considers the ever-widening space between the "haves and the have nots"–a gap frequently based upon race and sex/gender–the functionality of the Dream must be questioned. The inequity of the Dream has led some to prosperity, while others have been seduced and led down a road of destruction.

The American Dream as a Religion

One disciplinary resource for interpreting the American Dream is religious studies. I suggested in chapter 1 that religion is a system for organizing the world in which one lives. It is a belief system that allows one to feel safe by making life more controllable. While the Dream can be seen as having many religious attributes, the Dream can also be seen as being a religion. Following this line of interpretation, the Dream was not shaped and directed by God. An American aristocracy shaped and interpreted it by directing the muscle of an out-group (outsiders, the commoners) who identified with, and desired to become part of, an in-group (insiders, the aristocracy). If one would list the characteristics believed to be markers of a religion, those markers will find their expression within the way the Dream functions for many Americans.

Race and Privilege as Features of the Dream

The American context does not allow just anyone and everyone to practice the religion of the Dream. A basic qualification relates to what one looks like. Race, therefore, became one of the primary marks of member-ship. The members of this religion are called citizens. With race as a qualification for membership, racism is a significant force for granting or denying someone participation in the American Dream. The white supremacy rhetoric[4] claims, "The white man is no longer a citizen of these United States" and, "All these foreigners are coming here and taking our jobs." Such rhetoric identifies whom they believe the Dream was meant to benefit. The American Dream is a creed, and race is one of its basic doctrines.

Another important feature of the Dream is the idea of privilege.[5] Frequently linked to entitlement, privilege is a dominant feature of the American Dream and the American consciousness. We believe it is a privilege to be in the land of opportunity. It is a privilege to be a citizen in "the land of the free and the home of the brave." And it is a privilege to participate in the "American Dream,"…or is it? Not only is a dream a process of conscious hopes, it is also the unconscious vision of a "city that has foundations whose architect and builder is God" (Heb. 11:10). Remember, the process of identity formation includes identification with another, and it was the vision of heaven with which the American Dream sought to identify. Hence, the early colonists utilized Old Testament motifs and images of promise and deliverance to describe their activities. They began to identify with the exodus, determining a triumphal existence to be God-ordained. Like the followers of Joshua, they began to reenact the destruction of the Canaanites in their struggle to fulfill the Dream and find life's meaning in America.

The American Dream and the Enlightenment

The period that, perhaps, had the greatest influence upon the emerging American consciousness was the period of the Enlightenment.[6] This period was a time of great intellectual growth for some and the "headwaters" of degradation for others. The Enlightenment was the period in which prejudices were empowered by the establishment of the construct of race as well as the scientific rationales for racism. This era is significant because it declares the context in which the Dream took shape. It also has been identified as an influential factor in the development of American racism.

In America, Thomas Jefferson was the leading "intellectual child" of the Enlightenment. Looking at Jefferson and the Enlightenment through the lenses of psycho-history, we can come to understand the formation of the American identity and America's difficulties with racial identity and racism. In his book, *Dimensions of a New Identity*, Erik Erikson notes that a study of Jefferson is the study of "a life history synonymous with the creation of the new nation."[7] Erikson identifies this one man's personality, beliefs, and life story to be the same as the ethos of the nation. No one denies that Jefferson was a significant framer of the new nation. Jefferson's life and works were instrumental to the construction of an American consciousness. Those things Jefferson believed became embodied as the characteristics of the nation. To review Jefferson's life is not just a look at an individual, as a single voice, but through psycho-history, his life story is representative of the nation as a whole.

Through his writings and by his living, Jefferson defined and embodied the nation's position on entitlement and privilege. In the language of mass and popular culture presented in chapter 2, the nation's high culture principle of entitlement has been communicated popularly through the "American Dream." Jefferson offered a groundswell of hope by stating all are to be entitled as human beings. From his influence arose a popular culture of equality, opportunity, and prosperity disseminated through the language of "life, liberty, and the pursuit of happiness." He declared all these things from his entitled, high-culture social position. His declarations became American mass culture's articulation of the Dream. Since Jefferson's life history, according to Erikson, is synonymous with the life of the new nation, then the same cognitive dissonance present within Jefferson will be present within the nation.

Dreaming the American Dream

Americans have been encouraged to dream; but the features of the Dream were not shaped by a groundswell of public participation. The few aristocrats above ground shaped the Dream and injected ideas of entitlement. With the promise of the benefits of liberty, the Dream became high culture at work. Some of the most formative historical statements of the American consciousness—"Give me liberty, or give me death!" and "We hold these truths to be self-evident, that all men are created equal"—were made by the European aristocracy that settled in America. Adopting the Dream meant adopting the style and values of the first high-culture American dreamers and discarding one's own values. Unfortunately, many aspects of the Dream are projections. As with all projections, the Dream is a distorted, larger than life, denial of reality.

The American Dream was raised to consciousness and interpreted within the context of the struggle for freedom. The Enlightenment brought a shift in our understanding of human agency, causing the struggle for freedom to be understood as a human responsibility. The underside of the experience was the simultaneous creation of groups that were considered less than human, and therefore "unfree," based on the establishment of race, class, and gender lines. From our separate encampments of particularity, the unfree have been battling one another to claim a piece of the projected Dream. Our competition for acquisition of the Dream has us blaming other unfree groups for our individual and group lack of liberty. The nation's history is clear: The American Dream degrades otherness and thus creates dividing lines, battle lines that determine upward mobility. Those dividing lines, which continue to be sustained institutionally, are maintained through domestic terrorism. Every unfree group in America has experienced terrorism. Night-riders, police brutality, "trees with strange fruit," trucks with bodies in tow, fire bombings of churches and federal buildings, rape, and spousal and child abuse are the terrorist activities of America in the name of freedom and the Dream.

Because we all desire freedom from the various oppressive forces in our lives, we continue to attempt to acquire the American Dream in our struggle to be free. Desiring to live unfettered by the constraints of the underprivileged, we cling to the Dream of a better tomorrow as we face the challenges of the day. Today, we dream deliverance from the instability associated with our social systems, hoping to reclaim our families, traditions, neighborhoods, and nation. We dream deliverance from insecurities that have produced our growing intolerance. And, we dream of deliverance from diminishing economic opportunities that create the perception of fewer privileges. As we dream, we wrestle with our issues of privilege and entitlement while fighting to overcome our national and international esteem problem. Whenever these issues have combined in the past, they have been negotiated through nationalism, elitism, carpetbagging, and scape-goating, or they have been covered by theater comedy.

The American Dream as Assimilation

Participation in the American Dream stresses the denial of many valued cultural identifications. Typical of the identity formation process, the American Dream exerts pressure for people to conform to the preferred norms of society. Identity not only promotes a consistent sense of self, it also reveals "a persistent sharing of some kind of essential character with others–the maintenance of an inner solidarity with a group."[8] The Dream promotes a consistent sense of the American self. Hence, the American Dream is an organizing component of the American identity.

Through a process of shunning what is different and encouraging sameness, the American Dream promotes cultural assimilation and individualism. This shunning, which is sometimes a shaming, has been perpetuated by a preexisting paternalism. Perhaps more basic is an ethnocentrism that always considers all other cultures less mature and insignificant. The American Dream is an institution of the American culture that supports a number of idolatrous belief systems that flourish by oppression. To that extent, the Dream has become bankrupt of hope for countless communities. The American Dream may be another way to articulate notions of dominance and the justification for the mass destruction of others.[9]

The New American Dream

The shunning groups largely rely on stereotypical characterizations. The groups most often shunned either refused or were denied full participation in the American Dream. This is, perhaps, the primary reason why a "New Dream" had to emerge during the 1960s. The American Dream had a visible defect whereby it offered freedom and justice to a few. Most of the American resistance cultures had (have) been relegated to an inferior position. The "New Dream," however, imagined extending equality to all peoples. Since the emergence of the "New Dream," many of the stereo-typical characterizations seem to no longer be expressed in overt ways.

Although many have assumed that the greater struggle has concluded–that the errors of the stereotyping have been corrected–the stereotyping continues in covert movements and unconscious processes. What is more, the stereotypes are not new images, but the same images that have always been ascribed. Ethnic stereotypes have incredible longevity.[10]

The New Dream emerged out of a sense of crisis in American life. As I stated earlier, a crisis is a time of extreme vulnerability, as well as a time of heightened possibility. This means our vulnerabilities push us to regress, while our possibilities promote growth. Unfortunately, a state of crisis has a strong tendency to reactivate former defense mechanisms due to the strong desire for security and stability.

A story about domestic life, although in poor taste, can be instructive on this point. It has to do with having a bad day at work and "going home to kick the dog." Whenever the United States is in crisis or experiences a bad day in the world, many label someone here at home a "dog" to be kicked. It is just easier for folks to "go home and kick the dog" than it is to find new ways to cope with life's discomforts. As we continue to negotiate with the crises of difference and indifference, will we progress to new ways of relating, or regress to previous atrocities?

Racism in America Defined

Racism is one of those former defense mechanisms to which we regress. We especially activate it in our times of crisis. Because racism expresses itself in cyclical fashion, at times it appears to be less threatening than at other times. Thus finding ourselves in a lull period, we should not assume that racism's power has been diminished by our efforts alone. Think of it this way: While a particular hurricane may cease to exist, such as hurricane Ivan that caused so much devastation, hurricanes as a force have not become extinct. During the next hurricane season, Katrina developed, as hurricanes always have, moving with destructive force even greater than Ivan and Camille and Andrew and others.

As I reflect on the collective consciousness of North Americans, based on psychological and historical factors,[11] the past atrocities of racism are, once again, becoming the present. Race issues are being substituted for human issues. Hiding behind the idea that we are no longer the racist society we once were, race issues are regarded as a card to be played when the justice chips are down. Hate groups are resurfacing and gathering support. Xenophobia has become the controlling motivation for violence in the name of justice.[12] Notwithstanding the multitude of phobias that have "blinded the eyes" of many, racism remains a significant oppressive force.

> Of all America's exclusions, none approaches in strength that of the black people by white people, the distinction of a self and an other according to the mysterious quality of race, especially as

revealed in the mark of skin color. Nothing looms quite so large, both as an endless source of crisis and as the sign of a deep cultural malaise, as does racism.[13]

Racism, as I have come to understand it, is a regenerative system of victimization that justifies, multiplies, and diversifies itself. Racism is a system that degenerates, subjugates, and annihilates the undesirable in the name of religion or some other system of human ascent. It is a destructive, life-denying system predicated on the issues of identity and survival. Racism is the oppressive force that devours the divinely created human image; therefore, racism is fundamentally a theological issue.

Racism as a Regenerative System

Racism is regenerative in nature. Just when you think it has been clearly defined, understood, and terminated, racism mutates and revives itself. The words of Koheleth provide insight into the historicity of this system.

Is there a thing of which it is said,
> "See, this is new?"
It has already been,
> in the ages before us.
 The people of long ago are not remembered,
> nor will there be any remembrance
of people yet to come
> by those who come after them. (Eccl. 1:10–11)

Although one can consider the origins of racism at a particular geographical location, the dynamics of the system of racism seem to be timeless. Racism seems to possess an existential quality. Its existence seems to be resident in human nature, in the deep recesses of the soul. It is this existential quality in combination with humanity's perpetual longing for salvation that give racism its incredible power.

Fundamental to racist expressions is the act of making value determinations about perceived or observed differences. A few of the prominent dynamics of racism are color, economics, religion, and dominance. The most popular definition of racism to be found says racism occurs when institutions encourage and empower color prejudice to exercise leverage or dominance of one race over another (color prejudice + institutional power = racism). One group considers itself to be the "superior race" and the bearer of history. It always writes the story describing all others to be inferior. It is in this way that egocentrism and racism are functionally the same. That self-declared "superior race" always understands itself to be the conquering lord and destroyer of evil. When one group understands itself to be superior, it usually declares itself to be the standard or the norm in life by way of some ultimate authority.[14] This is why religion tends to be so important to racist ideology.

Racism vs. Prejudice

People sometimes confuse racism and prejudice by purporting that anyone can be a racist. The critical concept differentiating racism from prejudice, however, is institutional power. All racial groups do not have equal access to those structures of power. Institutions are the systems that guide and maintain our social interactions. An individual may have power to make things happen, to enforce one's opinion, or to disrupt social relationships. But individual power does not compare to institutional power, neither does everyone have access to the institutions that exercise control over social relations.

Anyone can be prejudiced. Prejudice is an attitude, opinion, or feeling formed without adequate prior knowledge, thought, or reason. Prejudice can be prejudgment for or against any person, group, sex, or object. Race prejudice involves positive attitudes toward one's own race and negative attitudes toward other races. Anyone within any racial or ethnic group can be prejudiced, but not all prejudicial attitudes or statements made by any racial or ethnic group can be racist. The distinguishing element of "institutional power" is essential for describing a racist action. To this, some people want to argue that African Americans now have access to institutional power. Those arguments have tended to make individual power synonymous with institutional power largely by defining institutional power as economic. Some people have confused other forms of abuse of power, such as a supervisor's capriciousness, as institutional power and thus concluded that Blacks can be racist. "Redlining" is an example of color prejudice combined with institutional power that results in a racist action. A person may have the individual resources (i.e., the power) to move anywhere that person desires. But if there is a desire to maintain a neighborhood's ethnic composition, then the institutional powers influence the processes to enforce the prejudices as normative.

The Psychology of Oppression

The psychology of oppression is a look at the dynamic relationship within and between the oppressor and the oppressed. Like looking at the psychological factors that create and sustain the dynamics of alcoholism, the psychology of oppression describes the factors that create and sustain the dynamics of oppressors and oppressed. Oppression is a burden to all who participate,[15] and everyone is affected and/or participates at some level. The wisdom of Koheleth is particularly helpful for understanding the pain of any oppressive system: "Again I looked and saw all the oppression that was taking place under the sun: I saw the tears of the oppressed–and they have no comforter; power was on the side of their oppressors–and they have no comforter" (Eccl. 4:1, NIV). Hence, if change is to take place, it must be an affective change that involves both the oppressed and the oppressors of the racist system.

When I first began to review the dynamics of racism and the psychology of oppression, I experienced profound frustration. The dynamics seemed to be quite a vicious cycle, without any change in their course. I became overwhelmed by feelings of hopelessness that frequently tapped into a deep rage. When I shared those feelings of frustration and rage with my mentor, Arthur Pressley, he simply said, "Before you can fix it, you have to know what is broken." What I understood him to be saying to me was that I needed to experience all the complexity and pain caused by the system if I had any hope of transforming this horrific system. I had to know the pain that it has caused me as well as the pain others have experienced as a result of this system. The words of Koheleth became very helpful as I reflected on the dynamics of racism and the experience of the oppressor and the oppressed.

Although the dynamics between the oppressor and the oppressed are hierarchical, the psychology of oppression says that everyone experiences pain and suffering regardless of whether one is the oppressor on top or the oppressed on the bottom. In fact, oppressors endanger their souls with every act of dominance. They have the power "to steal, kill, and destroy," often without any greater sense of security; yet they rarely change their ways on their own accord. The experience of the White minority of the Republic of South Africa is a good example for this point. During the latter days of apartheid, the White government exercised extreme control of the lives of Black African peoples, yet they never felt safe enough to live without razor wire and bars around their homes. A contemporary voice among the Whites now says, "We had no choice but to work to end apartheid because the system was destroying us."[16] This voice recognizes that the inhumanity expressed through the continued efforts to control or destroy Black life would have resulted in the destruction of their own humanity.

Koheleth's observation indicates that both the oppressor and the oppressed experience pain and desire a comfort not readily available. The particular points of pain and suffering will differ for the oppressor and the oppressed, but the human longings remain consistent. Both sides try to understand their condition in the face of the other. Interestingly enough, both sides will often present themselves to be the standard bearers of ultimate truth, claiming God as their help. While both groups need to be changed, the tendency is to place the burden of transformation on the oppressed.

People tend to encourage the oppressed to educate the oppressor into change. The lesson is a simple one: relinquish the power. This well-known lesson has caused many to walk away sorrowfully and continue to oppress. The more common disposition, however, is the idea of the redemptive suffering of the oppressed for the benefit of the oppressor. Yet if the suffering of the oppressed is to be redemptive, it must redeem the oppressed, not the oppressor. Hence, my primary concern is the oppression African Americans have experienced and how we might bring our suffering to an end.

Racism as a Historical Phenomenon

As I consider in more detail the psychic and historical factors that have established racism in America, the words of Sidney Mead are instructive:

> From a historical perspective, an individual is an animated focal point of traits resident in a community that transcends him in both space and time…This suggests that if we are to understand an individual's unique personhood, it is necessary to study the complex of traits that make up his community. As the ancient wisdom would have it, "you who pursue deliverance" must "look to the rock from that you were hewn, and to the quarry from that you were digged."[17]

We are constantly being presented with history as "the facts," unmingled and unadulterated. The presentation of "the facts," however, is not always the truth. The compilation of the facts precedes the narrative presentation of history.. The selection of facts is always a search based on a particular perspective or predisposition. Then comes a process of interpreting the selected information and organizing the material into a case to be understood as "the way it was." This understanding of history as narrative raises the question, "What is the 'real' story (history) in the United States as it relates to why race has been such a prominent issue of American consciousness?"

Because racism is a very integrated part of the fabric of this country, as seen through the historical events of slavery, Reconstruction, Jim and Jane Crow segregation, and resistance to integration, the nation's basic assumptions must be critically reviewed. The first assumption, perhaps, is whether or not the United States of America is a "Christian" nation, and whether it has been founded on Christian principles? The extent to which racism is such a prominent feature of the United States, the questions could also be raised, "Is Christianity a racist religion?"[18] The ideal of a Christian nation implies a theocracy, but that is not what is being communicated when people speak of the United States as a Christian nation. More accurately, America functions as a nation-state based upon civil religion:

> America [is a] nation with the soul of a church…assum[ing] its own form of Christianity, fusing "the spiritual tradition of the new and secular nation with the spiritual tradition of the old Christian society. Thus the essentially spiritual society of the nation was in effect Christianized by partially digesting into its spiritual core a particularized version of Christianity."…Nonconformists came to America and had "their view incarnated in the constitution and legal structure of the United States…[t]he course of [American] history exhibits the slow, strong power of high generalities get[ting] incarnated in actuality, and our institutions are primarily

incarnations of the constellations of myths and ideas that dominated the thinking of the eighteenth century in which the nation was born."[19]

The nation-state, as such, made it easy for Christian truths to be subverted by an American civil religion[20] that was motivated by dominance and supportive of racism.

Is racism a central character trait of the collective American consciousness? The history of racist activity and ideology in the United States. is clear, but the issue of whether or not this behavior is a character trait is another matter. The history of legislation, both state and federal, is clear evidence of racist activity and ideology. The mere fact a prejudicial attitude can be institutionalized through legislation reveals the racist character at work. And even if it is an unjust law, large numbers of people will conform and follow that law. Furthermore, in the absence of a law to support a prejudicial position, laws will be sought or created. This point is also what makes religion such an important feature of racism, because the laws are identified with the laws of creation, the laws of God, and the God-given power to have dominion. Claiming God's created order and natural law is important to racist ideology. Whereas important government legislation on racial separation has changed, the vocalized attitudes have remained the same due to the prejudices that produced the laws. This is perhaps why it has been virtually impossible to uproot racism from American soil.

Christianity vs. Racism

Although many of the colonists professed Christianity, something within the psyche does not respond affirmatively to a Christian gospel of love for otherness. For this reason, George Kelsey[21] in *Racism and the Christian Understanding of Man* considered racism and Christianity to be incompatible. Racism, in Kelsey's framework, is an idolatrous faith—a religion that establishes one's human existence as god. For racists, God is not the supreme being whom they worship; instead, they worship the race itself as a god. Reverence and praise are given to one's own image in the name of worshiping God, in whose image all humanity has been created. If we see America functioning as a nation-state, we can easily see how its interpretation of Christian theology has often masked racist ideologies. Racist ideology masquerading as Christian theology is what allows racists to see themselves as "good Christians." For instance, one of the basic tenets for membership in the Ku Klux Klan is to be a Christian.

The Economics of Racism

When the colonials landed on these shores, indentured servants included both Black and White. We tend to overlook the fact that the indentured system is a type of slavery. Black and White together were enslaved when the nation was taking shape. A closer examination, however, reveals that the White servants' terms of indenture were often shorter, and their treatment more humane than their Black counterparts experienced. The difference in treatment and contract reveals that something was operating in addition to economic gain. Racial consciousness as an emergent feature of the American identity is why the indentured servitude slavery system ended for Whites. The decline of the indentured system stood in contrast to the developmental increase of the chattel slavery of Blacks.[22] I am convinced that the racial forces that encouraged the movement from indentured servitude to chattel slavery precedes 1550, when "black cargo" became a commodity for the English. The racialized inequities of the indentured system reveal the early colonial attitude of Africans not being considered fully human, which later transposed into Africans not being considered human at all.

The transition from indentured to chattel slavery is extremely important because many tend to reduce racism to a matter of economics. But if it was mere economics, why did the chattel system exclude Whites? Unfortunately, the major part of the answer is "all too clear." It was far easier to identify an escaped African as a slave than it was an escaped European as a slave. One could claim that that fact supports the economic argument. If all the slaves were White, they could have lost money through constant escape. Yet if you change contexts, other cultures in other parts of the world, where the people have been more homogeneous, have maintained slave systems. More important in the American context was the fact that the indentured Whites were too close in status, background, and appearance to those holding the papers of the indentured. Whites torturing Whites in America was too much like the masochistic torturing of the self and blasphemy against the god of race.

Economics, by way of the development of capitalism, did influence racist ideology, but economics represents an *influence,* not the *source* of racism. Cornel West in his book *Prophesy Deliverance* and James Comer in his article "White Racism: Its Root, Form, and Function"[23] both see racism in North America as the outgrowth of the social conditions of sixteenth-century Europe. Those social conditions influenced, and at times mediated, the European's encounter with Africa. West declares that capitalism is involved in, and is even a significant feature of, expressions of racism in America; but he is critical of the people who tend to focus upon economics and capitalism as the root of racism.

An understanding of racism solely based upon economics fails to take into account the xenophobia central to racism. Capitalism was one of England's prime motivations for the slave trade, but still West's historical overview of racism posits racism's foundational events and attitudes in the period that preceded the Reformation (1520s). The conditions of this period are significant because they have been identified as the primary catalyst for the formation of the capitalist system. According to West, although the category of "race" is a seventeenth-century phenomenon, racist ideology in the forms of myth, folktale, legend, and story predate the seventeenth-century. The clearest conceptualization of racism for West is twofold: culture and economics.

Comer's understanding of the formation of racism in the British (and subsequently the American) mind did not begin at the first encounter with the dark skin of the African. Anti-blackness ideologies were prevalent in English religion long before the initiation of the slave trade. Without a doubt, many pre-American ideas and beliefs supported the racist ideology that developed in the colonies. Like West, Comer believes that the origins of racism preceded the Protestant Reformation. He grounds this in a precondition of exploitation to achieve economic, social, and psychological security. He believes that "prior to the Protestant Reformation,…every race of [humanity] was subject to slavery, and the enslavement of women for sexual exploitation is as old as the institution of slavery itself."[24] What the Reformation did, in Comer's estimation, was to redefine humanity and thus to make it necessary to designate slaves as less than human.

Reviewing the historical development of racism psychologically, Comer notes that the earliest activities of the Atlantic slave trade revealed that "they supposed no natural inferiority in Africans, no inherent failure to develop and mature."[25] He, therefore, places considerable responsibility upon religion for fostering racism. Although I agree with Comer's assessment of the influence of religion on the development of racism, I disagree with his supporting assessment that Africans were not initially perceived as inferior. The European travelers of the fifteenth and sixteenth centuries described Africans in every foul way imaginable. Those chronicles became the sources for racist ideology:

> Richard Hakluyt was the foremost English chronicler…[whose] portrayals of Africans became an ideational standard by which the English generally viewed and judged black people. As the historian Winthrop D. Jordan writes, the English people "from the first [began] to set Negroes over against themselves, to stress what they conceived to be radically contrasting qualities of color, religion, and style of life, as well as animality and a peculiarly potent sexuality." Puritan minds latched onto these racist ideas of blacks as innately different from and less than white people.[26]

Comer attributes the perpetuation of racism to the psychic and social conditions that forced conformity upon the enslaved Africans. Furthermore, he identifies projection as a significant function of racism. Projection is an unconscious psychological process whereby the negative aspects of an individual are not accepted as a part of the individual self, but rather those aspects are "projected" or cast onto another as though the problem is the other person's negative attribute. The other person becomes a screen to express the unconscious negative aspects. The evil associated with dark skin has been projected upon Africans. Comer concludes that racism is always psychological in origin and is culturally transmitted through social interchange.

Racism as a Theological Issue

Popular opinion today frequently sees sexism and homophobia as more deeply theological issues for the Church than racism. I have even heard people go as far as to say, "Racism is not a theological issue." As astounding a statement as this might be for some, this statement reflects a popular church culture reality being fed by a societal mass culture reality that presents racism as an American "ism" of the past. To regard racism as a nontheological issue is to deny its influence as an oppressive force within the Church and America. Furthermore, to say that racism is not a theological issue is to disregard completely the rise of racist ideology within American culture. When people think racism is not a theological issue, perhaps they are simply toeing the mass culture party line of identifying racism as an economic issue or, like Comer, they are declaring racism a psychological issue. To allow such an opinion to stand unchallenged within popular church culture would be a blatant disregard of the ongoing African American human dignity struggle. Racism is the oppressive force that devours the human image; therefore, racism is fundamentally a theological issue. The preservation of African humanity has been the premier struggle of the African American community, and the preservation of humanity is always a theological issue.

Racism and Nationalism

Like all oppressions, racism can take many forms. If one reviews the development of this country in terms of developmental stages of life, racism was shaped and reshaped by every issue and incident that formed the American identity. As the nation struggled to assert an identity that differed from England, the requirements for citizenship became more stringent. The African presence was described in a way that kept them from experiencing the vitality of the new American identity:

> Racism, though partly an expression of the universal political exclusion of slaves, was also a reflection of its particular historical context in the modern nation-state. It is worth remembering that southern slaveholders not only played a leading role in the first great nationalist revolution that created the U.S., but that the American Revolution was also a major turning point in the development of scientific racism. The connection was not simply fortuitous, and Benedict Anderson's important distinction between racism and nationalism suggests why it was not. Nationalism is a

language of inclusion within what Anderson calls the "imagined community" that constitutes the nation. By contrast racism is a language of exclusion that "erases nation-ness by reducing the adversary to his[her] biological physiognomy." Thus it is not entirely surprising that the birth of the "first new nation" was accompanied by the disturbing articulation of a racist ideology. For the emergence of nationalism generated novel pressures to re-affirm the slave's place outside the "imagined community" of the modern American nation.[27]

Even as nationalism is the language of inclusion, it simultaneously promotes exclusion. In the case of the United States,, racism has been a consistent exclusionary force. The rhetoric of the contemporary "Christian nationalist"– a pseudonym for "a racist"–therefore, builds a community based on exclusion. From a historical view, this is clearly "nothing new." With this, I question whether we are less racist as a society, or, has racism adapted with the developmental processes?

Race as a Modern Construct

While racism is theological, psychological, and cultural, it is also important to recognize that the term "race" is a relatively new sociopolitical construct. As such, race and racism are products of "modern" Western society. It was not until 1570 that race developed as a concept. Francois Bernier first employed the category of "race," primarily denoting skin color, in 1684 for the purpose of classifying human bodies. The first authoritative racial division of humanity is found in the works of naturalist Carolus Linnaeus in 1735.[28] Hence, it was not until the eighteenth century that political, linguistic, and geographical distinctions became "race" issues. Theories such as the "Great Chain of Being" emerged, a hierarchy to creation. Such a hierarchy was conceived as a vertical chain with its links representing the various levels of creation. These vertical links, therefore, located some people as higher up and closer to God than others.

The American Dream, Thomas Jefferson, and Sally Hemings

I have been reflecting on many different ideas in an effort to deconstruct race and racism. I have presented racism as having many component parts that require a thick analysis. I have identified culture, history, economics, psychology, theology, and nation-state as vital categories setting the destructive power of racism. As I further deconstruct racism's role in the formation of identity, I return to the symbolism of the American Dream.

Historically, the American Dream projected America as the new Israel– the land where God would fulfill the covenant. Like the Hebrews subduing the inhabitants of the land of Canaan, the new Americans believed themselves to be participating in the work of the Divine. This belief persisted through the colonial and antebellum periods into frontier expansion and beyond.[29]

To better understand the metaphor of American Dream as a vision of hope and despair, consider the elusive nature of dreams from a psychological perspective. A "dream is a fragment of involuntary psychic activity, just conscious enough to be reproducible in the waking state."[30] And "even though dreams refer to a definite attitude of consciousness and a definite psychic situation, their roots lie deep in the unfathomable recesses of the unconscious."[31] Because dreams originate in the unconscious, the dream as remembered has a hidden meaning. This means the specifics of the dream may be a long way from the actual point of the dream.

Another way of looking at dreams is from the perspective of a guiding myth. A "guiding myth," like a guiding light, is a story that provides meaning to one's life circumstances and a framework for understanding and proceeding within a given context. A myth states some truth about the nature of human existence and provides the confidence for endurance. Here is how this point relates to dreams. Dreams are the guidance system of the psyche, and the American Dream is the guidance system of the collective American consciousness. Yet the American Dream, as a dream remembered, is filled with hidden meaning from the unconscious. Furthermore, if our unconscious dream life, heavily influenced by our conscious realities, perceives a sense of meaninglessness, then our existence becomes a tumultuous and frantic push to acquire meaning and stability. That push might begin to express negativity out of a sense of fear related to the future. Another possibility is to misinterpret the dream content in a wishful way.

One of the early dreamers of the American Dream was Thomas Jefferson. A closer look at his life reveals how the Dream has provided hope for some and a nightmare for others. Mass culture's reverence for Jefferson also reveals how America has accommodated racist actions for the sake of upholding a glorious American Dream. The subtext is to say that we uphold Jefferson's virtues as the nation's efforts to live its best intentions. But by only focusing on what we want to accentuate as the good, we regularly overlook those who have suffered and continue to suffer.

Ask Sally Hemings, Jefferson's enslaved mistress of African descent, how she was able to participate in the American Dream beneath Jefferson's roof. Ask her what she was entitled to according to *Master* Jefferson. According to his declarative presentation, she was entitled to liberty. But she never saw her freedom. On what grounds could he declare independence and enslavement at the same time? How could the inequitable ground upon which he stood be considered sacred and moral ground? Even today, what is Sally Hemings entitled to? The descendants of Tom and Sally are fighting to be recognized by the Jefferson family. Are the contemporary questions of paternity raised by her descendants about economic inheritance, or are they about the importance of family history and human dignity? A legal brief prepared in April 2000 by an attorney in Virginia concludes that the "Tom and Sally myth...is a tale that should return to its status as no more than a footnote to the Jefferson legacy."[32] *A footnote to the Jefferson legacy?...*what about the Hemings legacy?!?! What truths do we really hold to be self-evident? The Tom and Sally story, with all its race and gender implications, reveals the American inclination to preserve a heritage that does not include African Americans. We regularly cover this fact by our public praise of the biracial superstars of the entertainment world. But if those expressions were truly examples of America's intentions of the Dream being fulfilled for all, the Jefferson-Hemings legacy would have been embraced. Furthermore, Sally Hemings was never emancipated by Jefferson. She died as his enslaved mistress. And as a footnote to his life, we keep her in a separate, non-American grave.

Jefferson's Faith and the American Dream

I stated earlier that racist ideology often wears a Christian theology mask. As this relates to Jefferson and religious principles embodied in the Dream, Jefferson was a deist. Although reports do not indicate he was anti-Christian, he laid the foundations of this country as a deist. His faith stance also did not exempt him from the degradation espoused by the Enlightenment. His double standard of living was illustrative of the new nation-state. While he supposedly endeavored to eliminate slavery, he simultaneously supported slavery (by his relationship with Sally Hemings) and racist ideology. He made statements that justified the system, and his opinions are still present today:

> Thomas Jefferson reveals the depth of racism in the American South, not because he was an extremist but, on the contrary, because he was so moderate. He thought slavery an evil and he held blacks and whites equal in certain qualities of heart that he viewed as essential to a virtuous republic. It is in the light of such moderation that Jefferson's racism seems all the more significant. The difference between blacks and whites "is fixed in nature," he explained, "and is as real as if its seat and cause were better known to us."...Jefferson detected in blacks a "very strong and disagreeable odor," a greater tolerance for heat, and less need for sleep than was true for whites...Blacks were as brave as whites, but more reckless; they were more emotional, but their "griefs are transient" and "their existence appears to participate more of sensation than reflection." In memory, Jefferson wrote, blacks "are equal to the whites; in reason much inferior." Hence black intellectual and artistic achievements were "destitute of merit." Whatever the origins of this "distinct race," he concluded, blacks were "inferior to the whites in the endowments of both body and mind," and this

"unfortunate difference of color, and perhaps of faculty, is a powerful obstacle to the emancipation of these people."[33]

Racism and the Bible

The eighteenth century was not only the time when scientific justifications for racism emerged, it was also a time for extreme biblical "proof-texting" to affirm white supremacy. This era promoted in-group and out-group dichotomies. As the age of reason, the eighteenth century and the Enlightenment promoted a move from superstition and being controlled by the elements to a position of "dominion" and superior control. To accomplish that task, the scientific and philosophical thinkers set about determining that white was normative and that white social structures and traditions were far superior to others. This was done through studies of the slopes of the cranium, the conclusion that Adam was white, and even the removal of Egypt out of Africa (the idea that Egypt was not an African nation on the African continent).[34] Christian preachers were famous for preaching the texts, "slaves obey your masters" and the curse of Ham (Canaan). By the turn of the twentieth century, these ideologies were an integral part of the American psyche and were promoted by the educational system.

Racism is systemic and systematic. Racism's fire has not died. Current acts of racism are not race issues being rekindled in the way people wanted to declare that the verdict in the O. J. Simpson criminal case has opened old wounds. Our national response to the verdict only revealed what was present but not acknowledged. The destructive fire was simply burning more brightly from the smoldering coals. When an oppressed person is compliant, servile, and denied opportunities for advancement, the oppressor is expressing hatred through condescension. The oppressors' perceived loss of dominance over the persons who have been objectified and degraded exposes the deep hatred. Although hate groups are always attacking the oppressed, the assaults are the most heinous when attacks are made against an entire racial-ethnic group:

> Racism...is a plan of political action. "It is the dogma that the hope of civilization depends upon eliminating some races and keeping others pure." The elimination of some races has not, for the most part, been carried to its logical limit in Western history. The reduction of life by means of deprivation has usually been a substitute for the elimination of races. Accordingly, the chief political plan of the racists has been segregation, involving as it does, subordination, suppression, isolation, and deprivation. But despite the prevailing practice of segregation, the logic of racism is genocide. The logic of racism is genocide because that which is wrong with an out-race is its fundamental being. The alleged evil in an out-race does not lie in historical functions, events, and

relationships. It lies in the human nature of the out-race. For the racist, an out-race is not fundamentally a sociological problem; an out-race is a problem in the order of human being. It is a sociological problem only for the deeper reason that it is a human problem. The segregation and subordination of a people because they are defective in being as such is obviously an inadequate handling of the situation. The problem of defective humanity cannot be resolved by segregation and quarantine; it requires the final solution. The final solution is extermination.[35]

Evidences of the racist political plan of action in the United States have been noted from time to time over the course of history:

The issue of white racism was forced into the open in 1968 by the National Advisory Commission on Civil Disorder, popularly known as the Kerner Commission…The commission reported that the major cause of urban unrest was racism in the white society…these few sentences caused a furor among white Americans: "What white Americans have never fully understood—but what the Negro can never forget—is that the white society is deeply implicated in the ghetto. White institutions created it, white institutions maintain it and white society condones it. White racism is essentially responsible for the explosive mixture that has accumulated in our cities since the end of World War II."[36]

Racism in Theological and Psychological Perspective

Historian Winthrop Jordan's approach to the history of racism in the United States considers identity to be one of the central issues. I take that one step further and say that racism is a "soul" problem and that identity is its leading feature. As a theological and psychological construct, the soul is humanity's connection with the Divine, with the infinite. The soul is not bound by time and space in the same way that the conscious mind is bound. The soul is the source of ultimate truth. From its core, we experience life's deepest pains and highest raptures.

My Christian theological understanding of soul originates in the book of "Beginning"—in Genesis. There one finds that God was in the beginning, before anything was made. In a process of bringing forth order from chaos, God formed humanity from dust in God's "image and likeness." Yet after human beings were formed, the form was lifeless. Modifying the biblical imagery, it was not until God shared the "breath of life" that human beings became animated, "living souls." The human form became vital because of the internal presence of the wind of God. From the psychological perspective, psychologists tend to be more inclined to the Hellenistic approach, using the term "psyche." Although their understanding does not necessarily exclude the Hebraic understanding, psyche tends to be a transcendent reality, energized by an internal force, that makes humanity "who and what" it is and ought to become. Jung saw soul as synonymous with psyche and believed that the psyche is actually the "Imago Dei." Therefore, his psychological view saw the soul as permanently connected to God who has been from the beginning. African (Black) psychologists believe that human beings are spiritual beings and that the work of psychology is to participate in the discovery of our humanity as embodied spirits.

As stated earlier in this chapter, race is a modern construct. It was developed as a way of separating and controlling human interactions. Before suggesting another way of conceptualizing racism, I restate the common mathematical definition for racism, which is: color prejudice + institutional power = racism. Now I would like to offer a different equation, *race = racism.* I know this equation looks a little odd, but I believe it to be an accurate one. The construct of race produces and maintains the oppression of racism. As a construct, race is a category of language development. One might choose to argue that racial consciousness was present even in the Hebrew Bible and conclude that racism is from the beginning of time. The book of Genesis tells us that Adam gave a name to everything that he saw, so the construct of race is the result of humanity naming and labeling human beings. Early biblical distinctions and classifications of people, however, were tribal distinctions, not racial. Race is not the same as tribe. The act of distinguishing and differentiating human beings based upon physical characteristics automatically produces hierarchical understandings of human life. The creation of race, therefore, is the creation of racism.

I subscribe to Kelsey's conceptualization that asserts racism as an idolatrous faith.[37] The race itself is what becomes the idol. This form of idolatry can be subtle: most racists do not regard their behavior as race worship. But they have associated race so closely with God that they have made the race into a god. This means they no longer understand themselves to be created in the image of God but begin to see themselves *as* god. As they look up and describe God, their description reveals their mirror reflection. So their gaze is not upon God but upon their own image that has become the substitute for God. The contours and color of their faces have become the graven image of god in human flesh. Theological reflection for racists is reflection on their own history and development.

Although they have made themselves god, they do not declare themselves to be god. Instead, racists declare that God has foreordained that they are the supreme beings in the world and others should bow to their sovereignty. Following the creation story, they declare that God has made their race to be the only human beings and given them dominion over creation with orders to subdue the land. They also believe themselves to be responsible for maintaining the created order. Because they believe themselves to be the only true human beings, all others are the animals of their domain.

Racists have objectified Africans and reduced them to animals or to some variety of subhuman beings. Many outlandish historical statements identify Africans as apes and/or as copulating with apes. Enslaved Africans were considered chattel, 3/5 of a human being. We have always been considered genetically inferior.[38] Racists, therefore, believe it is their right and responsibility to control others whom they, like Adam, have named and identified as animals.

Upon closer examination, racists' habit of thinking of themselves as the only human beings reveals the human tendency to attempt to control nature for the sake of safety. Clearly, safety and survival have always been important human issues. Humanity, in some ways, has always seen itself as frail and vulnerable, as a finite being. In that self-assessment, animals have frequently been both feared and admired for possessing power we perceive to be greater than our own human strength. This has resulted in many actions to gain control over nature and the animals. A variety of rituals were developed to control nature and to acquire nature's and the animals' power. Human beings have a long history of attempting to acquire the power of an animal by sacrificing and/or ingesting the animal.

Humanity has frequently exhibited a thirst for power in its attempts to exercise dominion over creation. Some theorists have suggested that as alternative forms of power developed, humanity began to dissociate from the animals as the desired power and became the vengeful hunter to establish superiority. The racist has continued to live out this transitional phase. The racist maintains this legacy through objectifying others. Racists identify other people as animals to be hunted and killed as a statement of dominance and superiority. This has included the practice of sacrificing those persons identified as animals.[39] Such acts have given racists a sense of power and security. They do not eat the flesh of those persons they have identified as animals, but they have feasted their eyes upon bludgeoned and burning bodies. Their rituals of sacrifice have included shootings, lynchings,[40] rapes, and burnings.

I also think racism can be understood as expressions of primary narcissism and/or the narcissistic personality disorder. Conceptualizing racism as a neurosis or psychosis suggests approaches for reforming this evil system. Narcissism is most fundamentally defined as self-love. But according to Christopher Lasch, who interpreted American culture as narcissistic, narcissism is closer to self-hate than it is to "self-love."[41] This means that the person—being unable to accept all parts of the self and the responsibilities for decisions with unwanted consequences—engages in the unconscious process of reaction formation. Rather than hating the self, the person expresses the opposite and loves the self and hates the other. Racists have an inability to acknowledge what they hate about themselves, so they project hate onto others in the name of love for their own race (or self-love), which is characteristic of the narcissistic personality disorder.

Therefore, the racist engages in a racial group self-love motivated by a reluctance to reject self.

Racists are narcissistic not simply because their primary concern is themselves. They are narcissistic because they cannot understand the pain they inflict upon others. A normal aspect of primary narcissism is to see oneself as the center of the universe with everything revolving around that self. The only feelings and needs that matter are those of the self. As one grows, the realization comes that the self is a "part of" rather than the "center of" the universe. Racists, however, never grow beyond the point of seeing themselves as the center of the universe. This self-centeredness prevents them from seeing anything they do as wrong. Because they are the center, they cannot understand why their actions would offend anyone. Their self-centeredness also means that they are the only ones with feelings. This attitude contributes to the racist practice of reducing other human beings to a subhuman status. Nonhumans, they reason, do not experience emotional pain; and even if they do, it is not really important.

Another force closely related to racism is genocide. Genocide is the total annihilation of a people or a culture. Indeed, if you destroy a culture, you have destroyed a people. A people whose culture has been destroyed may still be declared alive as animated beings, yet without that sociohistorical, relational sense of self expressed through culture, they are dead to the world. We must recognize genocide as a critical feature of racism. Culture, as the life-force of a people, really cannot be controlled. Racist ideology demands that those things that cannot be controlled must be destroyed. Racism destroys life by destroying the value inherent in people. We can see this most clearly when rape is a strategy of war. In those instances, rape is a direct attack against the heart of the people. Destroy the relational fabric of a culture, and the culture will die. As racists declare themselves god, they simultaneously declare that others have no part with god. The only life that they will allow is the life that they attribute to their own being.

The Black Family, Black Religion, and the Legacy of Racism

Throughout the history of Africans in America, racists have placed the systems of the black family and religion––two vital systems of African American identity formation–under constant attack. The attacks have critiqued the functionality of the African American family and religion without considering their genesis. But then again, the idea has been the destruction of the vitality of life. Slavocracy promoted separation from family, history, and our indigenous religions to promote another's identity, economic growth, and personal security. Clinging to life against all odds, African American spirituality became the rich soil for forming a "new creation" with integrity, whose identity was firmly rooted in family, religion, and spirituality. African Americans have endured the hardships of life in America because of the integrity of identity derived from a vital soul. The reality derived from that vital soul was a survivalist religion with a spirituality of hopefulness, personhood, and community. That is the historical backdrop of the African American identity. Jung believed that each generation carries the collective memories of the previous cultural generations. Therefore, the African American has a psychic legacy of heinous oppression that extends back more than five hundred years.

The damage that has resulted from color prejudice is significant. I recall teaching a church school class on the development of African American Christianity at an all-White church in rural central Pennsylvania. During the course of discussion, I located the garden of Eden on a map of Africa, thus declaring the story of creation to be an African story. One woman responded, "I am a nurse, and I have never seen a Black baby born to two White parents." The color prejudice that is so much a part of racism so affected this woman that she could not accept that idea that her Christian faith was based on a Black African religious tradition. For her, the first people created by God in Africa were White. It did not matter to her that the only White persons who self-identify as Africans are those who emigrated to there from European nations. I will probe the issues of color in greater depth in chapter 4. For now, I will only say that the evil and inadequacies that have been attributed to blackness are pervasive.

The Bible has been used to support these negative notions of color, yet rarely has the Bible been used to counter those notions with the same zeal. As an example of a possible counter, most people agree that dark soil is rich in nutrients for growing plants. Topsoil is black soil. So if the garden of Eden was as lush as many believe, that soil must have been very rich. Humanity was made from the same black soil in the garden. The story also communicates that the beings formed from that dark soil were good (perfect). This interpretation seems far more reasonable than many of the "scientific" studies used to justify chattel slavery.

Regarding the economics of racism, a look at slavery demographically could easily lead one to conclude that slavery, and subsequently racism, was basically an economic phenomenon. The cost for skilled laborers was low compared to the cost of goods. Profits were very high because production costs were so low. The supply and demand of commodities sold in Europe matched quantitatively the supply and demand of the "black cargo" sold in the Americas. The trade was nurtured by greed and prospered by exploitation. One can learn a great deal by analyzing slavery from an economic perspective; however, an economic analysis does not go far enough. For instance, Haiti was a leading producer of sugar prior to the revolution and independence of the African Haitians. The sugar did not stop growing once independence came, nor did it cease to be a valuable commodity. Yet Haiti ceased to be a leading producer of the world's sugar. They still had the technology for growing and processing the sugar, but they were denied access to the market. The enslaved Africans of Haiti had won their independence. Why was their sugar after independence less valuable? Did the demand for sugar end? Because of the xenophobia in the eyes of a world economy, the new Haitians were not appropriate business associates. Economics may be able to explain some aspects of the evil of racism, but economics certainly does not explain everything. It does not address what is wrong with the human soul.

To the extent that religion structures the world for safety, racism is a religion. Because it often travels in a Christian disguise, racism uses many biblical texts to justify its existence. The curse of Ham is still among racists' favorite texts. A close examination of this text, however, will reveal the inappropriate usage of the text. They read that Ham's punishment and curse for seeing the nakedness of his father was black skin and eternal servitude. A closer reading of the text reveals the meaning and value of the text.

First, the curse was pronounced against Ham's son Canaan, not Ham himself, and says nothing about skin color. Second, and most important, the curse was pronounced by Noah, not God, so it was not an everlasting valid curse. Yet the narrative does contain a truth. Just as Noah felt it necessary to attack another as a result of his own shame and embarrassment from his drunkenness, racists also feel exposed, vulnerable, and embarrassed. They cover such embarrassment with aggression. The wine for the racist has been economic prosperity accompanied by the sobriety of poverty that either exposes or compensates for inferiority. Their "hangover" might also expose their sense of mortality, which they address through the primitive practice of human sacrifice–take a life to preserve one's own life. Whatever the case may be, in their perverted efforts to preserve their identities, they found it necessary to destroy the identities of Africans and African Americans. The continuous attack on the African being makes the race issue a central influence in the development of the African American cultural identity. Reminders of our skin color are constant, influencing our social intercourse. Racism is a dynamic life-denying system with many component parts. In the chapters that follow I will continue to consider the many component parts that constitute racism. Along the way, I will consider the influence of gender oppression. Both race and gender have been significant in the shaping of African American identity.

4

The Color of "the Self"

After about 1680, taking the colonies as a whole, a new term of (European settlers) self-identification appeared—white...In the United States, the racial category of "black" evolved with the consolidation of racial slavery. By the end of the seventeenth century, Africans whose specific identity was Ibo, Yoruba, Fulani, etc., were rendered "black" by an ideology of exploitation based on racial logic—the establishment and maintenance of a "color line."

MICHAEL OMI AND HOWARD WINANT

Among the many influences that have contributed to African American identity formation, the issue of skin color has been extremely significant. The contrasting shades of black and white have been, and continue to be, used to illustrate positive and negative attitudes and actions. For instance, angels are white; and demons are black. A southern idiom to "do it white," means to do it right. If a child has done something wrong, the idiom for punishment is to "beat the *tar* out" of the offender. People distinguish lies on a scale with "white lies" being the most harmless and innocent. Beyond these illustrations, the contrasting colors of black and white have been adopted and internalized by all Americans to some degree. These contrasts express a perspective on the nature of reality extending from the sacred to the profane.

The Color of the Enemy

Americans who frequently declare themselves nonracist are very fond of saying, "I don't see color, I see people." As much as Americans would like to believe we are a classless society moving toward color-blindness, Americans are very color conscious. I believe American society's color consciousness is due to the deep imprint of racism on the American psyche.

Color prejudice, which is deeply implicated by English religion's anti-blackness, is at the heart of the American approach to life. From our earliest existence on these shores to the present, we have emphasized a colorized relational struggle between good and evil. This struggle has been epitomized by our "hero and villain; cowboy and Indian; white hat, black hat" culture. We have always wanted to see ourselves as the "triumphant underdog" on the side of God and right. From this, many Americans have always declared that God and right are always White.

The process of identity formation is very quick to determine who one is like and who one is not like. Different attributes of the self are identified for the purpose of locating the self in the world. We cling to those we are like and scream at those we are not like. For the purpose of our safety, we never willingly choose to socially locate ourselves in an undesirable position. We always prefer to see ourselves above the problem. To avoid a demeaning social status, we spend a great deal of time and energy declaring that we are not like those who represent the most degraded population of the society. And no matter how low in status we find ourselves, we always identify someone as lower whom we believe ourselves to be better than. Often that degraded population has been identified as the enemy; and the enemy is always associated with evil and represented by a color.

Theologically, as well as psychologically, this has established an interesting phenomenon. Within the psychology of oppression, good and evil tend to functionally represent the oppressor and oppressed. Because good and evil are most often thought of as value-laden religious terms, they tend to be descriptive of our understanding of the cosmic struggle of God. The theological term used to describe this struggle is "theodicy," that is, the questions asked regarding God's goodness and sovereignty in the presence of evil. The evaluation of good and evil related to the categories of oppressor and oppressed suggests that the description of each changes according to the social location from which one speaks.

Constructing Good and Evil

Like race, good and evil are constructs. Since they are constructs, they, too, have been defined according to human observation and subjectivity. As a result, descriptions of evil can often be understood to be a construct to explain the human condition. Such descriptions attempt to locate the origins of certain types of suffering. Because a prominent understanding of God is as a loving parent who only desires good for us, our descriptions of evil are our attempts to locate the horrors and pains of life as originating somewhere other than with a benevolent and merciful God. Furthermore, we also do not like the idea that our own suffering is the result of our own actions. Jung believed, principally, the only thing wrong with the world is humanity. But who among us is ready and willing to accept that idea? In short, evil is an instrumental construct, an idea in the service of humanity, formulated under a value or judgment system to explain the origins of our pain and suffering.

While we prefer to see evil as an external, the construct of good tends to be seen as an internal reality, or it is seen as the prime attribute of God that evil or the "evil one" struggles to corrupt. Regarding good as an internal means that when a person perceives a threat, that which threatens is often labeled evil and must be conquered by good. Consequently, to take part with evil is to participate in one's destruction. And since evil is all around us, we are constantly being oppressed by evil. Yet with good so closely identified with God, one's defense becomes a stance for eternal goodness on the human level; and on the cosmic level, evil must be obliterated! Hence, fighting for good means oppressing or destroying that which has been perceived as evil. Since evil seems to be an unending phenomenon plaguing our human existence, a person is always the oppressor of evil and oppressed by its presence. This is, perhaps, why the apostle Paul wrote in his letter to the Romans that when he would do good, evil was always present and pressing (Rom. 7).

Color Prejudice

In his book *Before Color Prejudice*, Frank Snowden searched antiquity to assess the oppressive influences of the colors white and black. His basic thesis was that nature, itself, encourages and perpetuates the positive and negative aspects of these colors. He concluded, however, that black was most often associated with negativity, evil, and death:

> Among the Greeks and Romans, white was generally associated with light, the day, with Olympus and victims sacrificed to the higher gods, with good character and good omens; black with night and darkness, with the Underworld, death, and chthonian deities, with bad character and ill omens. In this the Greeks and Romans resembled people in general who, according to research on color symbolism, have a basic tendency to equate blackness with evil and white with goodness. Recent studies point out that there seems to be a "widespread commonality in feelings about black and white," that among both Negroes and whites the color white tends to evoke a positive and black a negative reaction, and that both colors figure prominently in the areas of human experience concerned with religion and the supernatural. C. N. Degler's observations on this subject underline the similarities between ancient and modern reactions to color: "It is surely more than a coincidence that in Africa and Asia as well as in Europe, black is associated with unpleasantness, disaster, or evil. Black undoubtedly evokes recollections of the night–that time when men, with their heavy dependence upon sight, are most helpless and in greatest danger.

White, on the other hand, is the color of light, which emanates principally from the sun, which in turn is the source of warmth and the other conditions that support life. Is it any wonder that white is seen everywhere as the symbol of success, virtue, purity, goodness, whereas black is associated with evil, dirt, fear, disaster, and sin?"[1]

Due to the impact of our positive and negative associations with the contrasting colors of black and white, the color prejudice surrounding us has shaped our perceptions of God, others, and ourselves. The valuation of the contrasting colors of black and white, which have come to represent the eternal struggle of good and evil, has been ascribed to skin color and the citizens of America. This has resulted in the application of dualism to the human creature. Color prejudice, combined with dualism, maintains a constant human struggle of oppressor and oppressed. White and White people have been equated with good; and conversely black and Black people have been equated with evil:

Early Christian writers referred to Ethiopians and blackness primarily in two major contexts, demonological and exegetical. From the Greek and Roman point of view, we have seen, the unusual and distinctive physical characteristic of Ethiopians was their blackness. And the color black, for the Greeks and Romans as for other peoples, evoked a negative, and white a positive image. The demonological references to Ethiopians and blackness, covering a very limited area, were obviously related to the Greco-Roman association of black with evil and the Underworld. In apocryphal and patristic literature black was the color of the devil and of some demons who tempted early Christians or troubled them in visions and dreams. As early as the "Epistle of Barnabas" (ca. 70–100 AD.) the devil was called the Black One; and the way of the Black One was described as crooked and full of curses because it was the way of eternal death with punishment where one finds the things that destroy men's souls. In an encounter with Melania the Younger, the devil disguised himself as a young black man. The devil is black, according to Didymnus the Blind, because he fell from the splendor and virtue and spiritual whiteness that only those who have been "whitened" by God can possess.[2]

Hellenisms that have been integrated into Christianity have contributed greatly to this human dualism of White people against Black people. These Hellenistic categories are observable in antebellum America. When the colonial identity was shifting from English and free to an American identity being simply described as White, all the Hellenic views on black and white were in full effect. As white was made to represent freedom and good, black became synonymous with slave, eternal servitude, and evil. We see this clearly in the interpretation of the curse of Ham. In this struggle of good and evil as oppressor and oppressed, the good understands itself not as an oppressor, but as a defender and protector of the sacred, a defender of God. The good perceive themselves not as attackers, but as those under attack, for that their soul survival is at stake. The struggle to maintain their status of goodness consumes their entire being. The good do not see themselves as oppressing people. They see themselves as oppressing the evil that oppresses them with equal vigor. Simultaneously, the spirit of the oppressed has a way of turning the process inside out by identifying the oppressors as the originators of evil and claiming preferential status in the sight of the Divine. The oppressed regularly accept the labels that have resulted from the oppressor's projected evil, yet the oppressed always transforms those negative labels into positives.

This social phenomenon has had a devastating effect upon how Africans have experienced America. Since Europeans have identified themselves with the purity they have ascribed to whiteness, they have projected as evil and slated for destruction everything that is not European, including Africans. A racist attack is not a personal attack, because the dark-skinned people have been objectified into evil. From the moment we have been transformed into evil objects, we lose all our human qualities. Objects, differing from humanity, exist according to their usefulness. When they are of no use, those objects may be discarded and destroyed. To make the situation worse, the belief system says that the "object" that is declared evil, cannot coexist with good. It becomes, therefore, a sacred duty to destroy the evil ones. The sacralization of this destructive process begins with self-aggrandizement. Although European Americans have tended to project their evil on to African Americans, African Americans have either internalized or exorcized the evil. Internalized evil causes us to oppress one another through violence and alienation, self-hatred, and self-destruction. Exorcized evil allows us to transform the evil and claim preferential status with the God of the oppressed.

The Color Line

Because of the phenomenological nature of oppression, as Koheleth has written, neither the oppressor nor the oppressed have any peace. The color line maintains a vigilant dualism of humanity. But this line also has been a bold dividing line of Americans for centuries. The color line has been the defining feature for good and evil. In effect, color has been the primary resource for identifying the enemy within that must be exorcised, and the enemy without that must be annihilated. Color, as the primary component for denoting race, has been the central catalyst for race prejudice among all. Color is to racism as gender is to sexism; and combined they form the quintessential barrier that prevents human unity.

The Double Standard of the Color Line

Although black is rarely seen as good, a double standard alludes to the ascribed blackness within. A deep, rich tan of "gold or bronze" (metals of wealth and virtue) on Europeans is seen as desirable, while the summer sun makes the Africans "blacker" and more undesirable. The "gold or bronze" tone may be the natural complexion of the African American. Although more acceptable, many consider this, too, to be undesirable. This double standard is an active feature of the American psyche and a "double-edged sword" of the African American identity. It suggests that a mulatto skin tone is the most preferable, yet by racial standards, a mulatto is African (Black), which is a debasement of existence.

Antebellum America also bore witness to this double-edged message in the "Fancy Trade." The Fancy Trade auctioned mulatto women exclusively for sexual pleasure. Because they were closer to white in complexion, they were more acceptable. Also, because they were Black, they were libidinously more desirable.

What was past is present. Today African Americans continue to live with the double-edged messages present during antebellum times. People, especially White people, assume that darker individuals will always seek to date and marry lighter individuals. Even with Black pride, the message is: Be dark, but not too dark. The darker your tan, the better…as long as you are genetically White on the inside. This has also encouraged images of beauty to be to be more European than African. As a result, the self-concept of African Americans is greatly influenced and monitored by the popular culture through media and social mobility:

> Since the end of slavery, blacks have been exhorted to "whiten" themselves as a prerequisite for acceptance as "real Americans" by whites, despite the clear evidence that most whites will accept blacks only to a limited degree and despite the persistence of institutional racism, particularly discrimination in employment and housing. The effects of such cultural pressures on black identity in America were pointed out by W. E. B. DuBois in 1903: "It is a peculiar sensation, this double-consciousness, this sense of always looking at one's self through the eyes of others…One ever feels his twoness–an American, a Negro; two souls, two thoughts, two unreconciled strivings."[3]

While awaiting a haircut one day, I became privy to a conversation between the barber and the mother of a six-year-old boy whose hair was being cut. The barber commented as to how "black" the child was becoming as a result of the summer sun. The mother countered that her son always gets lighter every winter. The conversation concluded with the barber's encouraging the mother to use sunscreen on her son and to keep him out of the sun so he would not get any "blacker." This conversation is exemplary of the impact of color prejudice and racial oppression central to American society. To be of an opal skin hue is far more desirable than to be as an onyx stone. Color prejudice is epitomized by the adage, "white is alright, yellow is mellow, brown stick around, black get back!" Wallace Thurman, in his 1929 novel, *The Blacker the Berry*, articulates color prejudice from the perspective of self-hate:

> In an environment where there are so many color-prejudiced whites, there are bound to be a number of color-prejudiced blacks. Color prejudice and religion are akin in one respect. Some folks have it and some don't, and the kernel that is responsible for it is present in us all, that is to say that potentially we are all color-prejudiced as long as we remain in this environment. For, as you know, prejudices are always caused by differences, and the majority group sets the standard. Then, too, since black is the favorite color of vaudeville comedians and jokesters, and conversely, as intimately associated with tragedy, it is no wonder that even the blackest individual will seek out someone more black than himself to laugh at.[4]

Thurman's illustration reveals color prejudice to be as irrational as racism, and equally as devastating. Colorism is truly comedy and tragedy wrapped into one. Just as vaudeville was black-faced, in one period in American history powdered white faces and wigs were vogue. What tends to be true about identity formation is the shunning of what is undesirable while one aligns with that which is most appreciated, and often most prominent, within the social setting. What is rarely emphasized is the lengths to which people will go to maintain a particular identity after it has been formed. And if it is not the maintenance of the identity, it is the maintenance of the value system established by the process of formation. Consequently, people tend to identify with the "norm" and find others perceived to be further away from the norm than themselves.

Color as a Character Trait

Color prejudice expresses its destruction in a variety of ways. Its divisiveness is like a cancer. Color prejudice's devious interaction with human nature promotes a search for the justification of its own existence. Snowden suggests that color prejudice, like racism, was a relatively young phenomenon. He concludes that although color contrasts were employed during antiquity, the colors and their ascribed meanings were not applied to people. But as others have suggested, it is such a short leap from objective color to objectified persons. To think of a time when color prejudice did not exist is almost unimaginable. Color prejudice tends to express and justify itself by ascribing traits through the usage of religion and hierarchies.

By ascribing traits to color, color prejudice identifies particular characteristics and determines them to be the true traits of a people for all places, for all times. The prejudiced person assumes the content of one's character simply by seeing the color of one's skin. This means that when a person meets another, even if for the first time, the behavior of the other is anticipated by virtue of the color of the new acquaintance's skin. Color prejudice determines the level and type of interaction. Ascribing character traits to skin color tends to make interactions more comfortable because the prejudicial classification limits the range of possibilities:

> Differences in skin color and other obvious physical characteristics supposedly provide visible clues to differences lurking underneath. Temperament, sexuality, intelligence, athletic ability, aesthetic preferences and so on are presumed to be fixed and discernible from the palpable mark of race...Skin color "differences" are thought to explain perceived differences in intellectual, physical and artistic temperaments, and to justify distinct treatment of racially identified individuals and groups.[5]

Color Prejudice as Self-defense

Human nature seems to express an insatiable need to insure psychic security. We have highly developed defense mechanisms to shield ourselves from pain and anxiety brought on by change. We determine our space relationships and our levels of involvement according to the labels and attributes we ascribe to a setting and the individuals within a particular setting. We control an environment by categorizing people with attitudes such as, "A person's character is thought to tie in with [their] slant eyes, or a menacing aggressiveness is thought to be linked to dark color."[6] Color prejudice is, therefore, another way in that we make our environment manageable to insure our security.

Religious Justifications for Color Prejudice

Americans have traditionally used religion to justify color prejudice. In the United States the primary sources for religious justifications are the Bible and the Jewish-Christian tradition. People achieve psychic security not only by objectification, but also by identification. As one perceives the nature of existence under the authority of a just and holy God, the unholy traits are projected into the external world onto people who have been objectified. This act of projecting the unholy produces for the projector a self-identification with the "Holy One." Psychologically, this is the process represented when Kelsey says that racism is an idolatrous faith. The identification unifies one's own race and then attaches race to the Divine. This union ultimately elevates one's status to the level of the Divine, thereby making one's race the holy one. One's race, by virtue of its color, becomes the focus and divine image for one's faith. God is replaced by the idol of race. This also contributes to the psychic legacy of the United States, which identifies Black (African American) people as the servants of White

(European American) people. White supremacists' interpr⟨
curse of Ham understands whiteness to be normative for
the divine color of God. This results in their claiming divinᴜ ˌ
themselves, which ultimately leads to a belief that they themselves aɪᴜ ᴜ
and, as such, are worthy of service from all Black people.

Twentieth-century historian J. A. Rogers suggests in his book *Nature
Knows No Color-Line* that the primary sources for color prejudice can be
found in the early rabbinic traditions. According to Rogers, the rabbinic
purpose was twofold: One was to elevate the Jewish faith tradition, and the
other was to justify their occupation of the land. He explains this by
examining the origins of the "curse of Ham" (Gen. 9).[7] This text, often
misinterpreted and miscommunicated, has been used to make Black and
servant synonymous in the American psyche. Lest we forget, under chattel
slavery, Black did become synonymous with slave.

American advertising has consistently reinforced the synonymic
relationship of Black and servant. During the Great Depression, in an effort
to stimulate business, the National Hotel Management Hotels advertised
with the image of the Black railroad porter as their spokesman. "The
portrayal of the porter is interesting in this ad, for beyond the obvious fact
that the only blacks present are in service roles, the spokesman's
subservience is visually reinforced by his deferential smile, slight stoop,
and bent knees."[8]

An Example of the Synonymous Link

I was attending a graduation at my college alma mater a year or so
after my own commencement of 1981. As people gathered for the pomp
and circumstance, I stood looking for old friends to sit with. I had been
standing for approximately five minutes when two European American
women, who were heavily engaged in conversation, came my way. Without
ending conversation or really looking at me, they paused and one woman
extended her hand for a program. But I was a guest like she and not an
usher! I stood and looked at her with her extended hand as she looked in
a direction away from me. When she had decided that her hand had been
extended longer than she should have to wait, she interrupted her conversation, and turned to me. Seeing that I was not ignoring her, she realized
that I was not an usher. Without apology, she lowered her hand, and the
two walked away. Not even the courtesy of an apology, because for her,
the mistake was an honest one.

Color Prejudice and Biblical Interpretation

Color prejudice not only participates in our religiosity by coordinating
a holy war between good and evil, it also offers an inappropriate key for
biblical hermeneutics. This is another example of human subjectivity and
phenomenology masquerading as an objective and divine truth. With the

colorized lenses of present experiences, people project themselves backward and reread history and the Bible through a reorganization of the facts. This approach is eisegetical and noncontextual. The result is a story from the perspective of the reader rather than the original writer. Through this approach, the cradle of civilization, even the womb of humanity, can be relocated:

> A more cautious and systematic racial hierarchy was established by J. F. Blumenbach, a professor of natural history at Gottingen. His *De Generis Humani Varietate Nativa*, published in 1775, was the first attempt at a 'scientific' study of human races of the type Linnaeus had written for natural history a few decades earlier… Blumenbach believed in a unique creation of a perfect man. In fact, Blumenbach's explanation for what he perceived as important 'racial' differences followed the Europocentric pattern set out earlier in the century by the naturalist Buffon. Buffon had argued that the *normal* type of species found in Europe had degenerated in other continents because of unfortunate climatic conditions there: individuals became too big, too small, too weak, too strong, too brightly coloured, too drab, etc.
>
> Blumenbach was the first to publicize the term 'Caucasian,' which he used for the first time in the third edition of his great work in 1795. According to him the white or Caucasian was the first and most beautiful and talented race, from which all the others had degenerated to become Chinese, Negroes, etc. Blumenbach justified the curious name 'Caucasian' on 'scientific" and 'racial' grounds, since he believed the Georgians to be the finest 'white race'…There was firstly the religious belief that man could usefully be seen as coming after the Flood and, as everyone knew, that Noah's Ark had landed on Mount Ararat in the Southern Caucasus. There was also the increasingly important German Romantic tendency to place the origins of mankind–and therefore Europeans–in Eastern Mountains, not in the river valleys of the Nile and Euphrates, as the Ancients had believed.[9]

"Theologians" use the Hebrew Scriptures as their religious basis for justifying prejudice. What is often misunderstood, however, is that the Hebrew Bible does not make racial statements. The various distinctions made in the Hebrew Bible are on the basis of culture, cultic beliefs, territory, tribe or ethnicity, and the history of relationships.[10] Race was first employed in 1684, approximately 2100 years after those first texts now considered race-related were written. Although Noah's sons are often regarded as the first ethnography, with each considered the progenitor of a different race of people, their origins were still the same. They were the sons of Noah and one wife, the sons of Adam and Eve. They were brothers…*homo-ousia*! Like race, good and evil, color prejudice serves a narcissistic self.

The Color of God

As I indicated earlier, color prejudice is a process of identifying with the Ultimate and Eternal Good. That Good has been conceived of as being white; and its polar opposite, evil, has been conceived of as being black. This Hellenistic dualism of humanity has really placed us in an awkward position. Dualized humanity has been a point of tension within the African American faith community for years. Due to the color prejudice that dominates American racial ideologies—which have often been misnamed Christianity—many African Americans have labeled Christianity a "white man's religion." On the other hand, many African Americans have been so profoundly influenced by the white/black dualism that their churches are filled with the images of an Aryan Jesus, never to consider any other representation. In either case, the influence of color prejudice has caused African Americans to buy into the ideology that the devil is the black one. The resultant African American identity is formed in opposition to, or in consort with, America's color prejudice, which means we either identify with or reject Christianity. We either identify with or reject an Aryan Jesus. Furthermore, we either identify with or reject an African Jesus.

> "As I was saying," Truman continued, "you can't blame light Negroes for being prejudiced against dark ones. All of you know that white is the symbol of everything pure and good, whether that everything be concrete or abstract. Ivory Soap is advertised as being ninety-nine and some fraction per cent pure, and Ivory Soap is white. Moreover, virtue and virginity are always represented as being clothed in white garments. Then, too, the God we, or rather most Negroes worship is a patriarchal white man, seated on a white throne, in a spotless white Heaven, radiant with white streets and white-apparelled angels eating white honey and drinking white milk."[11]

On the European American side, if God, who is white, is the Savior and Master, then it is easy to see how the English, during the formation of this country, were able to understand themselves to be the savior and master of all they surveyed. They literally believed themselves to be Lord of the manor.

The Color of Hierarchy

Once color prejudice has been associated with character traits and reinforced by religious ideology, it produces a third type of expression and justification: hierarchy. The human dualism manifests itself in this instance in the form of superior/inferior. Human color prejudice manifests itself as the struggle of a good, white god, who is superior, against an evil, black devil, who is inferior. The hierarchy of color prejudice is really quite Darwinian. According to Darwin, it is the destiny of the inferior to become extinct. Survival, then, becomes the purpose of life that is expressed by the color line. White supremacists thrive on this supposition of life. Their rhetoric insists that if Whites are to *survive*, they must maintain their purity as Whites.

Beyond the dualism of hierarchy appears the stratification of class based on color. The color hierarchy says that a tan is a symbol of wealth and prosperity, so there are major investments in tanning lotions and tanning salons. Yet, not all Whites can afford a year-round tan. On the other side, a tan on non-Whites is a symbol of human degradation and poverty. Those who experience this at the core of their being make major investments in skin fade creams and a religion that will wash them "whiter than snow."[12] Why would any dark person want to become lighter? The answer is that greater opportunities and privileges are afforded those who are more like the prominent culture in appearance.

The hierarchy of color prejudice involves negotiating with three mediating terms. They are "privilege," "complicity," and "relinquish." Some *privileges* associated with the American system purport to be distributed on a first-come-first-served basis. However, the argument of supremacists is that the Whites were here first; and there is much *complicity* for this system. Many people like things just the way they are. But they are the people with the advantages and the privileges. When given an opportunity to share, the tendency is to decline. People do not tend to willingly *relinquish* their privileges. If asked to change, the request is regularly experienced as a threat that causes a hostile reaction. This reinforces the color prejudice that stands at the center of the American identity.

Human Dichotomies and Conformity

Dualizing humanity, often discussed in terms of oppressor and oppressed, is a dichotomy that can also be conceptualized as in-group and out-group identifications. The color line is a powerful distinction for group identification and relegation. The in-group is the oppressor who sets the normative standard. The out-group is the oppressed who struggles to overcome the stigmatization of exclusion. Inherent in in-group and out-group dichotomies is the pressure of conformity. Whether in-group or out-group, one must conform to the characteristics associated with a particular group. Individuals and groups decide to conform or resist the opposing force based on a situational analysis and a personal level of integrity.

The foundation of conformist or nonconformist behavior is identity and security. A person's decision to conform is never independent of self-image, self-understanding, safety, or group identity. Conformity is understood as a process of consciousness whereby a person modifies his or her behavior to reflect identification with the admired group. It is an attempt to reproduce the behaviors of the admired group with the hopes of gaining the same privileges and power. On the other side, one might choose to conform to an out-group identity as a matter of survival.

The apostle Paul's letter to the Romans notes that believers should "not conform any longer to the pattern of this world, but be transformed by the renewing of (their) mind. Then (they) will be able to test and approve what God's will is–(God's) good, pleasing and perfect will." (Rom. 12:2, NIV). This text addresses several important issues related to conformity. First, the text recognizes that people must interface with the world in which they live. Second, individual change is a part of life in this world, so one can conform or be transformed. Third, to be a member of the transformed group outside the norm is a risk, but also an obligation. Fourth, the emphasis is upon internal locus of control. Locus of control identifies the source of causality. When things happen as a result of one's own behavior, the locus of control is internal. When things happen as a result of behavior outside the self, the locus of control is external. The implication of the text is that the world has an attractiveness for which people would want to conform, but the coerciveness of the world must also be recognized and not underestimated.

Conformity is regarded as "the change in an individual's beliefs or behavior as a result of group pressure. While this failure to remain independent of social influence may have negative consequences–e.g., when it leads people to violate their own moral principles–conformity is also an important force for social stability."[13] Conformity is the act of yielding to group pressure. Conformity takes two forms: compliance and private acceptance. Compliance means to conform by behavior, while private acceptance means to conform by private attitudes. More fully, compliance occurs when an individual, to receive a reward or to avoid punishment for nonconformity, gives in publicly to the majority but does not necessarily change his or her private view. Private acceptance, which is a process of internalization, is the acceptance of the influence of the group because it is congruent with the individual's value system. Since the individual is already predisposed to the ideologies, pressure is not required for this type of conformity. Hence, private acceptance is the most dangerous attribute of color prejudice. In fact, conformity can be another way of talking about complicity with a system.

Those researchers who have studied conformity to detect a conformist personality trait seem to conclude that the issues of self-image and the authoritarian personality are central. These researchers generally agree that people with low self-esteem usually conform more often than do those who are more self-assured. Also, some conformists resemble the orientation of the highly authoritarian personalities. Authoritarians tend to conform readily out of respect for convention. Conventionality is acting in a customary way. It is the adherence to the standard practices of traditions. The highly authoritarian is inclined to follow even the arbitrary and relative perspectives of group conventionality that can be different from societal conventionality. "The essential features of the authoritarian personality clusters are rigidity, conformity, conventionality, a belief in power and toughness, in the ends justifying the means—especially in dealing with out-groups—in the use of force and aggression, and in myth and superstitious ritual in so far as these referred to their own group's concept of leadership and power."[14] This is the type person who will follow the most unjust law without question because it is the law. Authoritarians require highly structured lives with limited space for social deviation.

In-groups vs. Out-groups

Everyone is a member of several groups simultaneously. Thus, each of us is a member of an in-group and an out-group. In an earlier discussion, I indicated that the oppressed have resources available whereby they reconstruct their condition and identify themselves with good, and label their oppressors as evil. The same holds true for out-groups. For example, high culture, or high society, is an in-group that frequently describes popular culture as the unsophisticated, as an out-group. But out of the popular culture emerges another group—resistance culture that has become a desirable in-group—that is equal or stronger in appeal when compared to high culture.

As groups are formed, they always come to develop positive, even self-glorifying attitudes toward themselves and to discriminate against out-groups. Personal identities deteriorate and the group identity becomes the focal point as the group becomes internally homogenized. When the authoritarian personality becomes a guiding trait for the in-group, the outcome is devastating. This is because "the [authoritarian] cluster also contains the tendency to use stereotypes, rigid in-group out-group discrimi-nation and projection of human failings onto others while remaining uncritical of one's own actions."[15] So, "stereotypes," "discrimination," and "projection" are all active components of color prejudice. *Stereotyping* involves ascribing character traits. *Discrimination* results in inequality and unfreedom, forcing servant roles upon Blacks, whereby servant and Black become a synonym. *Projection* exorcizes the evil within onto others, while the projecting group never questions their own perceived "god-like" actions.

Pressing these dichotomies of color prejudice farther, if one calls the prominent White culture the in-group, for which its authoritarianism is "white supremacy," then the resistant Black culture (and other peoples of color) is the out-group, which is the coerced victim of discrimination and projection. To hope for the White power base to be relinquished seems to be an impossibility. The resistant group is "encouraged" to stay in "his and her place." Neither conformity nor nonconformity results in a peaceful coexistence. The mere presence of otherness in America makes him or her suspect and threatening. This is the double-edge that color prejudice maintains.

Because the out-group is neither permitted to be conformed nor to be anti-conformists, the out-group constantly negotiates with both external and internal rage—rage from the in-group, rage from members of the out-group, and rage from the individual self. The out-group is not permitted to be like the prominent culture, nor are they accepted for a stance in direct opposition to the prominent culture. The rage intensifies due to the loss of a positive sense of self in the world. The self that stands forth is constantly being degraded. The identity that develops is a false self. The rage also intensifies due to a struggle either to maintain one's power base, or to eradicate the objectified evil through denial, self-hate, and self-destruction.

The negotiations with the rage tend to result in two reproductions of behavior being experienced. On one hand, the reproduction takes the form of compliant actualization of the projections of the in-group. Often this is simply because it can be salvific to fulfill expectations. On the other hand, the reproduction takes the form of establishing an in-group within the out-group that actualizes, by emulation, the attitudes of the dominant in-group. Consequently, in the early nineteenth century, there were mulatto social clubs within the African American community:

> Also in the 1800s a movement was started by blacks who worked as house servants, many of whom had white as well as black forebears. The term *colored* was used by these offspring to distinguish themselves from the Africans who worked in the fields. The light-skinned children who were the product of relationships between planters and house servants formed themselves into a distinct class. In Charleston in 1794 the Brown Fellowship was established, admitting members of mixed heritage. A similar society in New Orleans was called the Blue Vein Society; membership was based on skin color so light that the blue veins could be seen.[16]

Their self-perception prompted a need and gave them the means to become an in-group, not unlike the dominant in-group that rejected them.

> Thus in-groups are often recreated to fit the needs of individuals, and when the needs are strongly aggressive the redefinition of the in-group may be primarily in terms of the hated out-groups...This situation, it seems, can be best stated as follows: although we could not perceive our own in-groups excepting as they contrast to out-groups, still the in-groups are psychologically primary. We live in them, by them, and, sometimes, for them. Hostility toward out-groups helps strengthen our sense of belonging, but it is not required. Because of their basic importance to our own survival and self-esteem we tend to develop a partisanship and ethnocentricism in respect to our in-groups.[17]

What is absolutely clear is that the rage cannot be negotiated; it is a destructive force. Rage must be transformed into something new. More will be said on this point in chapter 9.

The end result is that we must be liberated from the color line of oppression if we are to achieve community.

> But the greatest reason for color prejudice is avarice. I said that the Arabs, themselves, of Negro stock, used their version of the Ham story to exploit and enslave Central African blacks. The mulattoes of Haiti were also cruel exploiters of the blacks. One factor contributing greatly to the success of the exploiters of the blacks is the inferiority complex of large numbers of whites who compensate for the frustrations of life by looking down on Negroes. They need someone to be better than in order to feel really alive. This in time develops into hatred and mob violence.[18]

Life and its consequences must be redefined if the color line is ever to be broken.

5

African American Genderism

It is perhaps in revealing that homophobia is actually contrary to the well-being of black life that black people might arrive at a more liberating view of the biblical tradition in matters of sexuality. It might allow the black community to lift the sacred canopy that it has placed over homophobia. To reiterate, the authority of Scripture is in large measure determined by whether or not a text supports the life and freedom of the black community. A sexual discourse of resistance should clarify that homophobia is antithetical to black life and freedom and thus disrupt the terrorizing manner in which black people have used biblical texts in regard to homosexuality.

KELLY BROWN DOUGLAS, *SEXUALITY AND THE BLACK CHURCH*

"Stay awake and pray that you may not come into the time of trial; the spirit indeed is willing, but the flesh is weak."

MATTHEW 26:41

In chapter 4, I noted that color is to racism as gender is to sexism. Colorism is a component of racism. Although color prejudice is an important part of what gives racism its destructive power, color prejudice is a destructive force in and of itself. In like manner, genderism is a component of sexism. While genderism supports sexism, genderism is also a destructive force in and of itself. This chapter will focus on the influence of sexism, heterosexism, and homophobia upon African American identity. Our understanding of ourselves as sexual, bodily beings has been radically influenced by our experience in America and our encounters with the Bible and with biblical interpretations of texts related to the body. I intend to argue that rather than using the Bible as a liberating resource as we have

'one related to racism, we have subscribed to interpretations
:ts that have encouraged and supported gender oppression
.. issues related to the body, we have yet to do what Randall
..cy encourages, which is to "resist texts that support oppressive
ideologies."[1]

Racism and Sexism

I attended a workshop at a professional conference that explored the
impact of racism on African American life. Fairly early in the course of
conversation, the workshop leader made a point regarding who is
"authorized" to speak for African American people on racial matters. The
leader was quite emphatic: If a Black person is married to a White person,
then that Black person "needs to go home and keep their mouth shut" on
issues of racism. There I sat, in silence, next to an African American woman
who was married to a European American man, who also sat in silence. I
recall thinking how unfair and inaccurate the leader's statement was. I
thought of challenging the leader but quickly concluded that the leader
would only try to belittle me in an act of self-defense.

I, however, really wanted to ask the leader, who I knew was heterosexual, if she had the right to speak out against the sexual oppression of
men insofar as she goes home to her husband every night? The leader's
perspective on who is authorized to speak for Black people is not a new or
unusual position. It is a perspective that says, "You have sold out, so get
out!" Likewise, a strong sentiment among African Americans claims that
only certain people are authorized to speak out against sexism, namely
women. Must solidarity mean uniformity? If a Black person is conscious of
racial oppression, she or he has every right to declare the inhumane
treatment that he or she has received. Likewise, anyone–in fact *everyone*–
has the responsibility to speak out against the oppression of sexism.

Womanists have made an invaluable contribution to the functional
understanding that racism and sexism have similar dynamics and support
one another as forces of oppression. The tri-dimensional force of racism-
sexism-classism as articulated by womanism is well-known. But here, I
only want to speak of the racism-sexism dynamic, and I only want to name
it at this point to highlight the analysis that I have applied to sexism. I
believe it is also important to identify the fact that the destructive force of
racism is reshaped, redefined, and more powerfully construed through the
racialization of sexuality. As a result, it is virtually impossible to talk about
sexism within the African American community without reflecting on the
impact of racism. Racism and sexism both attempt to define and declare
the origins of our humanity, the essence of our being, the grounds of our
condition and social location, the roles we fulfill, the realm of responsibility
and possibility, and the basis of our relationships. Both attempt to declare
that our identities and behaviors have been predetermined to be negative

and maladaptive. These oppressive forces always work together to impose upon us an inferior identity. And, like racism, sexism often has very perverse scriptural interpretations and distorted theological underpinnings.[2]

Black Theological Themes

The biblical question that was reshaped, redefined, and took up residency within racist ideology and literature is: "Can Ethiopians change their skin, / or leopards their spots?" (Jer. 13:23). This question attempted to lay weight to a perspective that considers changes in human nature, behavior, and character to be impossible. Africans, by virtue of our black skin, were *determined* to be a race apart, a nonhuman, even animal, race full of filth and guile. Through the years, other questions have arisen to reflect more positively on the origins of Black life. These questions have explored the nature of our existence, the hatred we have endured, and the struggle to be free. In redefining the origin of our dark skin to be the good black topsoil found in the very good of God, who molded and made us with the most gentle touch and tender kiss, we knew God was without and within us. When we looked at God, it was as though we were looking in a mirror that reflected that we were made in the image and likeness of God. In the early years, however, these reflections and descriptions were dominated by a male social perspective that regarded racism as the quintessential oppression to be unmasked as the premier evil assaulting the human soul.

The persistent themes of race and anthropodicy extend back to the very origins of Black theological discourse. The color-line has been a thick, unerasable line in America. The racist mind hears the words, "God is light and in [God] there is no darkness at all" (1 Jn. 1:5), and believes that God is White. Black folks corrupted by racism hear those same words, also believe that God is White, and begin to sing a song of redeeming hope with the words, "whiter than snow." Black theology has worked to reform our existential hope and restore us to a vision of God who is Black and on our side. Our failure to see that our full liberation requires embodiment is where we had fallen short. And we can claim no vision of embodiment if our full humanity as male and female is denied. One might assume that if sexuality is racialized then a fight against racism is simultaneously a fight against sexism. But the only way to fight against sexism is to fight against sexism. While we confronted evil through challenging the construct of race and the question of anthropodicy, we regularly ignored the evil we have molded with our own hands. By our hands, we have created "misogynodicy." This is the combination of misogyny and theodicy. The construct declares that our objectification of women is destructive of the female image of God. It is a recognition of the pain and suffering we have caused. Misogynodicy means: We hatefully, yet joyfully, declare women to be embodied evil.

Racism and sexism are cooperative oppressions. Both attempt to define the origins of humanity, the essence of our being, the grounds of our condition and social location, the roles we fulfill, the realm of responsibility and possibility, and the basis of our relationships. Both attempt to declare that Black identities and behaviors have been predetermined to be negative and maladaptive. Racism and sexism always work together to define and declare African Americans to be inferior and nonrelational. We must oppose the forces of racism and sexism at the same time if we are going to be free and see justice. Black theology had to learn this lesson, but learn this lesson it did.

Black theology now declares three well-defined generations of liberation theologians. With each new generation came a new analysis of the struggle, a new talking point on the essential nature of Black humanity, and an expansion on how to understand and participate in a liberating praxis. Although the foundations of Black theology were constructed around the oppression of racism, it has grown beyond pointing to racism as being the only evil that assaults Black life. Black theology has taken its critics seriously and has grown in spite of its detractors. While Black theology continues to hold racism as an evil to be confronted, it also acknowledges the other oppressions assaulting our people. To this end, many Black theologians, men and women alike, have accepted the challenge to confront sexism and sexualized blackness. Black theology now considers this challenge to be an important part of the Black theological project and enterprise.

The Body and Christian Identity

When most Christians are asked to think about body issues, notions of purity are frequently central to those considerations. The responses regularly coordinate body and bodily activities with a profound sense of bodily impurity by virtue of the influence of Augustine on Christian beliefs and theology. Augustine's theological systematics were greatly influenced by his struggles with sensual pleasure. His work, strongly representative of Platonic, neo-Platonic, and Stoic philosophies, placed a heavy emphasis on purity being the spiritual turning away from the body. So radical is that turning, however, that it actually encourages a view of spirituality as separation from the body.[3]

Down through the ages, embodiment has been a very serious problem to the formation of a Christian identity. Although Augustine's voice can be heard throughout Christian culture, today evangelical Christian theology maintains his legacy as a central challenge for the Christian life. Evangelical Christian theology is replete with ideas that present the body as fallen and incapable of doing good. Most Christians understand humanity to be comprised of body and spirit (or mind-body-spirit). But whether we see human beings as a di-part or tri-part reality, our basic understandings of what it means to be spiritual regularly exclude the body by virtue of our emphasis on the depravity of humanity resulting from "the fall." The Augustinian description of our condition has been applied to (or if you would prefer, combined with) the Pauline description of the body as flesh, which encourages American society's ideas of bodily impurity. This has resulted in the body being seen as the problem of life, a prison to the spirit and to Christian identity.[4] In the end, our efforts to be spiritually free have meant we must be disembodied, that is, we must escape the body.

To profess Christianity means that one has made an identification with Jesus as the Christ and become a follower of his teachings. In that identification lies a hope that one's being will match the being of Jesus. Put simply, we Christians want to be like Jesus of Nazareth. Our best efforts to live the faith are guided by a hope to inherit a place in God's kingdom where Jesus reigns at the right hand of God. Due to the ways we have understood the gospel to be a message against the world, our desires to live as true, believing Christians have been marked by our efforts to be Christ-like in all that we say and do. Consequently, as Christ's body was crucified and resurrected, our goals have been to die to this life, a life defined by the sensual pleasures and comforts of the body, and to be resurrected into a new body in the heavenly life that is to come. The theology of salvation that guides the lives of most Christians emphasizes escaping the body, escaping the death that the body represents, by being born of the Spirit. Without a spiritual rebirth, which we understand as a death of the body, we have no hope of a new life in this world or the world to come.

In chapter 4, I reviewed the impact of colorism on the Christian heritage and identity. One of the impacts of colorism has been the association of the color white with our understanding of spiritual salvation. According to Bailey, the transformation of the biblical curse of whiteness into a blessing is evidence of White supremacy at work in the translation and interpretation of biblical texts. The color white, which has come to signify purity, has been identified as a mediating force for salvation. Consequently, Christians have often forged strong links connecting color, purity, and embodiment.

Like Jesus wrestling with his fate in the garden of Gethsemane, Christians have struggled with issues of attachment to the body and "the world" and questioned whether it is better to be embodied or disembodied. This struggle sounds odd, especially when we emphasize that "the Word became flesh." But this is often contrasted with opinions that our most prominent physical associations with this world are described in terms of the negative physical pleasures of this life. Too seldom do everyday Christians recognize that the Incarnation means embodiment.

A common African American sermonic adage declares, "He became what we are that we might become what he is." However, our tendency is to think only of becoming what "he is" in the resurrection of the body at the rapture. So we focus, in many different ways, on crucifying the body, just as he was crucified. This attitude has been one of the sources of our sexism, heterosexism, and homophobia. We do what we can to escape the body in the name of holiness. It should, therefore, be no surprise that our physical preference is disembodiment in order to make heaven our home.

This impression of life and the body may be what led the Paul to contrast eternal damnation with marriage (1 Cor. 7:1–7); however, the contrast does not present marriage as a supreme blessing of human/embodied existence. The dominant sentiment is that we should prefer disembodiment, because from the letter writer's perspective, "It is better to marry than to burn with passion" (1 Cor. 7:9b, NIV), because marriage is for men who cannot control their bodies. Furthermore, within this framing, it is believed that women always lack sensual control: that is why women are always directed to be subordinate to the men in every way.

Embodiment vs. Disembodiment

The challenges of how to live in the body (or whether one should escape the body) have a unique history in the U.S. America's decision-making process on whether it is better to be embodied or disembodied has typically been meted out through comparing and contrasting bodily functions as good and bad. What follows is a hierarchy of differences. Every aspect of human existence, every function of human behavior, has been dualized and ranked, creating a list that provides a rationale for oppression. White has been identified as being over Black, and all the shades in between become degrees of goodness. Man has been identified as being over woman, and all the different body types become degrees of goodness. Heterosexuality has been identified as being over homosexuality, and all nonheterosexual orientations have been declared deviant. Hair color, length, texture, and style are ranked. National origin and ethnicity are ranked and then set the standard for what is considered the best in the world.

As we have sought to distinguish and differentiate people and things, we have been motivated and governed by a dualistic impulse to dissect life. Most of us have been socialized to believe that the best way to understand something is by cutting something open and looking at its internal workings. However, when we want to try to understand embodiment and the gifts of our creatureliness, the impulse to dissect is not for the sake of examination. On matters of the body, our impulse, in actuality, is to find a way to surgically extract or amputate that which we believe to be the source of our human corruption. Due to the ways we have tended to construct our theologies based upon spirit-body split, I believe we have a preference for disembodiment that always perceives our body to be unhealthy and flawed. Our dualistic impulse for dissection assumes a dysfunctional component to our being that must be extracted and discarded.

This is particularly true when we identify ourselves as sexual beings. Notions of sexual purity tend always to mean adding to life through subtraction from life. As a result, we have dualized spirituality and sexuality as the primary declaration for Christian living, and often have extracted sexuality from our Christian identity. Functionally, this has meant that oppressors have tended to project perceptions of the evil contained within the body onto the bodies of others. Oppressors have a strong inclination toward projection, believing themselves to be devoid of evil. Once there has been self-aggrandizement based on some appeal to morality, the destruction of the other is acted upon as a quite simple and justifiable task. Consider, for a moment, the legal assault on former President Bill Clinton. In the name of morality and justice, he was attacked in the name of defending the nation. The manner of the assault could lead one to believe that government, big business, and every American president before him were morally upright and without a spot or blemish. His accusers endeavored to prove that he was morally incompetent in an effort to destroy his image and remove him from office. Randall Bailey examined this phenomenon in his article, "They're Nothing but Incestuous Bastards: The Polemical Use of Sex and Sexuality in Hebrew Canon Narrative."[5] He argued that people will find a way to justify the killing of others through an attack on their sexuality.

On issues of embodiment, we have a tendency to focus on one sexual expression or sexuality in an exclusive way, and then we describe that exclusive act in a totalizing way, making the act descriptive of the whole. As long as we maintain the spirit and body as split realities, totally defining a person according to narrow views of sexuality will continue to be an easy way to eliminate an enemy.

As I stated earlier in this chapter, we have a preference for disembodiment and the destruction of the body. We regularly live out these preferential, destructive behaviors through colorism and sexism. Embodiment is not just a matter of accepting what one sees, as is so much the case with colorism. Embodiment is also about accepting what one feels, those inescapable pressures from within. It is, therefore, the nonacceptance of what one sees and feels that promotes disembodiment. To distinguish what is socially most acceptable, a hierarchical scale of social acceptance exists. The dominant governing image is White, male, and heterosexual. Although the prominent features of this image may vary from generation to generation, the image has been epitomized by the seemingly immortal sculpture of "David" by Michelangelo and any number of oil portraits of a fair-skinned, blue-eyed, Aryan Jesus with flowing light-brown hair. Many efforts have been made to change that dominant image, but an equal number of efforts have been directed toward preserving that image. While the preservation of the dominant image is at the heart of racism, the preservation of the image along with the domination of the one identified as "other" is the core of sexism. Furthermore, it is an idealized role associated with the image that constitutes genderism. So, in some ways, it is the image and prescribed roles that we must seek to understand if we are going to re-ascribe sex and gender identities.

Making the Identity Connections

Race, color, sex, and gender are all oppressive forces that affect our identity formation. Because the body is such an important part of what mediates how one answers the questions, "Who am I?"/"Who are we?" the body complexifies the relationships that determine identity.[6] Different aspects of our sexuality conflict and constrict our relational expressions so that we are engaged in a constant battle as we strive to know ourselves as spiritual beings. Because God's Spirit brought order out of chaos and created all life, to be spiritual is to be creative. Fantasy, like God's Spirit, is a creative energy. But because fantasy is associated with the body, fantasy is experienced as being a negative feature of our being. Fantasy, which is not the exclusive domain of sexuality, is an important part of the human imagination and helps to give rise to human possibilities. Yet, when fantasies of the body are directed by colorism, the fantasy tends to promote objectification and exploitation.

The human body naturally stimulates erotic senses that are supported by fantastic imaginings, but racialized sexuality exaggerates the erotic sensations through an identification of the exotic. When something is identified as exotic, it is usually associated with ideas of a lush and lavish paradise. The exotic is a constructed idea that is regularly accompanied by a bodily sensation. An exotic experience is thought to be more pleasurable than ordinary experience. The exotic is an extraordinary experience of erotic pleasure. A racist colorization of the body regularly results in black bodies being regarded as extremely exotic and extremely pleasurable. Through racialization of sexual differences, our black bodies are frequently thought to be the most erotic and exotic objects of sexual pleasure. Such thinking simultaneously makes African sexuality the most unholy, unclean incarnation of evil in America. Consequently, we African Americans sacrificially escape our bodies through an over-spiritualization of our lives. Many have projected the erotic and exotic onto Black sexuality, and we have introjected those fantasies as being prominent features of our lives. In an effort to escape our own racialized fantasy life, we have tended to either live out our fantasies as conquests, or we have tended to become disembodied servants of God who believe our absence from the body puts us in the presence of the Lord.

Escaping Black Sexuality

Black theology has done a wonderful job of addressing Blackness and the problematic associations with black skin. But in some ways, Black theologians have done more to cover the black body than to rejoice in its phenomenal beauty. Introjections of racism and White supremacy have caused many of us to experience our bodies as filthy rags covering our spirits. Standing opposite one another with a profound sense of bodily impurity, our desires to be pure have placed a heavy emphasis on spiritually separating from the body. So strong is that desire, it encourages spirituality to be understood as separation from the body, which supports our denial of the pain caused by sex and gender oppression.

Our embodiment problem is most keenly felt within the African American church. If we distinguish Black theology from Black church theology on a discussion of the body, we must conclude that Black church theology is winning the fight on how to understand the black body. Black church theology is replete with ideas that present the body as fallen and incapable of doing good. Black church theology's basic understanding of spirituality regularly excludes the body by virtue of its emphasis on the depravity of humanity. Although Black theology has been an effective champion for Black humanity, our discussion of humanity has sometimes concluded with a disembodied humanity.

Again, it is the problem of introjection. White supremacy declared black bodies to be dirty. But when the White racist began to feel "a rise at the thighs," black became sexy and "that ole black magic" became irresistible. Blackness being associated with arousal by the White mind resulted in black becoming the erotic and exotic. Once sexuality became totally racialized, the dirty black body became primal sexual pleasure, and the objectified woman's black body became "nasty," that is, the most sexually stimulating and desirable. Pure body and nasty body are the combatants of the war raging within the African American being. We have, therefore, preferred disembodiment as our spiritual answer to warfare. Embodiment is not just a matter of accepting what one sees, embodiment is also about accepting what one feels. The nonacceptance of what one sees and feels promotes disembodiment. Accepting Black sexuality as the next level of work has been the task of the current generation of Black theologians.

Finding Embodied Harmony

Although embodiment has a lot to do with how people relate to one another, we are not completely at peace with such strong urges within the body that call for relationship. As we look at the forces that inspire relationship, we enjoy declaring that opposites attract. We use this adage to explain all kinds of relationship. When we say, "Opposites attract," we tend to think of opposites as the positive and negative polarities of a magnet. We use this understanding to declare that, like magnets, the physical opposites of male and female attract, the temperaments of talkative and quiet attract, and the attitudes of serious and jestful attract. Just because polar opposites attract does not mean we have automatically established a harmonious union. Actually, most of our explanations suggest that the union of opposites affirms and supports sexism and genderism, and encourages homophobia. In fact, many of our relational statements related to what it means to live in harmonious union tend to be grounded on beliefs that men and women have irreconcilable differences.

As an illustration of what we mean when we talk about harmonious union, consider the ways most people talk about marriage. A major debate rages regarding what even "constitutes" a marriage in American society. Today, marriage is a constitutional matter, a matter of law, which declares marriage to be a governmental issue that should be legislated by a moral society. Within our current debates, marriage is a moral issue that has lost its spiritual potency. Spirituality and sexuality have been divorced while church and state have been united on the matter of marriage. Marriage declares that two people are joined together by the bonds of love, whereby the two become one flesh. Separate and distinct lives are knitted together to become one heart. Identified in our rhetoric as the oldest "human" institution, it has been defined as the matrimonial union of opposites. The defining rhetoric, however, has less to do with opposite temperaments and more to do with the union of the opposite sexes, that is, a man and a woman.

As battle lines are drawn and defensive positions are taken, we seem to have developed an historical amnesia on the nature of harmonious union and marriage. The legislative history of marriage in the United States shows that many people have been denied the sacred right of holy union in the name of preserving moral decency and social order. During the period of slavocracy, enslaved Africans were denied the right of legal marriage. Rights were for human beings, and chattel had no rights. It was illegal for Blacks and Whites to marry. The history reveals that marriage is about being human. Since we African Americans have continuously struggled to preserve and declare our humanity, we should be the first to respond to the human cry for justice. If we were able to cheer as our response to the O.J. Simpson verdict, which we understood as being different from cheering for O.J., surely we can decry discrimination in all its forms, especially when it identifies someone as chattel. This is no different from the psychological constructs that have supported racist ideology as discussed in chapter 3. To the extent to which we have declared salvation to be an escape from the body, our sexism, heterosexism, and homophobia vacuum the spirit of God out of the body. By sucking the breath of God out of the body, we thus through the objectification of the body declare the body to be an open cistern of evil, an animal, and no longer a God-animated "living soul." In this way we make the body void and nothingness, like the world before God began the work of creation.

Harmonious Union or Irreconcilable Differences?

Our most common descriptions of holy matrimony reflect our difficulty to conceive marriage as harmonious union. I regard our basic descriptions of holy matrimony to be expressive of the tragic victimization of our lives embedded within experience in the United States. Think, for a moment, about the "fuzzy math" we use to describe marriage. We say things like: "I was half and you made me whole"; or we make reference to a spouse being the "better half" $(1/2 + 1/2 = 1)$. "I was nothing before you"; or "I am nothing without you" $(1+0=1)$. "Always keep a little something on the side that he doesn't know about" $(1+1=1)$. "I always try on a shoe before I buy it," and, because shoes wear out, "a five year marriage is an old couple" $(1+1=1+1)$. Many of these statements present how easy it is for people to regard oneself or another person as being less than human or inferior in status.

When many declare the vital features of a harmonious union using holy matrimony as the prime example, the picture they generate is often a function of our efforts to preserve the ideal image of male supremacy (which is usually partnered with White supremacy) in conjunction with our dualistic impulse. It is far easier for us to split things and people apart than it is to maintain the integrity of wholeness. This splitting behavior means we are inclined to maintain corrupted images and to express misguided understandings of union. Our ideas of union tend to be expressed through the language of subservience resulting from an emphasis on a fallen state of being. Whenever we choose to argue the nature of things and who God put in charge of our relationships, we inevitably choose models that promote and support understandings of our brokenness and fallen nature. We tend to ignore the fact that scriptures tell us that Jesus came so that we might live the more abundant life, and that he declared that salvation makes all things new. Instead, we choose to live according to the judgment of the law and declare that that's the way God intended.

Although we declare we value the work of Christ and, as a result of salvation, we say we live according to the promise of new life, the influence of Augustine and evangelicalism actually have us living according to the judgments of the fall. As we describe the roles of husbands and wives, the basic descriptions of holy and harmonious union rest upon sex and gender differences that emphasize superior/inferior ideologies instead of stressing equality and mutuality. Through a puritanical "rule of thumb," meaning we calculate the weapons we will use to enforce our idealized images, we promote disembodiment and beat the life out of one another in the name of Christian virtue. Although we are not as unconscious about our dominating behaviors as many would like to assume, we are more naive about how our relational rationales diminish and degrade the lives of others. Ultimately, we tear our spirits out of our bodies as our way of declaring harmonious union. Rather than promoting a harmony based on communality, we tend to define harmony through a defensiveness based on separation. In the end such definitions offer a false sense of security regarding holiness.

Continuing to explore the issue of harmonious union, consider the myth of Lilith. This myth comes out of a medieval work entitled the *Alphabet of Ben Sira.*[7] As a commentary written for us to understand the biblical narrative, it does more to reinforce the existing social system than to allow the biblical narrative to critique our lives and hear God saying something different about the way we live with one another. According to the myth, Lilith was the first wife of Adam. Although their marital strife seems to be rather specific, the story has been interpreted to say that Adam and Lilith argued about everything. Believing the two of them to be equal, Lilith refused to be dominated in any way. But in the story—here is what actually breaks up the marriage—Lilith refused to be on the bottom during love-making. Because of Adam's lack of mutuality, Lilith left Eden. Angels of the Lord visited her, commanding her to return to Adam. She refused. Her refusal resulted in her becoming the lover of many demons, the seducer of men, and the source of crib death. Among the many things to be concluded from this myth: This story suggests that equality is not an option, that equality is not what it means to be spiritual, and that a body without spiritual guidance is destructive.

The myth suggests that the only way for a couple to live in perfect harmony and union is for one member of the partnership to be totally submissive to the other. Our descriptions of harmonious union seem always to be accomplished by one person being dominated by another. In this case, as in most cases, the submissive person is supposed to be the woman. Sadly, any time she voices her right to be viewed as an equal and be mutually affirmed and appreciated, her speaking is regarded as defiance and evil. When she speaks for her own right to life, out of her own integrity, she is pathologized, demonized, and made a pariah to the "will and plan" of God. The only feelings the myth valued were the feelings of the men. The only voices respected were the male voices. No matter what Lilith said or did, she faced continual efforts to dominate her.

Persons who seek to live with healthy self-esteem within a patriarchal society have a tendency to ground their esteem in oppressive behaviors. Oppressive societies socialize their members to be oppressive. This is not a new thought. It has been commonly recognized that most spousal abusers grew up in homes where domestic violence was commonplace. As oppression replicates itself, people frequently identify with their oppressors and step on those whom their oppressors would step on. The masculine steps on the feminine, and the "light-skinned" step on the "dark-skinned." Attacked by a racist society, the African American man frequently struggles for dignity and self-worth at the expense of the African American woman. But like Lilith, African American women have always declared they suffer as much as men, even as they work to affirm and support African American men. A more culturally specific understanding of the dynamics being explored in the myth of Lilith is the African American woman's legacy of "sass." Whereas Lilith sought to defend herself against subjugation through escaping her condition, sass has said, "Rethink what you say and do to me." Sass has been the resistant response to oppression that includes a declaration of self-expression, self-preservation, and the defense of those in her care. Sass has been the active maintenance of an integrative self.

Because voice and naming have been understood to be powers of dominion within God's creation, the denial of voice has been understood as the way to control the bodies of others. Through sass, African American women have kept spirituality and sexuality together by standing their ground and speaking their minds. Their ability to speak their minds in the face of dehumanizing oppression has led many to conclude that they are the cause of the breakdown of the African American social fabric.

The Spirit and the Flesh

Let's consider that question of harmonious union and the American preference for disembodiment in the context of the gospel of Matthew and the Gethsemane narrative. Jesus is in the garden, separated from his disciples. He throws himself on the ground and begins to pray. He stops praying. He goes back to get some moral support from his disciples, whom he has asked to stay awake. Finding them asleep, he says, "Stay awake and pray that you may not come into the time of trial; the spirit indeed is willing, but the flesh is weak" (Mt. 26:41). Think for a moment of the variety of contexts in that you have heard or said, "The spirit is willing, but the flesh is weak." What meaning did you intend? What did others mean as they spoke those words? The context for this statement, at the very least, has something to do with Jesus' struggle within life as the inevitability of his death drew near. While his statement suggests an awareness of death being imminent, a part of him was hesitant about actually "giving up the ghost." Our typical reading of this text, however, reinforces our notions of spirit power being more potent than physical power. We regularly conclude that spirit is superior to the body. This notion points to an idea that if the spirit simply dominates the body, or if we simply separate ourselves from our bodies, then the condition of the body is of no consequence. But to emphasize such an idea encourages the escapism that is a natural defense mechanism when we are physically assaulted. In the midst of experiencing the ultimate violent violation of the human soul, we frequently separate ourselves cognitively and emotionally from our bodies to escape the horrors of the victimization. In other words, as the victimizer dominates the body, the victim leaves the body, imagining he or she is in some other place. But if this becomes our way of addressing life—that is, separating what we perceive to be our "selves" from our bodies in the midst of struggle—what does it really mean to achieve a harmonious union? Is separating our spirits from our bodies really living?

Sex and Gender

Our tendency and inclination for disembodiment is largely encouraged by our understanding of sex and gender. These very separate and distinct terms are all too often blended and used interchangeably to describe our physical being. In a discussion of sexuality, when most people are asked, "What is sex?" invariably the answer has to do with sexual intercourse. Sometimes the answer suggests having to do with masculinity and femininity. My next question is always, "What is sexual?" At that point, there is often a scrambling of ideas to make clear that talking about sex and sexual are not the same thing. Frequently, people will say something such as, sex is the idea of intercourse, and sexual is the act of engaging in intercourse. When I begin to clarify the terms, I will often say something like: "When you are asked to fill out an information form, the answer to the 'sex' question is not, 'Yes, please.'" Sex has to do with our physicality, that is, whether one is male or female. And being gay or lesbian does not change one's sex! A gay man is still male, and a lesbian remains female. I understand that the answer to the question "What is sex?" is usually influenced by our understanding of what sexuality is, but the question and common answer, for me, also reveals our narrow views, if not our limited understandings, of our bodies in relationship.

Sex has to do with our physical being as male and female. Gender, on the other hand, has largely to do with our psychosocial attributes of feminine and masculine. Gender is determined and defined by society and suggests the roles that we play in relationship. Each gender distinction is ascribed a specific role, and maintenance of that role is declared to be the determining factor for the maintenance of the family and social order. So constructed by society are our gender roles that we even assume we can detect the nature and quality of relationships by observing what have been determined to be masculine and feminine attributes. Both sex and gender have an impact on our psyches and inform how we relate to one another as men and women. Our blending of sex and gender, however, perpetuates the oppressive attitudes we impose on one another.

In chapter 3, I talked about the way racism infantilized enslaved Africans. We were regarded as children and identified as boys and girls. We were objectified and seen as less than human. We were identified as libidinous animals. We live with and by the influences of racism on our lives. Likewise, we live with and by the guidelines of sexism. I opened this chapter by noting that racism and sexism support one another and have affected our self-understanding. African American sexism, supported by the racist ideologies we have introjected, has blended sex, sexual, and gender distinctions and expressed them as though they are one oppressive force of domination. Our sexist attitudes have us confused and locked us as combatants in the name of supporting harmonious union.

The interlocking oppressions of racism, sexism, and genderism have had an overwhelmingly negative influence on our gender identity formation. This has resulted in inappropriate understandings of womanhood and manhood. Although womanhood and manhood are consciously defined by chronological age, emotional maturity, relational responsibility, and physiological functionality, many negative ideas influence our definitions. All too often, we define our manhood and womanhood by our sexual prowess. We defend a definition and belief in male domination by arguing the inferiority of femininity. What I believe we so often fail to realize is that our definitions are based on immature definitions of sex and gender.

Our language has supported these claims for years. While we have the capacity for turning negative identifications into positives, like saying "my boy" to declare the bonds of brotherhood, we have also pointed at select gatherings and said, "They are boys who think they are men." Such a description often has nothing to do with chronological age. In fact, the description is describing the actions and attitudes of full-grown men who are being declared immature. Likewise, we have identified girls as acting "womanish" or commented that too many girls believe they are women because they have given birth to children. I am sure the immature descriptions of men far outweigh those attributed to women. Nevertheless, the term *sexual* tends to be determined quantitatively; and the term *gender* tends to be determined qualitatively. The more sexually active the male is with women, the more respected he is, and the more likely he is to be regarded as a "real" man who is truly masculine. The very nature of our sexism, however, doesn't hold the opposite to be true for women, except in those cases where her fertility and child bearing bring her recognition as being a "real" woman. And the more seductive she is, the more feminine she is thought to be. But these are all socialized constructions of gender designed to define social and relational roles for the maintenance of an oppressive system. We must remember, the ability to name and define particular behaviors as masculine and feminine is a way of exercising domination.

Racism, sexism, and genderism regularly impose influence on African American ideas of beauty and the feminine. It really is rather ironic. We have a tendency to live into the oppressors' ideas of masculinity while validating through competition the oppressors' ideas of the feminine. This is further complexified by the fact that we have tended toward defining sex and gender through the lens of an adolescent quest to declare our identity. Adolescence is that peculiar time of trying to become a responsible adult while at the same time trying to understand who one really is in light of who one has been to others. This time is often characterized by an acting-out in order to fit in. Consequently, as one seeks to act as a responsible and mature person, one's actions are often characterized by gender naiveté and sexual immaturity.

I admit, not all African American men and women are guided by immature images of maleness-femaleness and femininity-masculinity, but I believe a large enough percentage are guided by immature images to say it is something that needs to change. We make many statements to say, "*This* is what guides our understandings of identity." The problem is we are more powerfully guided by understated or even unstated ideas and images that actually speak louder in directing our conduct than do our stated ideas and images. If we do not address the power of the understated, we will always assume we are guided by things we are not.

Sex and Gender Testing

We have developed a variety of tests for determining the potency of sex and gender in women and men as we endeavor to dominate one another. Passing the test of sex, the quality of one's maleness or femaleness is often measured quantitatively by the sexual standards. The quantitative measure becomes the determinant for declaring the quality of one's masculinity or femininity. The most unfortunate feature of this evaluative process is that the tests are based on school-age and adolescent worldviews. The results of the adulthood tests are intended to produce the same results we strive for when testing children. That is, we want to be able to say, "He is all boy," and, "She is such a little lady." Therefore, the problem of gender construction is that we have immature, racialized, sexual images as our starting point for defining our gender identities.

Furthermore, because of racism's impact on our genderism, we regularly feel our very survival is at stake with regard to our identities as men and women. This sense that our very survival is at stake fuels our self-defensive and aggressive impulses, resulting in the scapegoating of others through heterosexism and homophobia. Our approaches to sex and gender are often the same old arguments "warmed over" regarding our humanity and what is most human and divine: masculinity or femininity. We must be careful not to recreate an oppressive patriarchal system of social intercourse modeled after an antebellum ethic of sex and gender that was, in fact, rooted in an idolatrous understanding of a man's place in the world. Until we are able to affirm the lesson in one of the creation stories in Genesis that women and men are "bone of bone and flesh of flesh," that we are a part of one another and both a part of God, we will continue to struggle to create harmony through gender oppression. A mature view of gender is a balanced and complimentary view that regards the feminine and masculine, manhood and womanhood, as two equal parts of the same, and contained within the same, being.

6

The Psychodynamics of African American Religiosity

Psychiatry as a discipline is floundering on its previously established conceptual and theoretical foundation imported from 19th century Europe. My continuing question to myself as a late 20th century precautionary...is, "Can a greater understanding be achieved in the study of human behavior as it is organized and manifested in the world's dominant power system/culture?"

FRANCES CRESS WELSING

In regards to African peoples, western psychology in general accepted as a basic a priori assumption that African peoples were inferior. The conduct of western psychology in fact proceeded as if this a priori assumption was a proven fact.

WADE W. NOBLES

Many within the field of psychology and religion believe humanity to be religious in nature. Not all, however, consider religiosity to be a central component of their self-understanding. If one dismisses or decentralizes African American religiosity—more particularly, spirituality, which I will review in chapter 7—from the matrix, the entire picture of the African American community is skewed.

When reflecting on religion from the perspective of psychology, people tend to be most familiar with the psychodynamic approaches to the psychology of religion. This chapter is devoted to an exploration of psychodynamic psychology theories and their evaluation of religiosity. I will spend a considerable amount of time evaluating the basic personality theories of Sigmund Freud, Carl Jung, and Erik Erikson. The significance of their theories within my work is due to the fact that these three constituted my introduction to psychology.

Not only have they influenced my intellectual life, they are also very important critics of Western life and American culture. I, therefore, must attend to the impact of their reflections upon my own reflections as a scholar and as one interested in understanding the American components of African American identity formation. Furthermore, reflecting on their theories proves valuable because each considered human religiosity, and all three maintained the importance of the same in their theories. Of course, each expressed religiosity differently, but they agreed that religiosity exercises a powerful influence upon the personality. As useful as they can be, we face limitations when focusing exclusively on their theories, especially when considering African American culture.

Of the three European psychodynamic psychological theorists I am considering in this chapter, I will emphasize Erik H. Erikson and his focus upon identity formation. Erikson's theoretical forefather was Sigmund Freud; but to fully appreciate his theoretical construction, a look at Carl Jung is also important.[1] These three constitute a "synoptic" with their individual branches of psychodynamic psychology originating with the psychoanalytic work of Freud, reshaped into analytic psychology by Jung, while psychoanalysis grounded and informed the psycho-historical/ psychosocial work of Erikson. I will coordinate and critique their psychological positions from a generational perspective—Freud as first generation, Jung second and Erikson third—by reviewing the central themes of their theories.

My argument will be constructed in such a way as to illustrate the way Erikson's work resulted in the consolidation of several theoretical emphases of Freud and Jung. I will highlight their points of theoretical overlap and tension, and note the value of their perspectives if one chooses to consider their ideas for reflecting on African American identity. While Erikson moved beyond Freud and noted several valuable contributions of Jung, critical areas remain in which Eriksonian psychology fails to be insightful for the African American context. In chapter 9, I push well beyond Erikson by presenting a framework for understanding African American identity formation. My considerations here will reflect my own journey and transition from the psychodynamic personality theories of Freud, Jung, and Erikson to Black (African) psychology and African American pastoral psychology.

Personality Theory and Psychodynamic Psychology

Basically, personality theories are conceptual perceptions that attempt to express the collective, consistent behaviors of human beings as they attend, perceive, and negotiate relationships and the world. Although personality theories are lenses for interpreting human development and relationships, they are not simply attempts to define human behaviors and processes. They are frameworks that promote human integration, both individually and collectively. The positive hope is that through the use of personality theory, persons will be better able to understand themselves and seek to be transformed.

Participation in a culture means that one is involved in a particular social matrix, a particular value system. The value systems, in turn, vary according to differing influences that called them into existence and established the culture. While the joys and pains of the human heart may remain the same, the living conditions that impact human beings and define different social contexts evoke different human responses. The differing responses have established separate identities. Because cultures do vary and present a variety of influences that shape perspectives and development, it is critical to recognize that psychological theories are contextual and not universal. Due to the fact that the essence of humanity is the same the world over, it is possible to modify theories to appropriately consider different cultures. Differing cultural identities, however, means no one theory fits all.

Culture and Psychological Theories

My emphasis upon the particularization of psychological theories is somewhat similar to the rationale employed by some women psychologists. They believe that psychodynamic theories are valuable but fall short because significant portions of the theories are based upon male life experience. The fact that the theories have been based upon the lives of men is not a problem, per se, as long as it has been clearly stated at the outset. Too often, the particularity of the theory is denied. When theories are resourced and referenced, they are often regarded as universal, especially since patriarchy and intellectual colonialism govern the day. However, males are socialized differently from culture to culture. A man is a man, but some variation will appear among men from different cultural settings. For instance, what may be taboo among men of one culture could very well be normative for another. So, I am suggesting that not only are many theories generally based upon the lives of men, they are also reflective of European values and interactions with the social environment. As a result, anthro-centrism combined with ethnocentrism produce another oppressive "ism."

Utilizing the psychodynamic personality theories to evaluate the African American community without making any theoretical modifications will result in inappropriate assessments and inaccurate conclusions.[2] African Americans experience oppressive forces that are not implicit in the psychodynamic personality theories. The theories, therefore, must be modified to consider the life of the African American community appropriately. Yet even with those modifications, the theories may not fully address the dynamics of the culture. This is where I take seriously the challenge of colleagues like Na'im Akbar, Carroll Watkins Ali, and Ronald Philips, who have questioned why I would choose to modify theories rather than making a complete departure to declare an indigenous theory. As I stated earlier in this chapter, my psychological launch came by way of the three psychologists I review and critique here. While my journey takes me to the place of departure, it is important that I identify the markers on the path. Another important recognition is that an indigenous theory is not intended to suggest differences in what it means to be human. Such a suggestion would cause me to fall into the trap of the racist who says "some are human and some are not," or "some are more human than others." An indigenous theory says there are differences in the human experience, not in what it means to be human.

In an earlier chapter, I reflected on the oppressive force of dualism. The psychodynamic theories I am reviewing are dualistic. Their dualistic framing, however, has tended to position Africans on a lesser and more problematic level of human relationships. Believing Africans to be developmentally inferior will always result in the misinterpretation of African experiences. One cannot see the merits of a group if one automatically assumes the group to be less meritorious. Humanity has a range of experiences that produce different understandings of life. A people indigenous to the desert sands sees the world differently from a people indigenous to a tropical island. Each has a different worldview.

Another way of approaching this issue—the necessity of an appropriate psychological theory of cultural identity—is from the perspective of the psychology of religion. One of my basic assumptions is: human beings are essentially religious beings. This means human identity can be accessed through the psychology of religion. Because religious traditions differ, the implication is that character traits also differ from culture to culture. Whereas one can study religious phenomena psychologically within a variety of contexts, the nuances of difference due to the variety of cultural institutions expose the variety of human experiences that make groups distinct.

Misconceptions abound on the relationship between psychology and religion. Psychology and religion are interlocking systems of human nature. Psychology has to do with psyche/soul functions, and religion has to do with psyche/soul expressions for communal survival. A few common myths seek to explain psychology's distance from religion. The myths I am presented with most often are: Psychology is anti-Christian, and all psychologists are atheists. Both myths, of course, are false. Psychology is not a belief system for which humanity is the divine; therefore, psychology is neither necessarily for or against Christianity. Furthermore, all psychologists do not believe theism to be a crutch developed by the psyche as a defense against the realization of mortality.

What Is Universal about Humanity?

Although psychodynamics is rooted in the fact that change is inevitable, it has promoted a sense that human responses to change are universal. Therefore, when most people think of psychodynamic theories of personality, the common, most basic, assumption is universality. Many people believe that theories can be universally applied without modification to the lives of people throughout the world. Universality, however, is difficult to prove within any theoretical discipline. The universality of psychodynamic personality theories is challenged by the influences of race, gender, and culture on the human psyche. At this point the only thing I am willing to say is universally true is that all of humanity wrestles with radical social change and identity. The more fluid and uncertain our social environment, the more rigid or resilient the human identity will be. A variation of the opposite can also be true. If the social context is extremely rigid, the human identity can energetically resist the inflexibility of the social context. This is essentially due to the fact that people do not like change and will go to great lengths to maintain consistency and certainty.

A Conceptual Understanding of Psychodynamic Psychology

While the psychodynamic personality theorists focused upon in this reflection had varying methodological approaches and emphases, each stands within the tradition of depth psychology that places emphasis upon unconscious motivation and psychic processes. Each had a different starting point with different rationales for interpreting behavior. Freud emphasized sexuality and the struggle between life and death. Jung emphasized genetics, religiosity, and spirituality. Erikson emphasized social interaction, psychic conflict resolution, and identity. All three stressed, in different ways, human relationality and psychic well-being.[3]

Each of the theorists *constructed* a framework for understanding human development and psychosocial/psychospiritual adaptation. The foundations of their frameworks were based upon their personal formative life experiences and their individual understandings of personality. With that, it is important to remember that personality is a construct. To identify personality as a construct is to speak in an organized consistent manner about complicated processes that are otherwise puzzling and intangible. As a psychological phenomenon, the personality has many features and levels of functioning; yet, those features are coordinated by particular identifications. Identity is, therefore, one aspect of personality.

Each theorist's formulation of human psychic processes had a relational component. All three saw personality developing in relationship to something or someone else, but their emphases were individual and not communal. Although each focused on relational development, each theorist was dedicated to defining what it means to be an individual in community. Extending this idea, while each theorist worked on the individual and collective levels simultaneously, it is vitally important to remember that each remained focused on individualism and individuality. Their views of identity formation emphasized distinguishing the self from other selves. From their understanding, a person declares, "This is who I am, and this is who you are. This is who I am because of who you are." This individualized construction is very different from the African American communal way of identity formation, in which the self is distinguished from other selves by stating, "This is who I am because this is who we are together and apart."

Freud, Jung, and Erikson have written volumes on multiple topics and behaviors. Each one had experiences in early life that became the formative, foundational experiences that informed the ways they constructed their theories. Each theorist interpreted life using Western dualistic categories that emphasized superior/inferior psychic functions. The ideologies that grounded their works delegated some persons to be superior and relegated others to be inferior. This represents a problem for African Americans, since dualistic ideologies sustain racism and color prejudice. This dualistic emphasis, so central to America, reveals the necessity for an indigenous African American approach to African American psychology.

Because I consider the basic theories of the three to be a synoptic, I maintain that a consistent strand connects the three. Erikson's considerations embodied the very best of his predecessors. Erikson took the practice of psychoanalysis from the office to a broader context.[4] Here I will critique and coordinate this synoptic to understand better the value and the limitations of psychodynamic personality theories. Because theory is grounded in experience, I will overview the life experiences of the three. The differing African American life experiences reveal the necessity for an indigenous African American framework.

Freudian Psychoanalysis

I begin with Freud, the father of psychoanalysis. His theoretical emphases are a direct result of his personal experiences. This is very important to acknowledge. Freud's personal experiences created a great deal of internal conflict. He sought to work this personal conflict out in his professional life. He suffered significant turmoil in relating to his father. A man of Jewish ancestry, young Sigmund did not feel his father was courageous enough to defend himself or his Jewish heritage. Feeling the responsibility of defending his father's honor meant he was not very proud of his father. This caused Sigmund to have severe anxiety after his father's death. These two points, relational turmoil and anxiety, became significant "documents" for his work. He articulated these struggles through his five-stage psychosexual theory and in his later emphasis upon *Thanatos*–that is, the death instinct. Indeed, physicality is a key determinant for self-understanding, and both the psychosexual theory and the power of the death instinct expounded that fact. The foundations of life experience are coordinated with social intercourse and the human struggle with mortality.

An important part of "who we are" is grounded in our understanding of sex and gender roles. Freud's understanding alluded to institutionalized sex and gender roles as restrictive of self-understanding. Freud considered one of the central problems of society to be sexual repression. This was probably a very accurate assumption considering the rigidity (or frigidity) of the Victorian period, but it is less likely to be true of the people living in the generations after the American "sexual revolution." Remembering, however, America's reaction to former President Clinton's sexual impropriety in comparison to the reactions of people from other nations, the American mass culture may still be greatly influenced by the Victorians. In spite of the sexual content depicted daily on soap operas, we still may be a sexually repressive mass culture with a popular culture persona of sexual freedom. Nevertheless, sexual repression combined with other concepts of unconscious motivation address much of what is at the heart of the psychosexual stage theory.

Although Freud emphasized Thanatos later in life, I do not believe he ever rejected his earlier categories. His later theorizing of Thanatos suggested that human beings have a "death instinct" frustrated by a "life instinct"– i.e., *Eros*. His foundational theorizing stressed that all psychic activities have their origins in the body. Drives and instincts are physical experiences that give rise to psychological activities that begin in the unconscious and work their way through to consciousness and then into the external world. The dualism of his approach assumes that the body-mind system always seeks balance. Following a homeostatic model, the build-up of pressure requires a release of pressure. A simple example is, if one is hungry, one eats. The body out of balance eats to have balance restored. He expanded these notions into the balancing of life and death, in which both impulses are present, but life tends to be the stronger of the two. I contend that if one is to understand Freudian theory, one must first grasp Freud's understanding of psychic processes and personality development. All of his work arises from his understanding of how the psyche functions and of psychosexual theory.

The first three stages (the Oral, Anal, and Phallic) of his five-stage theory cover the age range of 0–6 years. In Freud's estimation, those early years are very tumultuous. At the conclusion of those years the personality is well established. Freud believed that from the ages of 6 years to puberty (the Latency stage), a person experienced no major changes in the personality. In his fifth and final stage (the Genital stage), the adult attempts to work out the unresolved issues of the earlier stages. Consequently, Freud understood the human experience in terms of the dichotomy of childhood and adulthood. Freudian theory is very dualistic as evidenced in his notions of the psyche-soma (mind-body) split. Even his basic understandings of human development reflect polar opposites–i.e., life/death, pleasure/pain, build-up/release.

Not unlike the rabbinic tradition expressed by the apostle Paul in his letter to the Romans, Freud also identified humanity as having a tri-partite nature. Paul identified human nature as being natural, carnal, and spiritual. In like manner, Freud presented the psyche in terms of three levels of consciousness (conscious, preconscious, and unconscious) with three component features (super ego, ego, and id). Stage theories are linear and hierarchical, with one stage following another. Based on his theoretical dualism and polarities, I have reconceptualized his stage theory and divided (or dichotomized) the psychosexual stages into two halves of a life story. Freud's first four stages are on one side and the fifth on the other.

Freud's psychosexual stages, combined with his understanding of psychic construction and processes, led him to theorize life as a series of conflicts. Because many of these conflicts have taken up residency in the unconscious, resolving life issues is a matter of making unconscious motivations conscious. Facing the challenges of life is either experienced as, or is mediated by, a human struggle among life, death, and immortality. Each of his theories were framed by his views of the power of instincts and mythology. So for him, the Oedipal complex was central. This life and death struggle between father and son became a central sexual issue and challenge to living as a responsible adult. The myth of Oedipus Rex was further nuanced to express the totemic practice of cannibalism through the incorporation of a part of the father's self. Yet all the crises a *man* experiences (because his theories are overwhelmingly male) are related to his physical being in the world. Consequently, the genital stage is a reproduction and a deconstruction of one's childhood in adult form.

Jungian Analytic Psychology

At the beginning of his career, Jung was a student and devotee of Freud. At one point, they were so close that it was "understood" that Jung would be Freud's successor to maintain the tradition of psychoanalysis. The two, however, went their separate ways. Given Freudian psychology, the breakup between Freud and Jung was almost "in-Oedipal," ("inevitable")! Therefore, Freud and Jung ended up sharing no common theoretical ground. Jung made the most radical break possible from Freudian theory. Ironically, given Freud's father-son legacy, it was not a son (either biological or adopted) who carried on the tradition with his emphases, but his daughter. Although Jung credits Freud with the introduction of "psychology into psychiatry," he felt that Freud's views on the nature of the psyche and the interpretation of human activity were limited. His major contention was that all human activity cannot, or at least should not, be reduced to sexuality and psychosexual stages. This was the essence of their "inevitable" breakup.

Jung's father was vicar of the small village of Kesswil, Switzerland. I believe there are two points of critical importance for understanding Jung's later theorizing, and both have to do with his father's influence. The first, very available to Jung, was his father's library, with its volumes on world religions. The second was that Jung was quite disappointed with his father's refusal to broaden his categories of God. Given these two points, he appreciated his father for his library and the range of his interests, but he also was critical of him for being bound by convention and church tradition. This resulted in Jung's considerations encompassing world religions and refusing to associate with any single tradition. His foundation was organized in accordance with his father's, but he did not want to be like his father.[5]

Jung based his theorizing on the anatomy and functioning of the psyche. His understanding of the component parts is coordinated by the regions of the conscious and the unconscious. He believed the most influential part of our being to be our unconscious. Like Freud, Jung believed our unconscious to be rooted in our physical being; however, that rootage was not understood to be in our biological being. For him to emphasize biology as Freud did, he would have been too dependent on Freud's sexual emphasis. Jung, therefore, posited the unconscious promptings to have their origin in human genetic coding and not in instinctual urges. From this, he developed his theory on the "individuation" process:

> Consciousness should defend its reason and protect itself, and the chaotic life of the unconscious should be given the chance of having its way too—as much as we can stand. This means open conflict and open collaboration at once. That, evidently, is the way human life should be. It is the old game of hammer and anvil: between them the patient iron is forged into an indestructible whole, an "individual." This, roughly, is what I mean by the individuation process.[6]

I also coordinate Jung's process of individuation with Freud's dichotomized stages. Jungian psychology is a psychology of adulthood with its major theories of psychical processes occurring in adulthood, not childhood. Jung spent a considerable amount of time unpacking what he identified as the individuation process. He presents a picture of many human processes that direct human growth according to a psychical timetable programmed by nature. He believed that genetics plays the most important part in the human experience of the psyche. He stressed that the human future is determined on the basis of the information stored in the genes. "In so far as no [one] is born totally new, but continually repeats the stage of development last reached by the species, [everyone] contains unconsciously, as an a priori datum, the entire psychic structure developed both upward and downwards by their ancestors in the course of the ages."[7]

Jung theorized that humanity has an existential longing to find the Eternal within itself and that, indeed, the Eternal does unite with humanity. He sought to explain the biblical notion of "living soul"—that human beings are bodies animated by the spirit of God and bearing the image of God. He did this through a universal investigation of mythology, cultural anthropology, and religions East and West, as well as by exploring his own memories, dreams, and reflections. My feeling is that he determined that if he were going to be clear that he was doing something different, it was imperative that he not work with biological categories. To maintain sexuality, which he disagreed with, would have necessitated considering early life experiences. As compared to Freud's later focus on the death instinct, Jung pursued issues of the death of the spirit.

Continuing to demarcate the tradition, the most that can be said about the correlations between Freud's psychosexual theory and Jung's individuation is that Jung regarded the first half of life as "ego formation," which is the basis for the *personal unconscious.* Since Jung's understanding of "unconscious" included the primordial experiences of humanity, he understood a region of the psyche to contain only the personal experiences of an individual's life. One of the most important features of Jungian psychology is the individuation process, that is, becoming a centered "Self." The issues that Jung addressed in his discussion of individuation are grounded in the formation of psychic processes and experiences of an earlier period in life. The reasons for individuation, and the negotiations that result from the process, are no different than those issues addressed by Freud. Individuation is an internal process initiated by nature, not social forces. It is a process whereby we relax our dependence upon our ego defense mechanisms and become freer to be what God has intended. God-images, which Jung regularly identified as *mandalas,* emerge from the "Collective Unconscious." Mandalas have a variety of presentations, but the foundation is always a circle within a square. These images recenter the self into an individual with an integrated identity. Jung concluded that "the individuation process subordinates the many to the One. But the One is God, and that that corresponds to [God] in us is the Imago Dei, the God-image. But the God-image expresses itself in the mandala."[8]

Eriksonian Social Psychology

This brings me to Erikson, whom I feel best explicates the identity issues. His theoretical framework also grows out of his personal struggles with his formative experiences. The works of Freud and Jung gave him a language to talk about these experiences. Erikson's emphasis grew out of his own sense of displacement because the father whom he had known as "dad" was in actuality his stepfather. His biological father abandoned his mother before he was born.[9] This knowledge made him a stranger to himself and caused him to wonder who he was. His wanderings led him to Vienna and the study of psychoanalysis.

Like Jung, Erikson's earlier works are clearly psychoanalytic. But desiring to place emphasis upon the ever-widening social relationships that influence the individual, Erikson theorized the psychosocial stages of development. Unlike Jung, Erikson remained committed to the tenets of psychoanalysis. He believed that individuality is the result of relational conflict resolutions that occur at different stages of life. Basically, as we gain mobility and venture into broader relational contexts, we are challenged by the new social milieu. He was greatly influenced, as Freud was, by a belief that life is a series of progressive changes. That is, perhaps, one of the principles of stage theories. But like Jung, who did not develop a stage theory of psychological change, Erikson concluded a different guiding principle for the changes in life.

Following the psychodynamic tradition of dualism, he formulated his perspective around the ideas of conflict and crisis. The concept of polar opposites became critical to much of his thinking. He theorized that throughout life we encounter predetermined conflicts that we experience as crises. These crises have been established by social demands. The outcomes of the conflicts/crises, either positive or negative, are retained as a permanent imprint within a person. Therefore, no conflict is ever completely resolved nor forgotten during the course of a life. Furthermore, all of our life experiences influence all of our relationships for the whole of our lives.

Erikson constructed his stage theory around the stages of the life-cycle. He proposed eight life-cycle stages of human development with corresponding ages. Although allowing some latitude on the age range that demarcates each stage of the life-cycle, we can still ascribe an age range for the purpose of generalizing the issues faced at each stage. The ages I share here are more the traditional ranges than what may be the developmental case today, since the hormonal changes that signal adolescence seem to start earlier and retirement now comes much later—along with people living longer. Erikson's life-cycle stages, with their ages, are: infancy (0–1), early childhood (1–2), play age (2–4), school age (5–12), adolescence (13–18), young adulthood (18–39), adulthood (40–60), and old age (above 60). Erikson theorized that a psychological crisis exists at each of the eight life-cycle stages. Each of these crises is the direct result of changes in social interactions and new relationships that develop with age. He ascribed an issue that he believed focused the crisis of each stage. In every case, he viewed the issue he ascribed as a positive issue. Because he was operating out of a dualistic understanding, he also ascribed a negative pole to each of the positive issues. This means that the conflict resolution of every stage could have a positive or a negative outcome. His eight stages are:

1. trust vs. mistrust
2. autonomy vs. shame and doubt
3. initiative vs. guilt
4. industry vs. inferiority
5. identity vs. identity confusion
6. intimacy vs. isolation
7. generativity vs. stagnation
8. integrity vs. despair

Just because one can come out on the positive pole at one stage does not mean that the resolution of the next stage will also be positive. His construction, however, did leave room for a person to revisit an earlier stage in life and rework the issues to come out on the positive pole.

I also coordinate Erikson's eight psychosocial stages with Freud's and Jung's theories. The psychosocial stage theory is also linear and hierarchical, but again, I divide the stages into two halves of a lived life. The two halves of Erikson's stages correspond as follows:

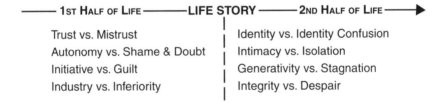

—— 1ST HALF OF LIFE ——LIFE STORY —— 2ND HALF OF LIFE ——▶

1st Half of Life	2nd Half of Life
Trust vs. Mistrust	Identity vs. Identity Confusion
Autonomy vs. Shame & Doubt	Intimacy vs. Isolation
Initiative vs. Guilt	Generativity vs. Stagnation
Industry vs. Inferiority	Integrity vs. Despair

The psychosocial stage theory is an eight-stage theory based on the epigenetic principle. This principle says "each stage of life, before it emerges specifically as such, is already present in a way in the earlier stages; and the development reached at a given stage must be redefined when envisaged from the vantage point of a later stage."[10] Erikson, not unlike Jung, believed that experience has both genetic and social building blocks. As the social circles of the child broaden, so does the child's self-understanding. Because those understandings are permanent imprints, childhood understandings become adult understandings in an ever-broadening adult world. Hence, the first four stages of Erikson's theory involve foundational issues that are never absolutely resolved and never discarded. The second four stages correspond to the first four in a one-to-one relationship. The basic issues of the first four are the same as the second four, merely more complex. The first three stages of both halves are essentially internal negotiations through experiences with the world, while the fourth stages of both halves are essentially external negotiations with internal ramifications.

While Erikson emphasized conflict resolution in human development, the primary focus of his work was psycho-history and identity. He believed that every person experienced more than one "identity crisis" that always culminates with an "integrity crisis" during the final stages of life. Erikson's theoretical focus concluded that life, as a cumulative, is organized around the search for identity through relationship. He saw humanity as the shaper of history and as shaped by history simultaneously. Consequently, the human legacy is both received and influenced by human hands.

A one-to-one correspondence exists between Erikson's first four stages and Freud's first four. The issues of Erikson's last four stages correlate with Freud's Genital Stage. All the issues, and even the age approximations, are noted by both Freud and Erikson. Since Jung's theories are not stage-oriented, the correlation of his perspectives is thematic rather than age-identified.

——— 1ST HALF OF LIFE ———		—LIFE STORY ———	—— 2ND HALF OF LIFE ——→		
Freud	**Jung**	**Erikson**	**Freud**	**Jung**	**Erikson**
Oral	Ego Formation	Trust	Genital	Individuation	Identity
Anal		Autonomy			Intimacy
Phallic		Initiative			Generativity
Latency		Industry			Integrity

A Conceptual Understanding of the Psychology of Religion from a Psychodynamic Perspective

Religions, according to many psychodynamic psychology theorists, function to meet a number of egocentric needs of people, including physical drives (as expressed by Freud), emotional needs (as expressed by Jung), and needs produced by social systems (as expressed by Erikson). The aforementioned areas have been conceptualized within the psychology of religion as bodily needs, psychogenic needs, and social needs. The bodily needs approach to religion describes religion as being a function of sexual desires and repression, as a desire for physical safety and comfort. This approach, however, leaves one wanting for fulfillment that is not physiologically directed:

> The theory of sex repression has its devotees. For evidence they cite the prominence of sex symbols in religion and the orgiastic nature of some forms of religious frenzy and mystical fantasy. Religion, they maintain, is a thinly veiled sublimation of the aim-inhibited sexual impulse. But this line of reasoning overlooks the even greater emphasis that religion gives to symbols of nutrition,

security, repose. It is likewise specifically guilty of confusing all forms of excitement with sex emotion, or else of darkening counsel by equating sex with completeness. In any case it overlooks the passionlessness that marks so much of religion. Also, we know, religion flourishes over the face of the earth in places and in epochs that know no sex repression.[11]

Psychodynamic psychology theories of religion tend to stress unconscious origins. The psychogenic needs have to do with the many human insecurities that originate in the unconscious mind. However, any theory of religion that focuses on unconscious origins is difficult to prove or to disprove. Yet, the force of the unconscious cannot be the whole story, for a large array of conscious causal forces lie also at hand.[12] These conscious causal forces push us from our safety zone into our creative zone and assist us in the reshaping of our reality.

Finally, social needs have to do with the fact that human beings are relational beings who need structure and order. This area does not operate independently of humanity's acute sense of finiteness. This is where the issues of survival and spirituality are most prominent. Religion constantly intersects with both survival and spirituality. From this perspective, implicit in the realities of mortality are the concepts of duality and dualism that aid in the structuring of religion:

> The sad truth is that real life consists of a complex of inexorable opposites–day and night, birth and death, happiness and misery, good and evil. We are ever sure that one will prevail against the other, that good will overcome evil, or joy defeat pain…It was precisely this conflict within [humanity] that led the early Christians to expect and hope for an early end to this world, or the Buddhist to reject all earthly desires and aspirations. These basic answers would be frankly suicidal if they were not linked up with peculiar mental and moral ideas and practices that constitute the bulk of both religious and that, to a certain extent, modify their radical denial of the world…When suffering comes…that is when people begin to seek a way out [of their life circumstances] and to reflect about the meaning of life and its bewildering painful experiences.[13]

Religion as an Illusive Struggle of Life Against Death

Freud believed that religion is an illusion, stating, "[It] is not rooted in a healthy, mature understanding of reality; it is an illusion, a neurotic symptom."[14] In religion, the adult preserves a piece of infantile, libidinous life. For Freud, religion was an indicator of unresolved issues. Religion, therefore, was considered an attempt to recreate a space of safety from an earlier time of safety and security in the midst of extreme anxiety. Part of the illusory nature of religion is the lack of recognition that the person is seeking to recreate the safety of the womb and infancy. His perspective implies that psychic survival is even dependent upon this space. The limitation of this approach is that it does not highlight the creativity of religion. Neither does it reflect the maturation that can result from religion.

The limitations of the bodily needs approach are perhaps why Freud later reshaped his inquiries of religion around the issues of civilization and illusion. Illusion, which he grounded in wish fulfillment, was a coping space for finding security in the world.[15] Neo-Freudians Robert J. Lifton and Ernest Becker refined this point by relating it to Thanatos. Lifton says that death has to do with "the idea of 'death in life,' of loss of vitality of feeling...Death becomes a model for life, life an imitation of death. Here death is a negative symbol for stasis, severed connection, disintegration."[16]

> A third aspect of death is perhaps the most neglected: death as a formative or constructive symbol, an element of creativity and renewal. Death then symbolizes the human capacity to confront in some way the most fearful aspects of experience and emerge with deepened sensibility and extended vitality and reach. This is what Heinrich Böll had in mind when he said, "The artist carries death in him like a good priest his breviary." Maintaining a psychic place for death, that is, enhances that that is most human, the imagination.[17]

According to Becker,[18] human beings have a preoccupation with death, which results in elaborate systems to conquer death. Constantly presented with our own mortality, the human spirit resists death and struggles for immortality. The struggle for immortality is the struggle for survival. In Lifton's terms, survival is rooted in "com[ing] into contact with death in some bodily or psychic fashion and remain[ing] alive...to 'touch death' and then rejoin the living can be a source of insight and power."[19] To encapsulate these points, the interaction between the realities of life and death create religion. Religion is the act of organizing the world in which we live by creating a safe space, both knowable and unknowable, for coping with the harsh realities of life. This includes rituals and the establishment of belief systems for controlling one's environment and perpetuating one's life.

A variety of other thinkers have influenced the psychology of religion. Two such thinkers, who were actually philosophers, are William James and Karl Marx. James defined religion as "the feelings, acts, and experiences of individual[s] in their solitude, so far as they apprehend themselves to stand in relation to whatever they consider the divine."[20] For James, religion was introspective and individual, therefore the only control is one's internal awareness. The limitation of his definition, like that of spirituality viewed only as sociopolitical action, is that it eliminates social religious activities and corporate worship. Marx believed:

> [Humanity] makes religion; religion does not make [humanity].
> [People are] the human world, the state, society. This state, this
> society, produce religion that is an inverted world consciousness…
> Religion is the general theory of this world…*Religion is the spiritual
> aroma of a corrupt people.*…Religion is the sigh of the oppressed
> creature, the sentiment of a heartless world, and the soul of soulless
> conditions. It is the opium of the people…[The human condition
> is a] vale of tears of which religion is the halo.[21]

For him, religion is illusory. Marx, therefore, in his understanding of religion,
would see spirituality as passivity, or what many would regard as spiritual-
ism. It is humanity's attempt to justify, and glorify, the horrendous life
conditions by imagining things are better and will get better naturally. But
if humanity is the world, the world is changed by first changing the self.

Religion as a Healing Resource

Jung believed that religion is a psychic process reaching toward wholeness. He understood psychic activities to be human finiteness groping for
the completeness of Divine Infinity. He believed the essence of all psychic
processes to be religious processes. Psychic and spiritual health are the
resulting activities encouraged by archetypes that are impersonal images
of the collective unconscious. The resulting activities and interactions have
established religion:

> What are religions? Religions are psychotherapeutic systems. What
> are we doing, we psychotherapists? We are trying to heal the suffer-
> ing of the human mind, of the human psyche or the human soul,
> and religions deal with the same problem. Therefore our Lord
> himself is a healer; he is a doctor; he heals the sick and he deals
> with troubles of the soul; and that is exactly what we call
> psychotherapy. It is not a play on words when I call religion a
> psychotherapeutic system. It is the most elaborate system, and
> there is a great practical truth behind it.[22]

For Jung, religion is an individual as well as a collective process. The
limitation of this approach, however, is that although it is keenly aware of
the life of the spirit (spirituality), the spirit can be seduced by corruption
yet not respond to overthrow injustice.

Religion as an Ideological Guide

Erikson believed that religion "elaborates on what feels profoundly
true even though it is not demonstrable: it translates into significant words,
images, and codes the exceeding darkness that surrounds [humanity's]
existence, and the light that pervades it beyond all desert or comprehension."[23] Due to Erikson's emphasis upon psycho-history and identity, he

also notes that religion is "a source of ideologies for those who seek identities."[24] In the context of Erikson's book *Young Man Luther*, ideology means "an unconscious tendency underlying religious and scientific as well as political thought: the tendency at a given time to make facts amenable to ideas, and ideas to facts, in order to create a world image convincing enough to support the collective and the individual sense of identity."[25]

> All religions have in common the periodical childlike surrender to a Provider or providers who dispense earthly fortune as well as spiritual health;...the insight that individual trust must become a common faith, individual mistrust a commonly formulated evil, while the individual's restoration must become a sign of trustworthiness in the community. This is the communal and psychosocial side of religion. Its often paradoxical relation to the spirituality of the individual is a matter not to be treated briefly and in passing...The religious layer in each individual abounds with efforts at atonement that try to make up for vague deeds against a maternal matrix and try to restore faith in the goodness of one's striving and in the kindness of the powers of the universe.[26]

Hence, Erikson's views are in many ways a combination of Freudian and Jungian understandings of religion to flesh out this very creative, life-orienting process. Religion is a summary of the life-cycle as we endeavor to determine who we are and to survive the world in which we live. The limitation of this approach is his emphasis upon positive parental experiences that form *faith*, which he conceived as being synonymous with religion.

Religious Experience

Since I have reviewed religion, it is also important to review religious experience. I have come to believe that a religious experience is an awesome moment of divine encounter. It is a moment, a brief encounter, of transcendent consciousness. It is not a trance, but a space of time when the layers of defense and the barriers of experiential pain are overtaken by an internal working of something more powerful than anyone's perceived sense of self. There is a self that stands forth as an integrator that unifies the fragmented individual in a moment of power and presence. A religious experience is a transcendent moment when one seems to clearly know one's place within the universe.

Thus, the ultimate problem addressed by religion is the human condition, on one level, and the conditions of a specific context on another. Religion orders a world that does not embrace, nurture, or care for the frailties of human beings. Religion is humanity's attempt to establish and maintain what it means to be human. Therefore, if religion is humanity's attempt to bring order as God brought order in the beginning, then "to be human at all requires that a person be able to act intentionally. In turn, what one intends in the world depends on how one attends to the world. After all, a person's image of the world can greatly affect his[her] sense of his[her] own place in the world."[27] Consequently, humanity religiously attends to the world by engaging and reshaping the context.

Moving Beyond the Limits of the Psychodynamic Psychology

Although psychodynamic psychology as embodied by the synoptic tradition of Freud, Jung, and Erikson is a very appropriate approach for assessing European American religiosity, it does not consider the African heritage to the extent that it ought in order to be an appropriate approach for assessing African American life. Freud grounded much of his theory in myth and symbolism. His interpretation and application of the myths and symbols have not reflected African or African American cosmology. His theories are more descriptive of European identity formation than they are theoretically inclusive of Africans. In some instances, those very myths have been resourced and have motivated some to acting violently against Africans.

While sexual repression may have been a problem during the time of his theorizing, that understanding would only have been true for the Victorian's. Nevertheless, within the Victorian context, sexuality was regarded as "bad," and bad (evil) must be eliminated. Also, since the pleasure principle was an important part of the anal stage, the elimination of what is "bad" from the body, urine and excrement, is pleasurable. Consequently, Western society has taken great pleasure in identifying Africans as excrement and eliminating us from humanity by projecting its sexuality problem and survival issues onto us.[28]

African American religious experiences tend to be very different from the European American religious experiences. If one were simply to consider the surface issues of this phenomenon, inaccurate and inappropriate assessments might be the result. An example of such assessments might be…It has been assumed that enslaved Africans learned monotheism and Christianity from European Americans. If such an assumption were true, then our worship practices should be the same as European Americans'. But the worship practices and expressions of European Americans and African Americans are not the same. Something different operates within African religiosity that makes our religious experience uniquely ours. Freud's attempt to illustrate that Christianity's sense of profound guilt emanated from Africa and the Egyptians rather than Jews reflects a high degree of moral development and religious sensibility on the part of Africans. Research into the religion and theology of the Egyptian pharaoh Akenaton reveals that Africans were monotheists prior to the American slavocracy. Acknowledging an African presence in the Bible declares we have been believers since the dawn of time itself.

Jung had a theory he called the "Transcendent Function," a psychic process whereby individuals move beyond a surface experience, allowing for the emergence of a truer, more historical, collective experience. The benefit of this function is that although Africans were removed from their homes and taught a "new" religion, former religious expressions can still emerge. Monotheism, for instance, was already a part of our African religious history and heritage. African American religious expressions differ from European American religious expressions because our experiences in America, our ancestral religious histories, and our guiding symbols are very different.

Where Jung does fall short is in his descriptive expressions of the archetypes and God-images. He claimed these symbols and myths to be universal and primordial; yet if the images and myths are primordial, then why are his representations predominantly European or Far Eastern, particularly since the "cradle of civilization" is African?[29]

Jung's critique of American society also cannot be overlooked. He clearly stated that many American problems are the direct result of White Americans living so close to Black Americans. He believed that Whites would be pulled down in nature unless their lives became more separate from African Americans. Although Jung tended to regard "black" as a negative attribute, his psychology maintained that both conscious and unconscious are of vital importance to individuation. This has profound implications when considering the identity formation of African Americans because it means that the impositions of certain social relationships are superseded by the internal mechanisms guided by the collective unconscious. As a result, there can emerge a true sense of self who has been guided by a "Historical Self." I will say more about this in chapter 9.

Erikson believed identity to be a consistent sense of self, the sum total of all social activity that has been promoted by the epigenetic principle. Although Erikson's focus reflected significant distinctions from Freudian theory, his foundational understandings of humanity were still dualistic. He continued to embrace the basic tenets of psychoanalysis and the idea of undoing.[30] However, unlike Freud, Erikson emphasized social relational changes rather than physiological changes to promote development. He continued to stress dualism through the psyche-soma relationship and the stage conflicts. The issue of every stage was described using positive and negative polarities. The resolution of issues means we fall on the positive or the negative side of the pole, preferably the positive side. The possibility for fixation is present at every stage.

Because Erikson hoped for the positive resolution of every crisis, his theoretical framing always left room for renegotiating the crisis of a particular stage. Within his thinking, renegotiation was almost an imperative. For example, much of American society has been directed toward forcing African Americans to the negative side of the pole. But within the confines of the African American community, African Americans have reworked each stage to develop a positive self-concept. While the broader context was saying, "slave," the smaller community was saying, "child of God."

Renegotiations have been an African American way of life. During the Enlightenment, Africans were not considered fully human. The basic understanding was that the Divine had marked Africans for permanent servitude. The "enlightened" citizens of these United States of America believed that God had cursed Africans to be slaves forever and that the sign of the curse was the color of our skin. The oppressive European landholders in America considered themselves to be fully human and regarded Africans as less than human. They validated their views by believing their misguided perceptions that Africans were happy in their enslavement. They thought we African Americans were happy in our misery. In their view, Africans were animals, the cursed of God, and well-suited to be "slaves for life." They shared a common thought that the more harsh our hardships, the more determined we would be to party through the night.

Unfortunately, many sons and daughters of the Enlightenment continue to maintain that legacy. This idea was one of the premises for titling the television sitcom *Good Times* during the 1970s. Living in poverty in an urban, subsidized housing project with "temporary layoffs" was a good time. During the 1980s, when the *Cosby Show* sought to counter that image, one of the common critiques of the show was that it was "not realistic" and did not represent African American life in the eyes of many European Americans. It challenged all the stereotypes. The show presented an African American professional couple who were affectionate and supportive. Their problem-solving dynamics were neither patriarchal nor matriarchal. They had strong family values with well-adjusted children.

Now, more than twenty years later, popular culture continues to project the age-old stereotypical images. Today, however, many of those images have been presented from the other end of the stereotypical spectrum. In chapter 4, I talked about black being identified as bad and white being identified as good. Popular culture's pendulum swing still presents black as bad, but it also now does more to present Black folks who aspire to live the American Dream as good. Often the issue is not in aspiring to live the Dream as much as it is the case that living the Dream tends to be based on Whiteness as the norm.

Take, for example, the show *Kevin Hill.* One could look at this show and regard it as a "breaking all the stereotypes" kind of show that presented the new generation that regards itself as not having the racial difficulties of former generations. The main character, Kevin Hill, was an established African American lawyer working at a firm led by an African American woman. He became a single parent by adopting his deceased cousin's daughter. He hired a gay white man to be the nanny. The basic setup took on some of the leading social justice issues we confront today–sexism, classism, homophobia, and single fatherhood; yet it positioned itself to say that racism is an "ism" of the past. The show's presentation of what is normative revealed racism's influence. Although Kevin Hill was far from friendless, he had no African American friends. None of the women he dated were as dark as he. All his love interests were very light African Americans, or they were not African American at all. As a result, European American categories and standards of beauty were what this show presented as the norms for success and living. In fact, if the lead actor, Taye Diggs, had been replaced with an European American actor, this show could have gone on without skipping a beat. For all intents and purposes, *Kevin Hill* was a white show with a black face.

Although race–which primarily denotes color–is a construct, it has been a prominent means of classifying humanity. People have used racial classification as a way of predicting behaviors. Consequently, issues of color and religion have constructed many hierarchical relationships that require liberation. Both racism and religion have had an incredible impact upon the African American psyche and African American identity formation. Resisting the negative classifications has been a significant expression of African American religiosity. Our religious experience promotes claiming human dignity. What Jung called individuation, African American religious experience calls salvation and freedom.

The Freudian understanding of religious experience, which has been expressed here by the term *freedom,* is the maintenance of infantile dependence. Yet completely opposed to this negative interpretation, one can say this religious "illusion" is a creative space that has given rise to a collective integrity. Hope, according to Erikson, develops during infancy. Even when life in America has been at its worst, we have had a faith and hope that life will get better. Erikson noted in his writing that hope is a fundamental strength and a foundation of faith.[31] African American religious history resounds with statements filled with vivid imagery such as, "when the chains of captivity have been removed by King Jesus, we are free forevermore."

By comparing individuation and religious freedom as two salvific processes, the African American religious experience is an indigenous approach to change. Individuation is a process whereby the dependence upon the defense mechanisms of the persona and the ego are relaxed so the true individual "Self" can be expressed. The "Self" is an archetype that acts to center the personality and is expressed within the psyche through figures like Jesus or Buddha. Through the rise of the "Self," the individual becomes free. From a psychoanalytic understanding of religion, one might conclude that freedom comes by turning from sin and becoming new creatures in the likeness of the Son as one is restored to community. Individuation is a process of nature; it is not initiated by the individual's hands. Freedom comes not by works but by the grace of God, for "while we still were sinners Christ died for us" (Rom. 5:8b).

This expression might be viewed as reinforcing Freud's description of religion as infantile; but this view does not fully express the way African Americans understood freedom activities. African Americans have developed not as a result of the Enlightenment but *in spite* of the Enlightenment. Although I would not say that psychology is religion, I say that religion has been the psychologist for the wounded African soul in America. This is also a view of religion from the perspective of traditional religions. Within traditional African religions, the healer was also a priest who served the psychophysical and psychospiritual needs of the people in the community.

A Resistance Culture

I stated earlier in this chapter that these synoptic theorists were valuable critics of American culture, but they knew little or nothing about the heart and soul of African American culture. The dominant culture of the United States is balanced by a variety of countercultures. Each one, in many respects, stands in sharp contrast to, and in defiance of, the historical values espoused by what generically tends to be called American culture. Americans have an international description. Through an evaluation of the leading tenets of American life, the description is a fairly accurate one. The leading tenets, however, do not describe all quarters of American life. Even within our borders, many aspects of American life are challenged and countered. A variety of ethnic groups are still American and resist the central value system that established our international reputation.

Occasionally, ethnic group expressions are identified as popular culture, but many of those group expressions have emerged as countercultural expressions. As Jesus has spoken in the gospel of Matthew, "But to what will I compare this generation? It is like children sitting in the marketplaces and calling to one another, / 'We played the flute for you, and you did not dance; / we wailed, and you did not mourn'" (Mt. 11:16–17). Refusing to be dominated by an opposing value system, a resistance culture clings to rituals, traditions, and relationships independent of the forces that compel people to conform or die. A resistance culture declares, "My experience is different from yours! We are who God has made us to be." For these groups, conformity would be death. The resistance culture understands its identity to be rooted in an historic "Self" that transcends this present time and space. This historic "Self," guided by a spirituality to choose life, resources the group's courage and commitment to live humanly, defying dehumanizing aggression and demoralizing expectations. Frequently seen as uninformed and immature, the resistance culture is spoken against by a critical voice that says, "Once they grow, they will see and believe like me." A resistance culture, however, resists the need to be a replica of the opposing culture and stands on its own historical sensibilities and encounters with the Divine.

African American culture fits the description of a resistance culture. I am not identifying the cultural diversity of the United States as subcultures.

Instead, I will continue to use the term *resistance culture.* This is done as an effort to avoid the trap of labeling all ethnic U.S. cultures as somehow inferior (sub-) to European American culture. By virtue of their existence, most ethnic cultures in the United States are resistance cultures. Through an identification with a national homeland, many groups cling to their ethnic heritage, celebrate their ethnic traditions, and pass on their ethnic rituals for the purpose of communal preservation. The maintenance of the culture is the living legacy passed on to future generations. While they identify with their nation of origin, they also proclaim their allegiance to their nation of citizenship. These ethnic cultures exert a countercultural force in order to resist the value system that is experienced as oppressive. Many of the values that define American life are as oppressive to some U.S. citizens as they are to others in an international context.

Not only have African Americans historically been deprived of the opportunity of full participation, but particular national attributes are contrary to what we have believed as a people. Our survival in the United States has not been dependent upon how well we have fit in, but on how well we have been able to resist the dehumanizing forces that have sought to destroy our sense of God, family, and community. A significant part of our resistance activities has been organized and directed by our religiosity and the African American Christian church. I am of the opinion that the heart and soul of African American culture took root and grew out of the religious experience of Africans struggling to maintain their humanity in America. By integrating African culture with our American life circum- stances, we resisted the chattel experience as the description of our souls. The hope of human freedom and dignity inspired us. We believed God was for us and with us, so we resisted ultimate despair. Those early resistance activities fostered and nurtured African American church and culture.

African American Christianity as a Resistance Culture

African American Christianity is grounded in our human struggle for freedom and justice. Although the majority of Black believers have identified with the Protestant denominations, those of us who are Baptist, Methodist, Presbyterian, etc., are Protestant only to the extent that we have faithfully resisted the oppression we have known in America. We did not participate in the Protestant Reformation and owe no debt to the culture or comments of the reformers. The founders of the mainstream denominational traditions did not fight to improve our standing in the world. Their message did not contribute to our efforts to maintain our full humanity. Nor did the message of the reformers positively influence the standard of life we were forced to endure on these shores.

The Protestant slavers of North America considered Africans to be soulless servants. For generations, we were thought to bear the mark of Cain or the curse of Ham. "Faithful" Protestant believers regarded Africans as chattel to be used for their personal pleasure and economic gain. A legacy such as this is hardly the foundation for the African American faith tradition that has nurtured generations of believers, nor is it the most valuable resource for interpreting African American religiosity.

The Christian church in the Americas has rarely acted on behalf of Africans in our quest for freedom and justice. I don't deny that some European American Christians joined our struggle for freedom and justice, but their numbers were never great enough to describe their efforts as representative of the Christian church. Racism and economic enterprises have frequently existed by a "hand-in-glove" relationship. At the beginning of the Atlantic Slave Trade, the Church had an opportunity to speak the words of peace and love on our behalf. Instead, the "missionary to the Indians," Bartolomé de Las Casas, made Africans the sacrificial lambs for the slaughter in order to end the Amerindian genocide.

In 1517, Bartolomé de Las Casas, also known as the "Apostle of the Indies," after watching thousands of Indians dying in corrals and burned alive, returned to Spain and pleaded with Charles V to spare them. Las Casas begged the King, as an act of mercy toward the natives of the Indies, to import Africans to be slaves, twelve for each colonist. In 1518, Charles V of Spain granted license (*asiento*) for importation of four thousand African-born people to be enslaved each year to the Indies. The license was sold to the Portuguese. This was the beginning of the enslavement of West Africans and the Atlantic Slave Trade.[32] Since the enslavement of Africans had nothing to do with Christianizing Africans, no one should ever see African American Christianity as having its heritage linked with the Christianity as it was practiced in the Americas. Christian mercy was not shown to us as our captors contemplated our enslavement. Consequently the foundations of African American Christianity are not found in Europe or in missionary evangelization. Its foundations are African religions, African spirituality, and our struggle to maintain our human dignity in the face of evil. The force of African American Christianity as a resistance culture is located in its maintenance of a heritage of unity and rituals of sacrifice for the greater good.

African American Christianity as a resistance culture refused to be dominated by the basic American religious value system. The system valued individual survival and "White only" privileges. Yet our survival system was based on communal and familial wholeness with privileges emanating from our human compassion and regard for one another. Our conversion experiences were so powerful and persuasive that turning away from the truths derived from those experiences would have meant death. We endured many brutalities to show the convictions of our beliefs. Guided by our spiritual heritage, we resisted becoming what the American religious context told us we were. Through resistance, we sustained our identity as the children of God and maintained the community relationships that supported our being.

Because of the limitations I have noted, it is more important to me to develop an indigenous approach than to continue to adapt psychoanalysis, analytical psychology, or social psychology. Because of the influence of African American religious experience, it is imperative to move beyond a mere Western or American approach. The next "leg of the journey" does not depart from making use of psycho-history; rather, it includes the theological understanding of faith and the activities of spirituality. Chapter 7 is devoted to a discussion of African American spirituality.

7

African American Spirituality
as Survival

Perceptions of God and Jesus paved the way for the slaves' notion of a God-given humanity; African American chattel were created in freedom. White theology and white Christian ethical practices not withstanding, black folk maintained that they were not livestock but sculptured by divine hands and made in a human image of God.

DWIGHT N. HOPKINS

Some years ago, I was consulting with an organization interested in developing ministries that partnered the council of churches and the African American church. Once we engaged in discussions concerning this desire, it became clear that the director saw the Black church as having a spiritual vitality he desired for his own. When I shared my concerns with a friend not affiliated with the organization, he took my analysis in a different direction. I suggested that the director was like Simon the Magician, who wanted the power he had witnessed among Christians but had no under-standing of the faith. My friend agreed with my assessment but went on further to say that spirituality is the crowning glory of the Black church, and also its greatest weakness. This chapter will examine African American spirituality. I will present an understanding of spirituality that describes it as a resource for survival.

Spirituality and Religion

Spirituality is one of the most influential forces within the African American community. It is the core resource that has shaped the community from within. African American spirituality, with its roots in African spirituality and African traditional religions has influenced the consciousness, directed the relational existence, and promoted African American survival for generations. The variety of interpretive approaches for understanding spirituality have ranged from power to pathetic, and from action to passivity. The spirituality of the African American is perhaps best understood from the perspective of religiosity.

To the cynical, religion is typically regarded as an invention of humanity, a coping mechanism to shield oneself against the harsh, uncontrollable realities of life. The African American religious experience is often considered the epitome of that understanding. Consequently, African American spirituality has been looked upon as being superstitious and escapist. These critical ideas have tended to spring from opinions of that religion as having been an inhibitor of Black progress as we have journeyed toward freedom. Although it may appear on the surface that religion promotes escapist attitudes from the world, religion has provided the African American with a worldview and an integrity that enable us to continue living against all odds.

The essence of human nature propels humanity to create a belief system that nurtures integrity and security. Even the person who professes disbelief in a higher being will have a highly ritualized belief system that has many of the same characteristics as the theistic believer's system. In North American history, religion, *generally,* has been the primary force for polity and policy. For Africans in America, religion, *specifically,* has been the primary force for integrity and survival. Religiosity has been the central feature of the African American self-concept. Therefore, an African American theory of communal identity must be developed from a psycho-theological framework. Spirituality is an essential feature of this critical framework. I regard it as the energy that organizes the identity.

Religion and Survival

Reviewing African American religious life requires attentiveness to avoid oversimplifying our religious experience. The sense of integrity that develops out of our religiosity is not an invention of the intellect, but a reality of our soul. Historically, Africans in America have been able to endure horrendous living conditions because of the integrity of an identity that was derived from a vivacious psyche/soul. The African psyche/soul developed a system of survival that has articulated a spirituality of hopefulness, personhood, and community.[1] This systemic perspective did not begin as a conscious process, but as an unconscious stirring.

The term *survival* is very appropriate for a discussion of African American communal identity formation. While I am aware of the problems associated with using the term, it is, nevertheless, an appropriate attitude for African Americans. Those who tend to argue against this attitude (one that argues for the idea of survival for African Americans) tend to base their disagreement on the hope that we will not merely survive but thrive. For those persons, survival tends to connote living hand-to-mouth and day-to-day. This approach regards survival as a human weakness rather than the courage of one's humanity. That is not what I intend when I speak of African American survival. One can only thrive after one has survived and overcome the trauma. The extent to which we are living with Protracted-Traumatic Stress Disorder,[2] surviving and thriving are inseparable. Survival is "the capacity of men and women to live beneath the pressure of protracted crisis, to sustain terrible damage in mind and body and yet be there, sane, alive, still human."[3] The maintenance of our humanity is the maintenance of our relationships and our community.

The people who have tended to negatively associate the term "survival" with African Americans have often understood survival to be a reactionary response within a powerless condition. Instead of regarding survival as the most human response, they exhibit a knee-jerk reaction that seems to be an unconscious response to the term. This response aligns survival with the evolutionary struggles of the animals. In that sense, survival implies a struggle to dissociate from the animals rather than acknowledging humanity's strength of spirit to remain human beneath the most adverse conditions.

Darwin has had a strong influence on our understanding of survival with his notion of "the survival of the fittest." That was primarily the context for my usage of the term in chapter 3 when I spoke of the racist who understands his or her racial preference to be a fight for White survival. I use the term survival here not in the Darwinian sense, nor do I use the term to indicate a life of mourning losses. I use the term "survival" to describe our creative strength to confront, with great courage, the life-denying forces we face daily. Survival means learning how to thrive in a socially and emotionally hostile world. It means constructing a worldview that acknowledges suffering, lives with losses, and transforms limitations into assets.

Survival in the United States of America

As with dominant traits, life also has a dominant experience. For the purposes of this discussion, one either has a dominant experience as oppressor or oppressed. In the broader scheme of American history, African American life has been the experience of the oppressed. We have only been included in the vitality of America as part of the underpaid or nonpaid labor force and as objects of pleasure for the enjoyment of the sadistic. Darwinian notions of survival were the order of the day for the colonials and later for those who forged into the West. As an ideology, Darwinian survival powerfully shaped the collective American consciousness, producing an attitude of "never yield and never lose."

We Americans understand ourselves to be survivors, to be revolutionary "underdogs" who struggle against the odds. This has, perhaps, been one of the underlying appeals of the reality television show *Survivor.* Due to the ideological "rugged individualism," the survival of self has meant the annihilation of other. Frontier survival produced systematic genocide and oppressive labor practices. The American lust for life and land are expressions of a lust for power. This individualistic desire for power promoted cruelty in the name of safety, security, and progress. This version of survival, by interpreting the actions of the oppressor, is the most prominent experience, but it is not the only interpretation of survival.

Survival for Africans in America–from the colonial period through Western expansion–was not guided by denying life, but by an understanding of the sanctity of life and the connectedness of all things. African survival, which became African American survival, has been guided by African spirituality. African Americans have been the victims of every life-denying activity actualized on these shores. The racist system called us animals and established conditions to force an animal's response. Rather than surrendering to the evil, however, the oppressed diasporadic Africans redefined their humanity, galvanized as a community, and chose life over yielding to the forces of death. "By choosing not only to live, but to live humanly, they took upon themselves the burden of an action requiring much will and courage, much clear sightedness and faith in life."[4] It was our faith in life, our spirituality, that made our survival creative rather than destructive. African spirituality provided a passion for living in relationship, helping us to resist a life defined by rugged individualism.

African Spirituality

African spirituality is commonly defined by the saying, "There is no separation between the sacred and the secular." The force of African spirituality is that it does not dichotomize the living. The energy of African spirituality brings unity to life. Larger than any one religious system, spirituality is an integrative process and the driving force for living humanly. It holds life as the highest value and promotes life as the deepest expression. Spirituality unifies all of one's individual parts into a whole self. All relationships are brought together into a harmonious community.

In an age marked by nihilism, spirituality is the answer to the longing in life that people experience. Because it is a process larger than any individual religious tradition, spirituality also has different conceptualizations of purpose and focus. Within America, spirituality can range in meaning from spiritual disciplines, such as prayer, to social justice to shamanism to escapism. It can mean reflective charisma or aggressive activism.

Generally, American connotations of spirituality have two manifestations. Spirituality either manifests itself as being active or passive. The active understanding considers spirituality to be activities that seek to reform living conditions. This is typically understood to be sociopolitical action. The passive understanding considers spirituality to be activities that seek to transform personal and individual emotions to endure harsh living conditions. This is frequently regarded as meditative, or the "inward journey." I believe it is important to know that ways people tend to describe spirituality as active and passive are both expressions of spirituality. Furthermore, I believe it to be imperative that both descriptions are held together as a single expression.

Spirituality as sociopolitical action is understood as actively seeking to bring God's justice in the world. The proponents of this perspective believe that spirituality does not exist or function outside of an activist context. So, righteous indignation, marches for peace, and rallies are active manifestations of spirituality. The limitation of this view is that worship does not qualify as an expression of spirituality. Therefore, this view tends to overlook the ongoing spiritual transformation of the protestor who is seeking justice. This is the activist form of spirituality.

Spirituality as meditative is understood as attending to a person's inner life. This perspective maintains communion and prayer as its central expression. Spirituality helps one to transcend the suffering and to resist evil in the world. This approach emphasizes the inward journey. It could ultimately manifest itself as sociopolitical action, but primarily it is a struggle to encounter the Eternal. Spirituality, in this sense, directs one's entire being to be in relationship with the spirit of God. This is the charismatic form of spirituality.

African American Spirituality

From an African American perspective, to separate charisma and activism within spirituality is to create an artificial worldview.[5] Our spirituality has promoted our survival in America since we landed in 1526. It has encouraged human life in the face of and in resistance to death:

> Spirituality seeks to connect and maintain the connection between all aspects of our living. It is the charismatic stirring within the soul that stimulates and perpetuates our commitments to living wholly holy lives. To be spiritual should not mean that we are disconnected from the world. Spirituality should mean that one is fully engaged in relationships and life. Spirituality leads us to have an active public witness that seeks justice and liberation as well as a vital personal relationship with the Divine. Spirituality is the active integration of our humanity. Through its expression, we cease to function in parts and begin to live up to our potential as whole human beings. Spirituality results in a singularly directed effort to be in communion with God, self, and others.[6]

In chapter 6 I attempted to present a theologically and psychologically balanced view of religiosity. The pains of life and the protracted suffering (that we identify as evil) we African Americans have experienced in America have organized our religion. We have a long legacy of suffering that has stirred our souls to seek the face of God. Although Hellenistic dualism and Western European intellectualizations encourage Americans to be religious stoics, our spirituality is far more emotive. Spirituality integrates passion and compassion. This means our spiritual activities are emotional, intentional, and relational.

African American spirituality has directed our response to our encounter with the life-denying forces of racism and death. Because the source of spirituality is the eternal reaches of the soul, our survival is God-inspired. Through our spiritual activities, we have a foundation for relationships that has supported our survival and preserved our humanity. Through African oral tradition and the art of storytelling, African spirituality carried all things from the past–the particularities of our cultural history and of our previous conversations with God–into the present. This gives us help in the present, and hope for the future. The premiere symbol of African American spirituality is the Black church. Whereas we could have become individuals and died in isolation, the Black church helped us to maintain our relationships and the ties of community.[7] The spirituality of the enslaved African constructed a worldview that resulted in the development of a survivalist religion that articulated hopefulness, personhood, and community.

The Middle Passage

The atrocities of the Middle Passage"–or the *Maafa,* –which ranged from maiming to murder, have had a profound impact on the identity formation of the African American. The Middle Passage was the voyage from West Africa to the Americas, and the *Maafa* is Kiswahili, meaning "the great disaster."[8] Those degrading and de-humanizing experiences have caused us to feel isolation, despair, and rage. To have an appreciation for the resilience of African Americans, it is important to know something of life in Africa before the great disaster of exportation. Too often people make an unfortunate connection between African deportation and deliverance. The connection is to believe that Africans were saved by slavery in America, that we were delivered from our superstitions into the light of God through our suffering in slavery. Such thinking lives on in racist illusions that suggest that the Middle Passage, commonly referred to as the "Slave Trade," brought salvation to Africans. But remember, we were enslaved, not slaves.

We need to be very clear! The majority of the West Coast African nations were far from being "naked savages." Many cities were nearly as large as the largest cities in Europe. Some African kingdoms and commonwealths compared in size to many European nations. "Many of them

[Africans] possessed flocks of donkeys and great herds of cattle, sheep, and goats. They were skilled workers in wood, brass, and iron, that they had learned to smelt long before the white men came."[9] Slavery in African society was radically different from the slavery fashioned in the Western hemisphere. In some places, those enslaved within African culture could be married, own property, and grow food for themselves. In other parts of Africa, the enslaved functioned as soldiers of the military, or as administrative officers. The *chattel* slavery, however, was a far cry from what Africans experienced in Africa. The New World confronted Africans with a dehumanizing ethos with which they were largely unfamiliar.

In 1441, ten Africans had been shipped to Portugal as a curiosity, after a trading expedition. Three years later, 235 Africans were shipped to the Portuguese port of Lagos. Initially, Africans were secured by banditry and kidnapping. By 1456, the prominence of kidnapping had given way to African and European exchanges. In 1518 the slave trade proper began. Ships landing in the West Indies carried the first Black cargo direct from Africa. Bartolome de Las Casas' initiated this with his plea to spare the Indians of Hispaniola from total genocide by enslaving Africans instead. Wars produced a population for enslavement for the Atlantic slave trade just as they had for the domestic African trade. Many wars were fought solely to secure persons for the Trade. What were termed wars in this context should more appropriately be classified as raids. This also meant that kidnapping continued to be a means for supplying the Trade. Individuals found in isolated places were often victims. Because women could not effectively resist capture, they were frequently targeted. Women constituted about one-third of the human cargo aboard most ships. Sometimes women of importance to the tribe were targeted to lure the men out into situations in which they could be easily captured. Eventually, the growing demands were largely met through other means.

People in Europe and North America carry a not so unconscious idea that Europeans brought civilization to Africa. The fact is, they did not introduce manufacturing plants, agricultural methods, business communities, political systems, or Christian ideas, as they were trying to do in the New World. What they introduced were muskets, gunpowder, dry goods, and rum, all means of advancing the enslavement of Africans. The slavers encouraged warfare by providing arms and munitions to both sides on the condition that they return with human commodities at low prices. On this front, the multiple languages of the numerous tribes proved to be a valuable asset for those who traded in death. "One tribe could not understand another. There were 264 Sudanic languages, 182 Bantu languages, and 47 Hamitic languages. A single people, such as the Wolof of Senegal, might be divided into two or three hostile kingdoms; the Yoruba of Nigeria had ten separate states. Neither these little kingdoms nor the warring tribes around them would join together against a common enemy, and hence it was easy for the slavers to set one group against another."[10] The described separation remained the case until the voyage.

African captives were gathered in castles/dungeons and slave markets at various ports to await transportation. Prior to their voyage, their heads were shaved. They were branded with hot irons to distinguish "ownership." Portuguese slavers baptized their human cargo captives before sailing. They held the belief that all captives had to be christened. Such an idea was so ridiculous: to baptize a soul for the purpose of demoralizing and exploiting a soul.

> In truth those wholesale baptisms must have been ludicrous affairs, yet they were not without meaning. They showed that the Portuguese at least regarded Africans as human beings with souls to be saved, and they help to explain why slavery in Brazil, though as cruel as slavery in the British West Indies, was in some respects a more liberal institution. The English were not in the least concerned with the souls of their black cargoes, and, unlike the Portuguese, they did not even send missionaries to Africa until the end of the 18th cen.; they sent only drygoods, gin, and firearms. In their practical way, and with their genius for large-scale undertakings, they probably inflicted more suffering on the Negroes than any other nation. On the other hand, they were also the nation that changed its heart, or found its heart, and did by far the most to abolish the trade. In the end it is hard to assign the chief guilt to any national group. English, French, Dutch, Danes, Branden-burgers, Portuguese, Mandingos driving slaves from the Niger to the coast, the absolute kings of Dahomey, Yankee skippers, Congolese middlemen, and Egbo merchants in Old Calabar–the trade brutalized almost everyone who engaged in it. The guilt for it rests not wholly on the white race, or partly on the African kings and slave merchants, but beyond them on humanity itself.[11]

African captives were stripped naked and marched single file at night through dark, narrow corridors to be boarded on ships. Men and women were put into separate holds–the men chained below deck in leg irons, while the women and children were on the upper deck. The height of the lower deck racks averaged between four and five feet. All the Africans were forced to sleep without covering on bare, often unplaned, wooden floors. While men were chained below, the women were frequently brutal-ized and exploited. A woman's nakedness was a constant reminder of her sexual vulnerability; rape, therefore, was a common method of torture and control. "An observer of the slave trade documented the prevalence of rape on slave ships. He asserts, 'In those days many a negress was landed upon our shores already impregnated by someone of the demonic crew that brought her over.'"[12] The women who were pregnant prior to capture or purchase were forced to endure pregnancy without any care, diet, or assistance. The number of women that died during childbirth, the number of stillborn children, or the number that flung themselves into the sea is unknown.

The Middle Passage was the place where brainwashing and indoctrination began. The slaver's job was to transform a free, spirited being into an unfree, "docile slave" for a lifetime of servitude. The slavers' goal was to destroy human dignity, remove names and status, and disperse groups so that persons of the same language group would not be together. Their task, fundamentally, was to remove any signs of an African heritage. This devious process was the foundation for the false identity of "Slave American." Because spirituality was such a vital part of the African being, the resources to survive the horrors were initiated, and the motivation to adapt and overcome was stimulated:

> During the process of their becoming a single people, Yoruba, Akans, Ibos, Angolans, and others were present on slave ships to America and experienced a common horror—unearthly moans and piercing shrieks, the smell of filth and the stench of death, all during the violent rhythms and quiet coursings of ships at sea. As such, slave ships were the first real incubators of slave unity across cultural lines, cruelly revealing irreducible links from one ethnic group to the other, fostering resistance thousands of miles before the shores of the new land appeared on the horizon—before there was mention of natural rights in North America.[13]

The first enslaved Africans who arrived in Jamestown, Virginia, in 1619 were not considered chattel. At that time, indentured servitude was the dominant form of slavery and included Europeans, who were rarely identified as slaves. The difference between indenture and slave was service and term. The identity of slave had a total loss of liberty and humanity. Yet at the beginning of North American slavery, differences in term separated Blacks and Whites. Most Blacks were serving for life. Though not overtly stated, this was evidenced by price and by the lack of a defined term of service. The Portuguese dominated the Middle Passage until the seventeenth century when the main features of the Trade became fixed. While the suppression of the trade began in 1865, the last cargo of human carnage landed as late as 1880 in South America. The sheer numbers of lives lost over the course of the Middle Passage are shocking and horrifying. The bondage that followed the horrors of "exportation" (because they were dealing in commodities, and not transporting human beings) presented Africans with an overwhelming sense of powerlessness to change the circumstances of their captivity. They did attempt to change their captivity. Many revolts occurred onboard ship, and many more Africans jumped overboard into the sea.

Spirituality Maintains a Heritage

The Africans who survived the brutality of the Middle Passage had to construct a new world that gave them hope and made life worth living. Their survival became dependent on the maintenance of their humanity, the formation of new relationships, and the reestablishing of the village. All these efforts, mediated by spirituality, were actualized by the development of the Black church.[14]

If African American spirituality, which fostered survival and the preservation of humanity, is to be understood beyond a psycho-spiritual phenomenon, then its African antecedents must be acknowledged. A few cosmological understandings germane to West Africa ought to be identified. Although the tribal systems of the West African nations were extremely diverse in language and custom, numerous relational and religious similarities existed. It may be important to note that African diversity is not different from European diversity with countries like Portugal, Spain, France, Switzerland, and Germany. Even in this difference, European similarities are universally acknowledged. It is, therefore, not unreasonable to consider African cultural unity amidst the diversity.

West African Cosmology

West Africans regarded the universe as organized by the Creator–God–and life was to be lived out in an orderly fashion. God, as the Supreme Being, was understood to have a human form. God was revered as Father, sometimes Mother, or Parent. The people thought of themselves as the offspring of God. There was, therefore, an understanding of communality and family was the primary structure. Relationships were built upon the importance of communal responsibility, which became the foundation of moral development and the value system of African society. There was remembrance of and reverence for the ancestors, which has often been misrepresented as ancestor worship. They believed spirits could affect human relationships. They believed in a force, a power, an energy that could be tapped by humans to transform the world. It was believed this power could be used for good or evil, and this has often been misrepresented as a religion of magic.[15]

African Spirituality Expressed Religiously

Religion, as the centerpiece of the African worldview, was organized phenomenologically and metaphysically.[16] It had no sacred text to guide its system, and orthodoxy was a matter of ethics within a particular life situation. The tradition maintained a form and was developed through myths, stories, proverbs, riddles, ceremonies, symbols, and legends. John Mbiti noted, "African religion is very pragmatic and realistic…Changes are often brought about by new necessities."[17] This speaks clearly to the African American's religious history of accommodating the Christian faith to their life circumstances and faith understanding. This worldview grounded in religion also reflects a congruence between African religions and the Christian faith:

> In many ways African Religion prepared the way for the conversion of African peoples to Christianity. But their conversion does not mean that they [had] abandoned all their former religious ideas and traditions. Often their religious life shows a combination of African Religion and Christianity.[18]

This understanding of the retentions of Africanism and its influence upon American life has been a stimulating debate for many years.[19]

The combination of the spirituality (making no separations between God and humanity, heaven and earth, nature and spirits) and religion became the primary interpreter of life for captive Africans. Spirituality as a guiding force came to dominate the African American consciousness. Communality, expressed through spirituality, promoted the survival of Africans as humans in such an inhumane environment. This survival was founded on the spiritual principle that there was no division between the sacred and the secular. Although living conditions were experienced as radical suffering, captive Africans continued to see God as the Creator who was very near, while they saw their captors as functioning outside the will of God. Their spirituality allowed them to see God through the veil of tears, experience joy in the midst of sorrowful slavery, celebrate life in the face of death, and envision freedom through the travails of life. Our lives became our sacred texts. Our songs became our sacred music. Our gatherings, no matter what the activity, became our sacred ground.

> The division between the sacred and the secular, so prominent a feature of modern Western culture, did not exist in black Africa in the years of the slave trade, before Christianity made real inroads on the continent…This quality of African religion, its uniting of seeming opposites, was perhaps the principle reason it was considered savage by whites. It was the source of creative genius in the slave community and a main reason that whites and free blacks thought the slaves lacked a meaningful spirituality.[20]

A virtue of the human spirit is adaptability. When captive Africans were thrust into the same perilous and desperate situation, tribes who formerly had no relationship developed bonds in the wake of the harsh realities. Perhaps when they previously encountered one another on African soil, though they were of the same skin, they were not of the same mind. However, on board ship their spirituality was at work building upon common truth with the hope of a greater truth. A profound faith in the Creator allowed them to look through the horrors of the Middle Passage. The intense suffering they experienced forced the Africans to push beyond the boundaries of what had been believed about life and their enemy, who suddenly became their neighbor, and develop solidarity for the purpose of survival. Implicit in African life was a care ethic for the survival of the family and community. Within the context of this "great disaster" (the *Maafa*), the care ethic saw all Africans as family and part of the same community.

Laboring on plantations did not destroy the newly enslaved Africans' consciousness, that is, a consciousness of what it means to be African.[21] This consciousness and awareness of an African past was maintained even though the new environment was determined to destroy every vestige of personhood. Landholders enacted every atrocity imaginable against the African in an effort to separate him or her from the past, from the community, and from the freedom under God that Africans had previously known. But captive Africans, like the Jew of the Babylonian captivity, refused to forget everything of their native homeland. The newly developed folktales retained African words and the identity of a free being who longed to be liberated. The poems, prayers, and stories condemned slavery and affirmed a noble African past. A high value was placed on survival, life, and humanity. An uncompromising spirit of resistance developed, resisting death, total assimilation, and absolute degradation. From this resistance emerged a theology of survival that guided moral and religious behavior:

> The whole of their being was engulfed in a system intent on their annihilation as persons. Their response to this overwhelming fact of their existence ranged from suicide to outright rebellion. But few slaves committed suicide. Most refused to accept the white master's definition of black humanity and rebelled with every ounce of humanity in them. The black church became the home base for revolution.[22]

The newly enslaved African consciously strove to maintain his or her homeland identity by incorporating cultural and religious traditions and symbols into the prescribed lifestyle of slavocracy:

> By operating under cover of Christianity, vital aspects of Africanity, that some considered eccentric in movement, sound, and symbolism, could more easily be practiced openly. Slaves therefore had readily available the prospect of practicing, without being scorned, essential features of African faith together with those of the new faith.[23]

African symbols and imagery such as the staff-cross were reinterpreted. Bodies of water that were thought to have a netherworld beneath were translated into the new context. Consequently, the Christian cross and the act of baptism carried many hidden meanings for the Africans in exile. Many cultural practices were also maintained secretly. "Secretiveness was dictated by the realities of oppression and worked against whites acquiring knowledge of slave culture that might have been used to attempt to eradicate that culture.[24]

Rather than assuming the moral standards of the landholders, the diasporatic Africans developed their own code of moral conduct and judgment. Through their spirituality, they developed a keen sense of perception for detecting moral material. The enslaved could perceive the guilt-filled dread of their enslavers; and the perceptions were occasionally confirmed by the landholders begging the forgiveness of those formerly enslaved. Such requests were rare but did happen.

In addition to survivalist religion nurturing an African self-identity and moral stability, religiosity was, quite often, the premiere form of rebellion. "Religion itself [was] an assertion of slave independence, which sometimes required outright defiance of the master's command."[25] Just as the enslaved were perceptive enough to detect the immorality of their enslavers, they also recognized the limitations of White Christianity. Slave testimonies, in abundance, document their observed limitations. They distinguished the hypocritical religion of the enslavers from true Christianity, and rejected the landholder's gospel of obedience to master and mistress. In fact, "slaves believed there existed somewhere a true Bible from God, since all that they heard from it was 'Servants, obey your masters.'"[26] True to African spirituality, they chose to accept or reject the message of the enslavers' preachers based upon their intuitive senses from their souls and their experiences. For instance, sermons on the subject "Don't Steal" were always reinterpreted because the enslaved acknowledged themselves as stolen property.

Previously, I attempted to share a framework for understanding the relationship between myth, history, religion, and spirituality. The goal was to share a perspective that understands truth as an expression from beyond time yet also moves within time and space through spirituality and the human's experience of history. As such, the same methodology used by the enslaved to interpret the sermons was also employed to exact their hermeneutic upon the biblical narratives. Instead of assimilating, the enslaved appropriated the narratives to have relevance within their experience. The exodus narrative became their archetype[27] of a mythic past. It became the enslaved's way of articulating a sense of a historical identity as a people. Through spirituality, the inner world expressions stood in direct opposition to the enslaver's belief. Through spirituality, the Africans who became Americans gave witness to the immorality of slavery and exposed it as contrary to the will of God.

Just as the survivalist religion was a product of African spirituality that provided a new worldview as well as a stable identity within a very unstable situation, the music of the enslaved was a union of African rhythms and their experiences in America. "Spirituals were born as the religious vision of the larger society was caught, as by centripetal force, drawn to the innermost regions of black spiritual consciousness and applied to what blacks were experiencing in slavery."[28] The African of the American diaspora was a "living soul" in every way! "The genius of the black religious system is that it is alive. It is not a system that is a servant to print, media, or linear logic."[29]

Some people subscribed to a popularized belief that Christianity as practiced by the enslaved was not radical. To this extent, these critics seem to feel that Marx was looking directly at slave religion when he presented his views that "religion is an opiate." However,

> To describe slave religion as merely otherworldly is inaccurate, for the slaves believed that God had acted, was acting, and would continue to act within human history and within their own particular history as a peculiar people just as long ago he had acted on behalf of another chosen people, biblical Israel. Moreover, slave religion had a this-worldly impact, not only in leading some slaves to acts of external rebellion, but also in helping slaves to assert and maintain a sense of personal value—even of ultimate worth.[30]

Many features could be highlighted as distinctive of the African American consciousness and community. If someone would undertake the task of compiling a list and prioritizing those compilations, at the top of that list would be the statement: "The [African-American] community is a suffering community."[31] The African American consciousness has been greatly influenced by the suffering caused by the destructive instruments of oppression and genocide. But in opposition to the despair and chaos, African Americans have been able to creatively give form and meaning to formlessness and void. They have been able to transform the evil and corrupt side of a dualistic context into a duality that has helped to "stave off" despair and to bring victory over the forces of brutality. The many things meant for evil, African Americans have transformed for a good. They were stripped of family, home, religion, and dignity. In return, they have developed new systems. The extended family has become their strength, hope has become their shelter, a new religion has become their guide, and unity has supported their stature and humanity.

The African American consciousness, guided by spirituality, has placed the highest value upon human life. It esteems family, honor, community, sharing, fellowship, and worship. Through the struggle, we have developed an identity of integrity because our focus has been humanity—that is, inseparable from the Divine—in direct opposition to the most inhumane conditions in the world. Without most of the advantages that one presumes necessary to negotiate in the world, we have survived! This fact is due wholly to the vitality/spirituality of the African American. African spirituality has been the formative experience and primary force for the development of the African American cultural identity.

Spirituality in the Future

As a closing thought, I have attempted to illustrate that the early history of the African American reveals a great spirituality through the refusal to identify with the projected image of the oppressor. But as a twenty-first–century African American pondering the future, I wonder if we will maintain the integrity of the past? We are currently in a state of crisis. How will we resolve our current conflict?

8

Liberating Our Identity

In an extreme view, I would argue that Black people are fundamentally artistic, and that Black life is an expression of the celebration of life. It is a fluid, expressive, emotional, and passionate life that is bound to be misinterpreted or misunderstood or simply not comprehended by the controlled, impersonal, formalistic procedures of social science. Whereas a person imbued with a Puritan philosophy will behave in systematic ways that can be measured by the instruments of social science, Black people often are not so easily encapsulated. If there is any hope of providing a comprehensive account of the Black experience within the framework of the American experience, I suggest that there must be some fusion of the principles, beliefs, and practices of an artistic point of view with the controlled observations of scientific procedure.

JAMES M. JONES

African religions gave rise to a dynamic interplay between community and individual. Whatever happened to the communal gathering affected the individual, and whatever happened to the individual had an impact on the community. Such a theological view of humanity cuts across bourgeois notions of white Christianity's individualism and "me-first-ism." It seeks to forge a group solidarity and identity, beginning with God, proceeding through the ancestors to the community and immediate family, and continuing even to the unborn.

DWIGHT N. HOPKINS

Freedom and justice are historical categories of African American life. Both categories are central to what we mean when we speak of the liberation of African Americans. As I discussed in chapter 6, the work of liberation is simultaneously the work of resistance. Consequently, liberation suggests more than spiritual and religious freedom, which are historical features of what it means to be free in America. Because of the conditions of our enslavement, the African American experience of the religious freedom tradition has often been misinterpreted to be escapism. Our understanding of liberation, however, has always meant more than "pie in the sky" or freedom in "the sweet by-and-by." Spiritual and religious freedom has been the language of African American resistance. Liberation suggests more than physical freedom and compensation for loss, which are historical activities initiated at the founding of the nation. Because of the dehumanizing ideologies and the segregation legally imposed on our lives, African American liberation has meant experiencing the rights, privileges, and benefits granted to every citizen of the United States of America. We African Americans have always desired our "just deserts," the same as any other who sings, "This land is your land, this land is my land…This land was made for you and me."

In this chapter, I review several African American approaches to liberation. Each of the African American liberation approaches I have selected has sought to help us to know ourselves while articulating an image of freedom and justice. To best articulate what each approach holds as critical, I have selected a group of liberation thinkers. Each selected person within each selected field has grappled with the African American individual and communal identity from different vantage points. Each of the selected voices has conscientiously sought to reinterpret the African American story in the United States of America. Each of the selected thinkers identifies a constellation of issues that are critical to the liberation efforts of the African American community. My emphasis here, however, is more upon the disciplinary fields and their liberation approaches than it is upon stressing the value of a particular thinker. The liberation disciplinary fields I reflect upon in this chapter are African American theology, Black (African) psychology, and African American pastoral theology. Although I may might not be utilizing the most recent texts of the thinkers, I have selected texts I consider representative of each discipline's methodology, and of the thinker's work. I also see the selections as appropriate for explicating African American liberation.

Strangers and Estranged Relationships

African American lives frequently have been strangely interpreted. These strange and peculiar interpretations have regularly made us appear to be a sick, even deviant, people. The ways our history and belief system have been falsely interpreted have often made us strangers to ourselves, believing ourselves to be quite other than what we are at the very core of our being. I appeal once again to the dynamics of marriage to explain what I mean by being "strangers to ourselves."

When I share in group settings some of the dynamics that exist in the life of a married couple, I frequently talk about how a couple can, although they have been married for many years, awake one morning and look at one another and ask: "Who are you?" After ten, fifteen, even twenty years of marriage, a couple can still have the experience of being strangers to each other. How can it be that one can devote one's life to another and still not know the other? I frequently explain this act of "waking up to a stranger" as being a consequence of not seeing, or having lost sight of, the other person. The two persons have constructed a life together based upon false ideas of who one another is and what is most important to them individually and as a couple.

A basic human relational defense is self-preservation. As much as we want to be open in our intimate relationships, we have a built-in defensiveness that inhibits our desires to be known. Although we recognize that closeness and growth comes through our personal presentation of absolute vulnerability, our fear of being hurt activates our self-preserving defense mechanisms. Furthermore, life tends to teach us that it just makes good sense to be a little closed off and always to keep the most sacred parts of one's self to one's self. This basic attitude has often resulted in people frequently seeing another in a way that allows them to feel safe; that is, we package people in a manageable way for our individual and collective security. As long as the other is predictable, we can live our lives with a degree of certainty. Often, we see them for who they are at the beginning of the relationship. When we are delighted by the newness of the relationship, we only see and experience delight. Yet when the real stuff that life is made of confronts us in the life and social history of another, we quickly renegotiate the grounds for being together. Unfortunately, the mediating factor tends to be dictated by our need for personal security. Our self-preserving instincts rarely allow any of us to experience relational life in openness and vulnerability. The sad truth remains that we are truly able to experience intimacy and be changed for the better by the encounter only in those open and vulnerable times.

At times we have an inhibition, even a strong prohibition, to be open and vulnerable in our relationships. At other times, we experience a fear of growth that comes with sharing life with another. This fear of growth often supports a person's rigidity and keeps the individual from experiencing life and knowing herself or himself in the most complete way. The highly defensive person is frequently the most likely person to see the intimate partner as a stranger because the focus has been on self-preservation rather than on the growth that comes from intimately knowing another, which, in turn, reveals the self. As a result, one day we awaken to see that the person we have held in our minds is not the person who is lying beside us or standing before us.

We can look at this from the other extreme. Your partner may conceive no life or value as an interdependent being and thus completely yield the self to you. In this case, you become a mirror or screen for your partner's projected self. Your partner has the ability to see himself or herself only by looking at you as the reason for being. The partner knows you because the sense of self has been derived solely by being in relationship with you. Unfortunately, in situations like this, you never saw your partner. You saw only an idealized image that often had little to do with who your partner really is. If radical growth occurs, the stranger that is seen is the result of the emergence of a new self no longer dependent on the other for meaning. This would particularly be true if one had given up everything of personal value and fulfillment for the sake of the other. If a partner ceases to be an appropriate mirror, or if there is no longer a need to project the self, then seeing the other as a stranger can simply be a statement of self-acceptance. The partner becomes a stranger because the former self is no longer dependent on the partner, whom they now see without projecting an image, maybe for the first time.

It is imperative that we African Americans disengage ourselves from the racist and sexist ideologies that we have both projected and introjected. We must cast off the "strangeness" we have experienced within ourselves—a strangeness that is the result of conforming to the constraints of racism and genderism. Ceasing to be dominated by a sense of being strangers to ourselves is more than a simple change in behavior. This change must have a transcendent capacity that reaches the very core of our being and allows for the liberation to be actualized in our souls.

The Work of Liberation

Our liberation work is often expressed and experienced through our testimonies and stories. Our oral heritage in this regard is quite clear. We have a strong heritage of invoking the voices of the ancestors and past experiences through storytelling. The sharing of the narrative provides a living legacy of history, morality, ethics, theology, and spirituality. The Africans of the antebellum South, along with the African Americans of the Jim and Jane Crow South, experienced the liberating power of God through living the testimonies and stories they shared with one another. Today, our forebears stand among us as a mighty cloud of witnesses. Retelling their stories of battles fought and won connects us to the power associated with maintaining the continuity of life after death. One of our problems, however, is that we have begun to manipulate the narratives by renegotiating their undergirding principles. In effect, we have ignored the warning of Genesis 3:1–6 regarding transliterating the truth.

The myth reports that Adam and Eve were strolling through the Garden delighting in the beauty of creation when they came upon the serpent—that ancient symbol of wisdom and transformation—described in the text as subtle/crafty. Awestruck by the question of the creature, Eve, with Adam by her side, decided to engage the serpent as a dialogical partner. Because the serpent had a perspective on the truth, the problem was not that the couple decided to engage the serpent. The problem was that they chose to compromise their principles to accommodate their angst. Too large a segment of the African American community has chosen to defer to the voice of the demoniac rather than to maintain, with confidence, the integrity of our testimony. Here, I am suggesting that the conditions that declare our community crisis are the consequential results of an integrity crisis.

Traumatizing Cycles

Oppression has a life that is cyclical in nature—what goes around, comes around, and goes around again. We are, therefore, traumatized daily. I posit that African Americans do not live post-traumatic stress lives, but we live "protracted-traumatic stress" lives, whereby we are continually affected by racism, sexism, and classism. Our historical self is being distorted by the projection and introjection of false images that encourage individual and communal disconnection and ultimately result in relational dissociation.

Evil and suffering will continue to inform and impact our existence due to humanity's constant struggle to maintain consistency in all expressions of life. There seems to be something in the very essence of the human being that pushes in-group/out-group distinctions. Barriers are constantly being constructed to establish and justify relationships of domination and segregation, which ultimately promote an agenda of genocide. Through a sort of neo-Social Darwinism, humanity propagandizes for the extinction of those identified as "less than" by a seemingly indestructible targeting system. For every action that demands change, there is often a counteraction to maintain the familiar. By way of example, when antidiscrimination legislation was activated, it was soon countered by allegations of a phantom named "reverse-discrimination." Koheleth noted this phenomenon in the book of Ecclesiastes. Through a comparative reflection on nature and the human experience, he commented:

> A generation goes, and a generation comes,
>   but the earth remains forever.
> The sun rises and the sun goes down,
>   and hurries to the place where it rises.
> The wind blows to the south,
>   and goes round to the north;
> round and round goes the wind,
>   and on its circuits the wind returns.
> All streams run to the sea,
>   but the sea is not full;
> to the place where the streams flow,
>   there they continue to flow.
> All things are wearisome;

more than one can express;
the eye is not satisfied with seeing,
 or the ear filled with hearing.
What has been is what will be,
 and what has been done is what will be done;
 there is nothing new under the sun. (Eccl. 1:4–9)

A rather discouraging commentary on the cycles of oppression, yet there is a liberating insight. If we assume that acts of oppression are new and different, we can avoid the history of its development and not see the ways it has gathered strength over time. Seeing the oppressive force for all that it is allows us to develop more appropriate liberation strategies.

To our detriment and dismay, the American consciousness continues to correlate the "content of one's character and the color of one's skin." The "color-blindness" that so many liberals want to promote has not established equality among all Americans. Our society is still very race-conscious, and as I explained in earlier chapters, race in America is rarely understood as separate and distinct from color issues. In fact, race and skin-color consciousness are critical to identity formation within the United States To become "blind" to that formative reality is to ignore a vital component of what makes us who we are. To deny the imposing power of race and gender is to make illegitimate the suffering we experience as a result of racism and genderism.

Classism has racial and gender components that base stratifications on physicality, creating a social-political-economic-cultural caste system that limits upward mobility. The fact that our value system for accruing posses-sions has moved from a communal to an individual ethos of acquisition has sharpened our senses of class distinctions. Particular attributes are ascribed to each class to the extent that class identification is a *class-ification* system. When class is determined by observable differences, we ultimately declare barriers that form a caste system that denies any possibility of upward mobility—meaning, classification and social status are determined by physical appearance and are assigned a corresponding behavior. This same rationale was employed to say that Africans were marked by God to be slaves for life through the curse of Ham. Following this misguided rationale, the only way to become upwardly mobile is to change one's appearance. But just as the "leopard cannot change its spots," the African cannot change her or his skin nor the racist ideologies that are projected onto Africans. We must be liberated from such dehumanizing ideas!

African American Liberation Disciplines

African American liberation disciplines are contextual approaches to African American life. Black theologians, womanist theologians, Black (African) psychologists, and African American pastoral theologians have struggled for generations to liberate African Americans from the forces that oppress our being. Each approach focuses on a different aspect of our existence and seeks to make a clarifying statement about what it is that radically influences our self-concept. Allowing each discipline to speak, while encouraging an interdisciplinary discussion, will help us to better relate to our story. These approaches can encourage us to aspire for freedom, to affirm justice, and to know dignity. Once our dignity has been liberated, our souls can be restored.

To be clear about the work of the African American liberation theologian, I should first state my understanding of the work of theology. Many people like to begin with the simple, etymological definition that says: Theology is the study of God. Although this is a true statement, in the strictest sense, theology is more than the study of God. It involves more than God-talk on particular issues. Theology is the language and the concepts we use to describe: creation and the cosmos; the activities of God and the human spirit; the human condition; and the struggle to live humanely in relationship with God, self, and others. Theology is also the language and concepts we use to prescribe: Divine-human restoration, human-human transformation, human conduct, and the pathway to justice. Therefore, the act of doing theology is the practice of creatively and constructively thinking about the issues of life based on what we believe about God, humanity, and Divine-human relationships. Although theology expresses a range of concerns related to human life and relationships, it is important to recognize "that theology is contextual, and that any theology that claims not to be contextual deceives itself, and even runs the danger of falling into idolatry by claiming for itself a universal perspective, which only God can have."[1]

Black theology has been critiqued as being an African American *man's* approach to liberation. This theological perspective has understood the external world as being, essentially, a hostilely racist environment. At the same time, it has seen the internal community as a resistant community organized by a spiritual solidarity ascribing race issues as the primary oppressor. In his book *Introducing Black Theology of Liberation*, Dwight Hopkins notes:

> Theology serves as a critical conscience of the church's vocation to liberate the poor in their journey with God to full humanity. To believe in and witness to faith require the ongoing critical questioning about whether or not that belief and witness are in line with the God of liberation of the oppressed...Black theology, therefore, is an effort of African American people to claim their blackness and their freedom as people of God. Freedom comes when black poor folk, led by the African American church, live out their freedom because God helps them in their daily struggle against personal pain and collective oppression.[2]

Womanist theology is an African American woman's approach to liberation. It has critiqued the external world as a hostilely racist, sexist, and classist environment. The internal community, on the other hand, has been described as a resistant community organized by a spiritual solidarity that acknowledges race issues, yet is seen as being complicit with the external world on issues of sexism and classism. Delores Williams addresses the womanist project in her book *Sisters in the Wilderness.* Defining womanist theology, she writes:

> Today a theological corrective is developing that has considerable potential for bringing black women's experience into theology so that black women will see the need to transform the sexist character of the churches and their theology. The corrective—emerging among black female theologians, ethicists, biblical scholars, ministers and laywomen—is called womanist theology...Womanist theology attempts to help black women see, affirm and have confidence in the importance of their experience and faith for determining the character of the Christian religion in the African-American community. Womanist theology challenges all oppressive forces impeding black women's struggle for survival and for the development of a positive, productive quality of life conducive to women's and the family's freedom and well-being. Womanist theology opposes all oppression based on race, sex, class, sexual preference, physical disability and caste.[3]

Just as it was important to state my understanding of theology before talking about African American theology, it is important for me to state my understanding of psychology, especially since pastoral theology is the combination of theology and psychology. Psychology, when it expresses itself as a "hard science," is the "study of the mind" and human behavior through exploring consciousness/unconsciousness, cognition, behavior, and human social interactions. In the instances when psychology expresses itself as a "soft science," it is more philosophical as it explores human motivations, propensities, desires, drives, and perceptions of meaning and reality. The *Britannica Concise Encyclopedia* describes psychology as follows:

> [Psychology is the] scientific discipline that studies mental processes and behavior in humans and other animals. Literally meaning "the study of the mind," psychology focuses on both individual and group behavior. Clinical psychology is concerned with the diagnosis and treatment of mental disorders. Other specialized fields of psychology include child psychology, educational psychology, sports psychology, social psychology, and comparative psychology. The issues studied by psychologists cover a wide spectrum, including learning, cognition, intelligence, motivation, emotion,

perception, personality, and the extent to which individual differences are shaped by genetics or environment. The methods used in psychological research include observation, interviews, psychological testing, laboratory experimentation, and statistical analysis.[4]

Because of psychology's historical participation and support of scientific racism, most African Americans are suspicious of psychology. Most of its theories have been used to "prove" racist ideas of Black inferiority or to "prove" the racist assumption that Blacks are deviant by nature. Black psychology was developed to be an opposing, liberating voice. Black psychology, also called African psychology, is thought, by the uninformed, to be nothing more than a "Black" approach to psychology.[5] Black (African) psychology is, rather, a specialized field of psychology, with its own fundamental premises and tenets, committed to the particularity and liberation of the African American psyche. Contrary to what many believe, Black (African) psychology is not the "psychology of Blacks." It is not to be understood as the study of the Black mind, no more than Black theology is to be understood as the study of the Black God. Black (African) psychology is a field dedicated to the analysis of the systems of oppression that inhibit Black life for the sole purpose of liberating African people.

> Many thinkers, both Black and White, have viewed the development of African [Black] psychology as nothing more than the "need" of some psychologists who happen to be Black to create an area of expertise that gives them preeminence in some aspects of the general discipline of psychology...It is, in my opinion, not true that African [Black] psychology can be relegated to either general psychology which is being "blackened" or to a sub-specialty based on the race of the subjects. In either case, African psychology amounts to nothing more than a "perspective" or a passing orientation. More accurately, the development and reascension of African psychology should be viewed as the recovery of a mode of thought and analysis that has lain dormant in the beingness of African [Black] peoples. In fact, it is believed that the contemporary emergence of Black psychology is evidence of an original and older body of knowledge correcting itself.[6]

Black (African) psychology, which tends to be understood as an amorphous approach to the psychological functioning of African Americans, has critiqued the external world as racist, having hierarchically structured the world through White supremacist ideology. Through the tenets of Western psychology, African people are always subordinate and inferior to Europeans and persons of European descent. Furthermore, Black (African) psychology understands the Black community to have a symbiotic relationship with Western, i.e., European, culture whereby it has lost site of the beauty of African culture, and it declares this symbiosis must be broken.

Black (African) psychology is truly a specialization and not simply a contextualization of European and European American psychology. It is not what some critics would suggest as being the "blackenization" or "ebonization" of psychology. Black (African) psychology is not the practice of adding "shades of meaning" to universalized psychological theory. Black (African) psychology is as old as Black people. In some ways, it is more epistemological than it is scientific. It has more to do with ways of knowing and being than it does with the study of the mind or behavior. Yet, as a field of study, Black (African) psychology has to do with rediscovering and revaluing our age-old diagnostic and healing traditions. We have always had our psychiatrists, psychologists, psychotherapists, counselors, and caregivers who were dedicated to inspiring community health. The problem of acknowledging and crediting the knowledge of our traditional healers and theorists is that Westernization denigrated our traditions and practices by calling them superstition, evil, savage, witchcraft, black magic, etc. Black (African) psychology is, therefore, the reclamation and extension of traditional and historical understandings of the African psyche, especially as the African psyche expresses itself in America.

African American pastoral theology, which is a combination of theology and psychology, is an African American indigenous approach to pastoral theology. In her book *Survival and Liberation,* Carroll Watkins Ali identifies the leading traditional definitions of pastoral theology. She writes:

> Here are three traditional views of pastoral theology. (1) A theo-logical enterprise in the formulation of "practical principles, theories, and procedures for ordained ministry in all of its functions." That is to say, the purpose of theological reflection is to set forth an accepted process through which ministry in general is administered. (2) "The practical theological discipline concerned with theory and practice of pastoral care and counseling." This approach considers pastoral theology to be an arm of practical theology around which theological reflection is organized for the development of praxis for pastoral caregiving. And (3) "a form of theological reflection in which pastoral experience serves as context for critical development of theological understanding."[7]

In her work, she argues for a new definition of pastoral theology grounded in African American pastoral theology:

> Seward Hiltner, who is considered the founding father of pastoral theology as a discipline, defined pastoral theology as "that branch or field of theological knowledge and inquiry that brings the shepherd-ing perspective to bear on all the operations and functions of the church and minister, and then draws conclusions of a theological

order from reflection on these observations." Specifically, Hiltner's definition introduces the concept of the "shepherding perspective" as a way of thinking about "pastoral experience." In order to adequately address the needs of the African American context, a new definition for pastoral theology is defined as theological reflections on the experience of the cultural context as relevant for strategic pastoral caregiving in the context of ministry.[8]

African American pastoral theology mobilizes the concern, passion, and compassion of suffering Black folk through an emphasis upon communality with the intention of restoring Black folks to a life of relationships. At its heart African American pastoral theology is an interpretive dialectic between theological anthropology and psychology that results in a definitive understanding of humanity. This field believes that humanity's image and nature are connected to the Divine rather than founding our nature on the functional, reductionistic, or deterministic grounds of general psychology. The field's attentiveness to the divine relationship demands a concern for faith issues and the dynamic life of the faith community at-large. Because African American pastoral theology resources Black and womanist theologies and church life, African American pastoral theology relies on biblical texts, church doctrines, psychological theories, and human science research data as essential sources. This also means that every aspect of human and communal life is considered. As such, no topic is off-limits. African American pastoral theology has theoretical, academic, and clinical components that are communicated through pastoral care, pastoral counseling, and pastoral psychotherapy.

Interpretive Differences

While both Black and womanist theologies are liberation theologies, phenomenology is what distinguishes the two. They are consistent with one another on the oppressive dimensions of race, but the phenomenological experiences of sex, gender, and social/economic status are radically different. The womanists state quite emphatically that the phenomenology of the African American woman differentiates their approach and perspective from White feminist theology and from Black theology.[9] Black psychology is in agreement with the perspectives of black and womanist theologies that hold that the phenomenology of race needs to be acknowledged. The foundations of Black psychology's critique, however, differ slightly in that they seek to critique a White supremacist system and correct the social scientific perspectives of Western society. To this end, it seems to not emphasize sex and gender issues but lifts social/economic status as it relates to the circumstances that cause one to orient one's self to a particular location. Because African American pastoral theology resources and dialogues with Black and womanist theologies as well as Black psychology, it reflects the sensitivities of each and also presents similar limitations in critique and analysis while holding race, sex, and gender as vital features of our humanity and social/economic status as an influential feature effecting our relationships.

Liberation Voices

The scholars whose ideas I will consider are James Cone (Black theologian), Cornel West (philosopher and culture critic), Delores Williams and Jacqueline Grant (womanist theologians), Frances Cress Welsing, Na'im Akbar, and Wade Nobles (Black psychologists), Edward Wimberly, Carroll Watkins Ali, and Homer Ashby Jr. (African American pastoral theologians). Each represents but one perspective within his or her respective discipline. Although each has a slightly different understanding of how African Americans develop their cultural identity, as well as the forces that influence that formation, combining all the voices helps to present a more complete picture of who we are and the challenges we face. The purpose here is to review the forces that these thinkers consider to be preeminent for the development of African American cultural identity.

Black Theologian: James H. Cone

James Cone[10] is one of the best-known, and perhaps the most historically controversial, theologians in the field of Black theology. Acknowledged as "the father of Black theology," Cone continues to be a prolific writer, sharing the many nuances of the discipline and subject matter. Acknowledging my own leaning and emphasis upon foundational life experiences and the ways those experiences give rise to self-concept and identity, Cone's testimony, *My Soul Looks Back*,[11] is a natural choice.

In that text, he reflects on his first attempt at formulating a theological position on the relationship between "Christianity and Black Power." He shares his remembrances of the primary tension he experienced between his Christian identity and his Black identity. Although his stated priority was to his Black identity, I believe his Christian identity, though negotiable, was not expendable. His encounters with racism and the complicity of theologians made Christianity negotiable; but unrecognizable to him at that moment, he also had inherited a legacy of religious accommodation that was a significant part of his Black identity. Both identities were vital parts of his being, and both, therefore, had to be expressed with integrity.

He is an active dialogue partner with many different oppressed peoples the world over, but his focus is African America. He grounds his work in the experiences of his personal past and the collective past of Black people in America and identifies racism as the hermeneutical key for interpreting the African American past:

> ...I promised myself that I would never again make a political or theological compromise with racism. Racism is a deadly disease that must be resisted by any means necessary. Never again would

I ever expect white racists to do right in relation to the black community. A moral or theological appeal based on a white definition of morality or theology will always serve as a detriment to our attainment of black freedom. The only option we blacks have is to fight in every way possible, so that we can begin to create a definition of freedom based on our own history and culture. We must not expect white people to give us freedom. Freedom is not a gift, but a responsibility, and thus must be taken against the will of those who hold us in bondage.[12]

Cone's personal metamorphosis became the model for his expositions on liberation. The insidiousness of racism countered by the power of Black history and Black culture provided him the existential context for doing theology. His approach to the identity formation of the African American holds racism as a primary catalyst that has shaped our experience and vision. Along with this, he acknowledges that the African American culture retains many African antecedents, particularly the African communal structure and religious experience.

Liberation Philosopher: Cornel West

Although he is not a Black theologian, the work of Cornel West[13] has been invaluable to the Black theological enterprise. As a cultural critic, this democratic socialist philosopher's analysis of racism was vital to my own deconstruction of racist ideology. West approaches the crisis of the African American community as a democratic socialist acknowledging that most socialist theory occurs within a Marxist framework. A general overview of West's works reveals an interpretation of African American identity and liberation through his critique of racism, which he nuances through a critique of Western philosophy and intellectualization. His purpose has been to show that a struggle against racism is both a moral and political necessity. In *Prophesy Deliverance!*,[14] his primary assumption declares Marxism as indispensable for uncovering the capitalistic and class influences upon racism. However, he does acknowledge that a strict adherence to the Marxist critique of racism is inadequate because it fails to probe the psychological and cultural spheres.

Although he recognizes the variety of oppressive systems that impact racism, he concludes that racism has a life of its own. The Marxist critique tends to be reductionistic in focus because it pushes everything to class struggle. Hence, West contends that while racism can be critiqued by general and specific working class exploitation, some xenophobic attitudes are not reducible to class exploitation.

West's analysis is critical for expanding the anti-racist assumptions that declare racism to be purely economic and greed based. He helps us to see that racism cannot be so narrowly defined. In fact, West is critical of people who tend to focus upon economics and capitalism as the roots of racism.

In his historical overview of racism, he posits racism's foundational events and attitudes in the period that preceded the Protestant Reformation, an event credited as the primary catalyst for the capitalist system. West believes that capitalism is involved in, and even a significant feature of, the expression of racism in America. He stresses, however, additional influences that make racism so deadly. The clearest conceptualization of racism for West is twofold, culture (which includes religion) and economics. He argues for an expanded view of the long history of racist ideology. West is committed to an interdisciplinary approach as critical to an understanding of racism, but he maintains a close critique of racism as a historically social and ideological phenomenon.

Womanist Theologians: Delores Williams and Jacquelyn Grant

Womanist theology, although a relatively young disciplinary approach, has been making a very important contribution to the understanding of African American identity formation. A womanist is defined as:

> From womanish (opp. of "girlish," i.e., frivolous, irresponsible, not serious.) A black feminist or feminist of color. From the black folk expression of mothers to female children, "You acting womanish," i.e., like a woman. Usually referring to outrageous, audacious, courageous or willful behavior. Wanting to know more and in greater depth than is considered "good" for one…Also: A woman who loves other women, sexually and/or nonsexually. Appreciates and prefers women's culture, women's emotional flexibility (values tears as natural counter-balance of laughter) and women's strength. Sometimes loves individual men, sexually and/or nonsexually. Committed to survival and wholeness of entire people, male and female. Not a separatist, except periodically, for health. Traditionally universalist…Traditionally capable…Loves music. Loves dance. Loves the moon. Loves the Spirit. Loves love and food and roundness. Loves struggle. Loves the Folk. Loves herself. Regardless.[15]

The womanist approach is phenomenological. Womanists work from the perspective that liberation comes by confronting the diverse oppressions of race, class, gender, and, sometimes, colonialism simultaneously. Black theology tends to emphasize race and racism as the primary evil, but the womanist considers race and racism as only part of the evil that she confronts. A womanist identifies racism, sexism, and classism as the forces that oppress her being. Not only do White and Black males act upon her in sexist ways, the White female is not excluded from oppressing her through supporting sexist male aggression and classist discrimination. Furthermore, classism, for her, is experienced through socioeconomic oppression and cultural imperialism.

For centuries, African American women have been abused and overlooked, misrepresented and misunderstood. Because race is indeed an important part of her identity, over the years an African American woman has found herself in a position of sacrificing other essential parts of her identity—namely, sex and gender. She has been manipulated and abused by White male patriarchy, ostracized and brutalized by White female rage, subordinated and emotionally isolated by Black male patriarchy.[16] Onlookers have inappropriately labeled her way of functioning as a matriarchy. Her survival needs have often required her to take the lead, but her high level of responsibility has often been first and foremost directed toward the survival of the family, by any means necessary. The essential reason she has been identified as matriarchal is due the fact that a patriarchal society regards any system different from itself to be deficient.[17] She has historically been denied her womanhood through a systematic process of masculinization. Her body has been objectified as the source of carnal sin, as the scapegoat of misogynists, as other than woman.

This is the context out of which the womanist speaks. Through a phenomenological focus, she becomes subject rather than object. Her self-understanding begins with her body in relationships—which also acknowledges her color—then advances through a legacy of survival. She engages in a "functional separation" from Black men because we have contributed to her dehumanization as have other oppressors and have not consistently fought for her liberation. Her liberationist view is not myopic, however. She acknowledges and honors the clear linkages she has with the other liberation efforts, but she also knows that the limits to those alliances. Therefore, the womanist aim is to liberate her womanhood, her people, and the world in which she lives.

The women's liberation movement often wants to claim the unity of sisterhood. The womanist, however, also engages in a functional separation from her White female counterpart, especially when White women do not acknowledge their participation in White racism. The Black woman's color has often been a barrier to the White woman's understanding of sisterhood. I still have the vivid memory of witnessing these dynamics while attending a plenary session at an annual meeting of the American Academy of Religion. The Academy runs on a very tight schedule, with one session flowing into the next. It is, therefore, important that every session conclude its work on time in order for the next group to occupy the space, keeping everyone on schedule. Mary Daly, the pioneering radical feminist, was the plenary speaker. The room in which she spoke was scheduled to be used by a session of the womanist group immediately after Daly's presentation. Daly spoke beyond the allotted time and didn't appear to be closing her address in consideration of the group that was to follow her in that space. Finally, Daly was reaching the climax of her address and declared, "I know your pain," a phrase she kept repeating as she attempted to identify what she perceived to be the experiences of all women. I noticed the co-facilitators of the Womanist Approaches to Religion and Society group, Katie Cannon and Emilie Townes, move with deliberate steps up the side aisle to the platform where Daly was speaking. They very politely let her know her time was up, and it was their time to use the room. Declared within Cannon's and Townes' action was a declaration, "If you knew our pain, you would have been more respectful of our time and ended your address at the appointed hour." During their session, they spoke truths that did not mirror those spoken by Daly the hour earlier.

Black theology tends to represent a dominant male perspective that, for balance, necessitates womanist theology. Delores Williams' critical reflections on Cone's *A Black Theology of Liberation* in the twentieth anniversary edition makes her a natural choice for consideration here. She critiques his personal reflections related to his growth as he expressed in his Preface to the 1986 edition. Williams says, "All the inspiration, wisdom, and advice contained in the material Cone quotes comes from men like Malcolm X and, on occasion, W. E. B. DuBois and Martin Luther King. Not a single woman is named, quoted, or given credit for contributing to the transformations Cone says he has made in his thought and style in the last twenty years."[18] Williams further contends:

> Just as Womanist Theology has an organic relation to black liberation theology, so does it also have an organic relation to feminist theology in its various strands: Hispanic, Asian, Jewish and Anglo-American. This means that black male liberationists, womanists and feminists connect at vital points. Yet distinct and sometimes hostile differences exist between them precipitated, in part, by the maladies afflicting community life in America—sexism, racism and classism. Consequently, womanist god-talk often lives in tension with its two groups of relatives: black male liberationists and feminists.[19]

Williams is a womanist theologian who approaches the human condition as a systematic theologian and whose hermeneutical categories often emerge within the context of popular culture. Beginning with the woman's body, she challenges the perspective of Black liberation theology that says God is a Liberator of the oppressed. A woman's first line of vulnerability is her body, and the biblical tradition clearly reflects her lack of control and vulnerability:

> A womanist rereading of the biblical Hagar-Sarah texts in relation to African-American women's experience raises a serious question about the biblical witness. The question is about its use as a source validating black liberation theology's normative claim of God's liberating activity in behalf of all the oppressed…The Hagar-Sarah texts in Genesis and Galatians, however, demonstrate that the oppressed and abused do not always experience God's liberating power. If one reads the Bible identifying with non-Hebrews who are female and male slaves ("the oppressed of the oppressed"),

one quickly discerns a non-liberative thread running through the Bible. In the Genesis stories about Hagar and Sarah, God seems to be (as some Palestinian Christians today suggest about the God of the Hebrew Testament) partial and discriminating. God is clearly partial to Sarah. Regardless of the way one interprets God's command to Hagar to submit herself to Sarah, God does not liberate her. In Exodus God does not outlaw slavery. Rather, the male slave can be part of Israel's rituals, possibly because he has no control over his body as Hagar had no control over her body.[20]

Due to the lack of control the woman has had over her own body, "survival" is one of Williams' theological concerns. She reviews the survival skills of African and African American women and incorporates their legacy into her perspectives on liberation. Williams explores the depths of the passion and compassion of Black women's survival and illustrates how she has been a major source of strength and inspiration for her family and community. Williams' focus seems to be that survival has been the Black woman's salvific preservative in the past and will be the Black woman's salvific deliverance in the future.

Insomuch as she focuses upon survival, Williams acknowledges the depths of racial and sexual oppression that has existed for centuries, and in the case of sexual oppression, for millennia. There is, for her, a sense in which the legacy of survival is an intuitive trait within every African American woman. This intuitive trait provides African American women with the resources to know when and how to resist or to endure. While resistance and endurance are, from Williams' perspective, two dominant traits of the African American culture, given the peculiar position in which the Black woman has found herself, those survival traits have been highly developed.

Another womanist theologian, Jacquelyn Grant, identified as "the mother of womanist theology," is somewhat more religiously conventional than is Williams. Grant seeks to reflect theologically upon the conditions of the faithful and to be prophetic in her liberationist efforts. In addition to stating a case for a phenomenological understanding of reality, Grant reveals how voices have been very subtly consumed in the name of sisterhood. Always before her are the phenomenological differences between Black and White, male and female. These differences have compelled her to critique those guiding paradigms and themes. Her nuancing of voices, so that all perspectives can be heard demonstrates the necessity for doing the same on a variety of issues and concerns.

In her book *White Women's Christ and Black Women's Jesus*, Grant explored the differences between White feminist theology and Black womanist theology. She explained, from a historical perspective, why feminist theology has been an inadequate approach for the liberation of Black women and inappropriate for interpreting the experiences of Black women. This does not mean that there are no Black feminists, for indeed, there are many. One of the very subtle distinctions is that feminism has tended to be a political movement with spiritual implications while womanism has tended to be a spiritual movement with political implications. The long and the short of Grant's analysis is feminist theology has been White in its outlook and racist in its expressions. Although she acknowledges that to be White does not necessitate being racist, she notes that the structure of the system of racism and the behavior of Whites makes the differentiation of the system and behavior difficult to distinguish. Nevertheless, her position is that for the most part White women have produced the body of literature that constitutes feminism. Its research has not included the Black experience as a source but has made the White experience normative. Additionally, she asserts that the movement itself was organized under racist tenets.

> What is apparent in this historical context is how Black women's experience involves a convergence of racism, sexism, and classism. Within the limited arena of domestic labor, the sexist assumption that women's place is [only] in the home is reconfirmed, as well as the classist practice of paying those who do "menial" jobs little or nothing, and the assumption that such work is more appropriately done by those of the servant class. These patterns are compounded by the racist assumption that White women need protection from actual work and therefore should function in a supervisory capacity.[21]

She adds a further distinction between White and Black women's liberationist efforts. Due to the structure of the oppressive system in which we find ourselves and to the privileges afforded White women by the system, White women liberationists seek fulfillment while Black women liberationists seek survival. For Grant, experience makes all the difference in the world, and, in fact, shapes the worlds in which we live.

Black Psychologist: Frances Cress Welsing, Robert Guthrie, Wade Nobles, and Na'im Akbar

Although Black psychology purports many of the same emphases as Black theology and womanist theology, their presentations of the issues critical to the formation of an African American cultural identity are slightly different. Black psychology focuses essentially upon psychic processes as they have been influenced by racism. Of course, the discipline evidences diversity; yet, the discipline emerged as a result of a long history of research that has sought to prove the inferiority of Africans on the basis of race. In fact, psychology began to gain prominence about the same time as the emergence of scientific racism. Consequently, race and racism heavily influence the directions of Black psychology.

Two distinctive traditions declare the meaning of Black (African) psychology. Although the two traditions describe the focus of the field from different starting points, they have no disagreement on the necessity of the field for the life and survival of the Black community. Two voices that embody the traditions are Robert Guthrie and Wade Nobles. Guthrie defines the field as being germane and indigenous to the African American context and experience, while Nobles defines the field as being PanAfrican and Africentric.

Guthrie defines Black psychology as "an outgrowth of Third World" philosophies that are not committed to the authenticity of traditional European and American psychology, but are born out of a need promulgated through neglect rather than traditional theoretical stances.[22] He continues:

> I envision Black psychology as a scientific study of behavior attempting to understand life as it is lived. Black psychology should be involved in a most interesting, interwoven kind of investigation concerned with the struggles, pleasures, interests, desires, habits, aims, drives, motivations, feelings, actions, and wants…all those bits of behavior that have molded black people into complex, unique, living beings. Due to the urgency of our mission, Black psychology should not only attempt to understand behavior, it should strive to disseminate its scientific findings directly to the community as soon as possible, in a manner that lends itself to application. In this sense, it is a systems approach to psychological science.[23]

Wade Nobles, representing the other tradition, believes that to truly understand the African American context, one must be attentive to African antecedents. To this end, he states "that the discipline of African [Black] psychology is rooted in, and therefore must explicate and understand, ancient human thought. Accordingly, African psychology is an effort to recreate a psychology of human beingness and has the potential to revitalize or be an alternative to general psychology. In starting with ancient human thought, [I] recognize that the Blacks of ancient Egypt (KMT) were the first Black philosophers and psychologists."[24]

Nobles further states:

> Black psychology is more than general psychology's "darker" dimension. African [Black] psychology is rooted in the nature of black culture that is based on particular indigenous (originally indigenous to Africa) philosophical assumptions. To make black psychology the dreaded darker dimension of general psychology would amount to distorting African reality so that it will fit Western psychological theories and/or assumptions…For Africans, who believed that [humanity], like the universe, is a complicated, integrated, unified whole, concerns such as the mind-body controversy would never arise and theoretical development and/or analysis based solely on the explication of the "mind" or the "body" as separate entities would be useless…Certainly particular people

cannot be meaningfully investigated and understood if their philosophical assumptions are not taken into account.[25]

Frances Cress Welsing, in an historical sense, is probably the most controversial figure among Black psychology theorists. Both Cheikh Diop and Charles Long emphasized the importance of language to the assessment of the African American community. In like manner, Cress Welsing understands language to be a symbolic system that carries messages within messages pertaining to the identity and survival of individuals and collectives. Diop contended that a collective personality is revealed linguistically, and Cress Welsing offers a psychological presentation for that contention.[26] Her critique of the African American community within the context of a larger European American society has essentially developed out of her clinical practice. In her book *The Isis Papers*, she offers a structural analysis of the social conditions that plague her client population (and by extension the African American community) and charts the preconditions to their source, which she identifies as White supremacy (racism). Critical to understanding her framework is the acknowledgment of the highly symbolic nature of humanity. She grounds her work on the premise that without an accurate definition of racism, the African American will not find wholeness.

Cress Welsing's approach is crisis-oriented and emphasizes "counter-racist" activities for African American health. Her diagnosis of the community concludes that African Americans are plagued by a number of "Dependency Deprivation Syndromes" due to the oppressive system created by racism (White supremacy). She believes that many social manifestations within the African American experience are a direct result of responding to the survival efforts of White supremacists, whom she interprets as struggling for White genetic survival because of their lack of color. She theorizes that the origin of oppression in the world is primarily due to the lack of melanin that has made Whites strive for the preservation their of race.

> Is it not true that white people represent in numerical terms a very small minority of the world's people? And more profoundly, is not "white" itself the very absence of any ability to produce color? I reason, then, that the quality of whiteness is indeed a genetic inadequacy or a relative genetic deficiency state, based upon the genetic inability to produce the skin pigments of melanin (which is responsible for all skin color). The vast majority of the world's people are not so afflicted, which suggests that color is normal for human beings and color absence is abnormal. Additionally, this state of color absence acts always as a genetic recessive to the dominant genetic factor of color-production. Color always "annihilates" (phenotypically- and genetically-speaking) the non-color, white.[27]

Her theory, "The Cress Theory of Color-Confrontation and Racism (White Supremacy)," has a genetic and psychological basis. While she does not highlight sexism, it is included in her understanding of White supremacy, for her presentation combines power and genetic survival under the single symbol of the White penis or phallus. This patriarchal, White supremacist system is visible in all aspects of human interaction, including symbols of the Christian church and Christian holidays. Racism, expressed and responded to in unconscious symbolic language, influences character development, personality, and identity formation.

> The Color-Confrontation theory contends that all the above (i.e., the individual and collective neurotic need to focus on color, sex, genetics, numbers, superiority/inferiority, white supremacy and power) can be explained on the basis of the core psychological sense of color-deficiency and numerical inadequacy. The individual patterns of behavior that, over time, evolved into collective, social, institutional and now systemic patterns are seen as the origin of the "system of white supremacy," that operates at a universal level and is the only effective and functional racism existent in the world today. Further, racism (white supremacy), in this historical epoch, is viewed as a full-blown social contradiction and the major social dynamic superseding all others in influencing universal social practices and decisions. The Color Confrontation theory recognizes racism as one of the dominating forces determining character development, personality and formation type. Therefore, a functional definition of racism (white supremacy), is the behavioral syndrome of individual and collective color inferiority and numerical inadequacy that includes patterns of thought, speech and action, as seen in members of the white organization (race).[28]

Africentric psychologist Wade Nobles has offered a slightly different perspective. While he regards racism as one of the leading features of the miscommunication of information, he focuses upon the structural organization of Western civilization and how it produced the ideologies of White superiority that created an insane environment for African Americans. Like Diop, Nobles believes that if one is to understand Africa and African people, African history must be connected to and understood in the context of Egypt. Western civilization originated in Egypt, Nobles purports, and the foundations of psychology, which originally focused upon the human spirit, were established there. Hence, if psychology is to be helpful to African people, it must emphasize the foundational tenets of spirit and not the objectified views of dualistic Western European society. Although his work began with Kemetic studies, the focus of his work today is Ghana, West Africa. In some ways, his Ghanaian focus is still a Kemetic focus since some have hypothesized that the Egyptian kingdoms were established from the interior of Western Africa to the Mediterranean.

Nobles does not emphasize color issues. The foundation of his approach compels him to explore the racism that is implicit in most psychological theories and to reconsider issues of identity and spirituality, which he interprets as the spiritual force of life. Declaring that as early as the nineteenth century psychologists were designing research and organizing data to prove what they already believed to be true (that is, to prove Africans to be developmentally inferior), Nobles has constructed an approach that is separate and distinct from the legacy of social scientific oppression. His critique notes that European psychology has misunderstood the essence of humanity and that its focus has been to quantify human existence. He concludes, therefore, that European American psychology has no spiritual illumination. By researching the "true" origins of Western psychology and "reintroducing" Africa as the cradle of Western civilization, Nobles presents a contextual psychology that is more phenomenological than quantitative.

He contends that the horrendous conditions of the African American community necessitate the emergence of African psychology. Furthermore, if African Americans are going to be whole and complete, African psychology must lead the way. Nobles presents African psychology as a compilation of the spiritual traditions of African religions and Egyptian theology, a charge to understand human nature, and a deep analysis of racism, classism, and gender identity. African psychology is a study of culture and cultural history; it is a study in the true nature of the self. "Unlike the mathematical illusion of normality found in the west, normality that would be consistent with African thought is a notion of normality that is equivalent to one's nature."[29]

> If culture is the ultimate expression and definition of a people's capacity to create progress and/or determine history, then critical thought or science, that is the reconstruction of that culture, must be one of the mechanisms for expressing and defining the people's capacity to wage war (i.e. liberation struggles). It is in the reclamation of our culture and ancient African thought and in the creative reconstruction of them as African psychology that Black people can regain control over the interpretation of our reality and the process of our human development...liberation struggles must develop and utilize a system of critical thought emerging from our own ancient indigenous thought. As a reconstruction of the systematic and cumulative ideas, beliefs and knowledge of our people, the role of psychology is the mental liberation of our people.[30]

Na'im Akbar remains one of the most prolific, and, perhaps, best-known Black psychologists in the United States today. He continues to regularly address audiences at colleges and universities, churches, and national summit conferences on the state of the African American nation. As a peer and contemporary of both Cress Welsing and Nobles, Akbar looks at the same data and emphasizes many of the same points as his colleagues. His reflections include his acceptance of the psycho-genetic links that have imprinted our existence, and his regard for Africentrism as an invaluable resource for liberating the African American mind. But his work expresses a dimension of African American life missing in the works of his colleagues. Akbar not only focuses upon African and African American spirituality in his liberation activities, he also engages faith issues as a vital feature of his work and sees religious faith as another dynamic feature of who we are as Africans in America.

Akbar understands the African American community to be at a pivotal point in our journey. While he might say we have been socialized to have our "hands out" and to blame others for our crisis, he contends that we have the responsibility for saving ourselves and redirecting our future. His work identifies many psychological preconditions that encourage us to remain in bondage with our hands out. Yet, at the same time, he declares that many psychological preconditions encourage us to, and show us how to, be liberated from the enslavement of our minds and thus to live African self-determined lives. He believes Black (African) psychology has a responsibility to participate in setting the captives free. His work declares we must be restored to our African selves. Akbar describes Black (African) psychology in this way:

> African Psychology is not a thing, but a place—a view, a perspective, a way of observing. African Psychology does not claim to be an exclusive body of knowledge, though a body of knowledge has and will continue to be generated from the place. It is a perspective that is lodged in the historical primacy of the human view from the land that is known as Africa. It is not limited to a geographical place, neither a particular ethnicity nor an identifiable ideology. It is the view that led to the very dawning of human consciousness and it is the substratum of all that is uniquely human on this planet...It is rooted in the prototypes of Ancient Nile Valley Civilization and was probably spawned in the garden we know as the mythological Eden.[31]

The book he is best known for is *Breaking the Chains of Psychological Slavery*. His basic thesis is that our most prominent negative behaviors and community crises can be traced historically to the dynamics of slavery. He gives example after example to show how we continue to live the destructive patterns put in place by a system intended to do us psychological harm. The devastating impact of slavery is still being expressed by the African American psyche more than one hundred years after our emancipation from slavery. To some extent, our physical bondage has ended. We, however, still have restrictions placed upon our lives keeping us from moving about as freely as we might like. For example, we still must be conscious and cautious as we walk through department stores knowing that we are under heavy surveillance simply because of our Black skin. Within Akbar's analysis, even this is a vestige of slavery, during which we were constantly being told not to steal. He says we have internalized that idea and understand thievery to be a part of our nature. In a conversation with me, he further stated, "There are many internalized images from slavery and patterns of self-bondage that we engage in that had their origin in slavery...The disunity and sense of our own helplessness are the real post-traumatic symptoms that we struggle with." If we are going to change our behavior and be truly free, we must know the sources of our behavior and struggle to be liberated through the reclamation of the African Self.

This text is extremely valuable for its longitudinal look at the factors that have influenced our understandings of who we are today. He writes not for the academic community, but for the African American community. His writing style tends to be at a level that makes for very easy reading even for challenged readers. Many within the academic community regularly challenge Akbar's reluctance to follow scholarly writing styles. He is frequently criticized for his lack of citation. His presentation does not rely on statistical information and extensive footnotes to support his analysis. The rationale for his style of presentation is clear: scholarly writing styles will affect the clarity of his writing and will take him away from inspiring liberation with his target audience. He wants no one from that audience to be lost. He speaks to people where they live, challenging them to see that the choices they make for the way they live have been influenced by a system intent on their humiliation and degradation. He knows that the person struggling for survival will not be inspired or encouraged by adding statistical data or extensive notes. The fact is, adding statistics will not make his analysis any more true, and it will not bring Africans in America any closer to liberation. If asked, he might even suggest that if you need to get statistical data to test the analysis, feel free to do so. Just be aware that statistics can often say whatever you want them to say, for even statistics require interpretation.

Akbar is not unique in his declaring the traumas of slavery as having power over us today. But he does something in this book that is often missing from the analyses Black psychologists offer. Akbar spends a considerable amount of time reflecting on the consequences of African people placing their faith and trust in the benevolent God whom we have been conditioned to see as White. He says that as long as we place our trust and hope into the hands of a White god, we will forever remain psychologically enslaved by White folks. If we place all of our confidence and hope in a benevolent, White god who sits in a superior position, it will be impossible for us to not act in deferential ways to European Americans.

On an unconscious level, we will always see White people everywhere as our god incarnate. The result is we will always work for them, worship them, be controlled by the god we see as sovereign. The only way for us to be free is to have our minds liberated by seeing that we bear God's image and likeness as Black people, and cease to see a blonde-haired, blue-eyed God, who inevitably becomes every European American we encounter.

> The most obvious problem that comes from the experience of seeing God in an image of somebody other than yourself is that it creates an idea that the image represented is superior and you are inferior. Once you have a concept that begins to make you believe you are not as good as other people, based upon the assumptions we have already established, your actions follow your mind. If you have your mind set in a certain way, your behavior follows precisely the program of your mind. The content of this program determines who we are and what we are. So, if you have internalized the view of the deity and the Creator as being in flesh, having a nationality and physical characteristics different from yourself, then you automatically assume that you are inferior in your own characteristics. The sense of inferiority is not in the form of "national humility" that we discussed, but you begin to believe you have less human potential than one who looks like the image.[32]

African American Pastoral Theologians: Edward Wimberly, Carroll Watkins Ali, and Homer Ashby Jr.

When one begins to consider the bibliographic resources that introduce and reflect on the meaning of pastoral care within African America, only one name has become synonymous with African American pastoral care. The preeminent African American pastoral theologian is Edward P. Wimberly. Within the pastoral theological guild, Wimberly stands head and shoulders above the crowd. For those of us within African American pastoral care, Wimberly has been the consistent voice crying in the wilderness. Since the late 1970s, he has been on the front lines of researching and interpreting African American pastoral care for the church and academy. His first book, *Pastoral Care in the Black Church*, was published in 1979. Prior to that, we had no pastoral theology texts written by African American pastoral theologians that focused directly and exclusively upon the African American context. Since then, Wimberly has been recognized as the single most influential African American pastoral theologian. Wimberly does not claim to be the father of African American pastoral theology, a credit he gives to the late Thomas Pugh, first professor of pastoral care at the Interdenominational Theological Center in Atlanta, Georgia. Still, his stature earns him the right to be identified as the godfather of African American pastoral theology.

One key attribute of an African American pastoral theologian is a commitment to the Church along with a commitment to scholarship. True to the African American pastoral theological vocation, Edward Wimberly is truly an academician and a churchman. While many theological scholars hope their works will reach laypersons, Wimberly has successfully managed to write for the pastor and layperson while continuing to influence persons studying for ministry. This was, in fact, the task that he committed himself to while engaging and research for his first book. Near the end of the first chapter of that text, he writes,

> In the future, the black laity will need guidance, but the guidance will have to take more cognizance of the parishioner's internal abilities. The pastor's guidance will be less authoritarian and more enabling of persons' own abilities and potential for making their own decisions.[33]

Although he might make this statement differently today, I believe his commitment to be consistent. His work has remained "cognizant of the parishioner's internal abilities." He desires to encourage the communal care work that the Black church has always fostered. Implicit in his work is the consciousness that the way we care for one another as African Americans is directly related to the racist structures embedded in American society.

The focus of his first book, which incidentally became the thrust of his work, is a description of the Black pastoral care tradition in the United States. In that text, he described the purpose and practice of pastoral care within the Black church. But rather than launching out and describing the theories that are indigenous to our pastoral care practices, he articulated how African American pastoral care lives into American pastoral care themes differently than the way most European Americans practice pastoral care. Referencing the most popular theory of pastoral care he explained how we were *sustained* during the hard times and *guided* "through many dangers, toils, and snares." He refused to make the critical mistake of attempting to impose theory upon our community; yet he also did not theorize a new basis for engaging in liberation. Instead, he talked about the ways our caring paralleled the theory. In much the same way that African American Christianity relates to mainline American Christianity, Wimberly's approach maintains our connectedness to the larger pastoral theological enterprise without jeopardizing our independence as a people with our own care tradition.

Wimberly's methodology has focused on the practice of African American pastoral care. His presentation is always interlaced with theory without becoming theory laden. This is due to his commitment to dialogue with a cross section of the African American community. But I also think his reserve regarding theory-laden conversation is related to his sense of identity and his efforts to remain "true to [his] own pastoral identity and vertical orientation, that [he] inherited from [his] black Christian background and upbringing."[34] He speaks out of his own sense of pastoral authority and exercises the symbolic power of the pastoral office to encourage the faithful to continue to sustain and guide one another. In the places where he feels we can do better, he practices what he preaches by gently guiding the community into rethinking its practices while modeling a more effective approach. His interpretive efforts have been more Black-church–centered than African-centered; however, he does not deny African antecedents as a resource for survival. Nevertheless, his efforts have been governed more by the integrationist tradition in his usage of theory and resources.

Carroll Watkins Ali has sought to move in a very different direction. Her project has been to develop theory that reflects and enhances indigenous African American pastoral theology. Her book *Survival and Liberation* puts forth, quite convincingly, a case for a more theoretical body of literature within African American pastoral theology. Like all theological liberationists, Watkins Ali emphasizes praxis rather than practice. Praxis is the progressive revelation that results from conversing with the dynamic changes of context. It is the process of modifying theory based upon the challenges presented by the new social conditions. The idea that theory gives rise to practice is commonly assumed to be the basic process for sound pastoral theological method. I believe, however, that this understanding is a truncation of pastoral theology and ultimately inhibits its healing and liberative activities. The pastoral theological dialectic is not a conversation between theory and practice, but a conversation between theology, a psycho-theology, perhaps, and the human condition. By shifting the categories of conversation from theory to theology, and from practice to human condition, the reflective and motivational activities ultimately result in praxis, which I also believe should be the core agenda for every pastoral theologian. The absence of a praxis approach to pastoral theology eliminates the self-critical dimension necessary for pastoral theologians to appropriately engage culture and context.

Watkins Ali's understated critique within her text is that the focus of African American pastoral theology has been upon the practice of pastoral care among African Americans instead of working to develop a larger theoretical framework. To simply nuance existing theory to fit the context will help us to cope, but it will not help us to be liberated, especially when those existing theories encourage our imprisonment. Because of the deep existential wounds we bear, practice is very important; and theory and practice must be linked. But to only contextualize traditional approaches rather than to break new ground and build new theoretical structures does not encourage the praxis necessary for our self-determination. Watkins Ali boldly goes where the majority of African American students of theology and psychology have been encouraged not to go. She takes a liberationist's stand as a womanist pastoral theologian and speaks to the racist and sexist features of the American pastoral theological system. She leads an exodus from that house to a theoretical house all our own.

Her work is a radical departure from the way pastoral theology has been conceived for African Americans. Watkins Ali declares the necessity for an African American pastoral theology, rather than simply stating the need for more African Americans to do pastoral theology. The field of pastoral theology has encouraged African Americans to do "their own thing" without cultivating the ground for a new generation of pastoral theologians and pastoral psychologists. Watkins Ali advocates for a specifically African American theoretical approach to doing pastoral theology that emphasizes the themes of survival and liberation. This is a departure from what has tended to be emphasized by American pastoral theologians. The tendency has been to develop a "Black perspective" on some traditional pastoral theological themes. Watkins Ali, however, argues that we can no longer afford to "blackenize" traditional methodology.

Although Watkins Ali is arguing for a shift from perspective to "indigenization," she is still squarely located within the discipline of pastoral theology. Her skeletal frame continues to make use of the same general disciplinary categories of pastoral theology. She continues to integrate theology, psychology, anthropology, history, and the like. Her point of departure, however, is the specific resources that are engaged within the various disciplines that not only regard, but validate, the phenomenological and existential realities of Black people. Consistent with womanist methodology, Watkins Ali turns to African American literature to explicate the groanings of Black people and further illustrate the needs for this indigenous approach.

Watkins Ali pushes for a critique of not only African American life, but also of America in light of the African American experience. Oppression still looms large in the lives of African Americans. While "melting pot" is no longer our societal language, the dominant social movement is the "melting/blending principle." To continue to reduce our experiences of racism to the extent our experiences are labeled classism, or to deny the structural social and economic inequities that are motivated by race and sex and to argue that affirmative action is unnecessary not only dishonors our feelings but promotes forgiveness without confession. It promotes reconciliation before mutual respect or liberation. To this, Watkins Ali encourages the development of new strategies for the survival and liberation of African Americans. She wants to strengthen and heal the Black psyche and help to transform American society at large.

Homer Ashby Jr. takes the next logical step in the development of an African American liberation praxis. He starts with the prime narrative of Black theology, the exodus story, also a central metaphor for the civil rights movement. Ashby suggests that we must take the next step on our road to freedom by crossing over Jordan and occupying the promised land. Rather than falling back on old images and traditional interpretations, he offers a new way of seeing who and where we are. His central thesis moves from the understanding that unless we accurately define and describe our current context, we will not be able to experience freedom and justice. He believes that too many within the African American community have misdiagnosed our social location. We are still declaring we need to be delivered out of the house of bondage, whereas we have marched out of our enslavement. He further believes that—although we have marched out of "Egypt," a metaphor for slavery—we are still experiencing the impact of having been enslaved, which is why we continue to keep the exodus narrative alive. In like manner, to continue to sing "We Shall Overcome" in some ways also disregards our current social location. Many are attempting to understand the circumstances of our lives, and all too often, the picture that is described is viewed through the same jaundiced eyes and offers the same conclusions for redressing our problems. Ashby believes we have also misdiagnosed our symptoms, which means we are working to overcome our problems in all the wrong ways. He says our liberation begins by recognizing that we have made the exodus journey and have crossed over Jordan into the promised land.

Recognizing that we have crossed over Jordan in no way means we "have arrived." To the contrary, recognizing we have crossed over means we face a new type of struggle. By lifting high the Joshua narrative and the African/African American tradition of conjure, Ashby is attempting to speak us into a new reality. His book *Our Home Is Over Jordan*[35] is his work of "Black Magic." No, he is not employing the works of evil to do others harm; but he is attempting to speak African Americans into a new way of seeing and being through conjure. Conjure is a way of taking control of one's environment, a way of controlling the elements to transform living conditions and manipulate the circumstances that inhibit one's life. Through conjuring Joshua, he is suggesting that we, like warriors in a conflict, take control of our available resources and fight the enemy head-on. Though our problems may seem insurmountable, we have the ability and resources to fight the good fight for our liberation.

Since I gave one of the endorsement blurbs on the back of *Our Home Is Over Jordan*, allow me to begin by quoting what I have already written:

> Homer Ashby has made a significant contribution to the field of African American Pastoral Theology. Lifting up Black Theology as a vitally important resource for our work, and critically engaging several significant, yet sometimes divergent, voices of the Black liberation perspective, Ashby encourages African Americans to reexamine our psycho-spiritual context by making a liberationist's

shift. We know where we have been; we know where we want to be; and Ashby describes our current space to say we must redefine where we are if we are going to truly be free.

His work of conjure is a powerful step toward the freedom and justice that have remained near and dear to the African American heart. Most of us still have the voice and the words of Martin Luther King Jr. echoing through our conscious memories. And for those of us who have not the consciousness of his speeches, we still have the unconscious stirrings of the images that Dr. King inspired. Deep within us dwell the words:

> I don't know what will happen now. We've got some difficult days ahead. But it really doesn't matter with me now, because I've been to the mountaintop. And I don't mind. Like anybody, I would like to live a long life—longevity has its place. But I'm not concerned about that now. I just want to do God's will. And He's allowed me to go up to the mountain. And I've looked over, and I've seen the Promised Land. I may not get there with you. But I want you to know tonight that we as a people will get to the Promised Land.[36]

So Ashby is pointing to a narrative shift that was encouraged during the civil Rights Movement many years ago. We had our wandering in the wilderness for more than forty years. Ashby is now attempting to stir our imaginations to sing, "There ain't no danger in the water," so, "wade in the water." In making this narrative shift, however, he emphasizes that the promised land is also the land of struggle. The victory may be won, but the battle is far from over.

Conclusion

Freedom and justice are wellsprings within the African American soul. We must tap those waters if we are to know true liberation. Although the liberation traditions I describe are very different, they have some tenets held in common by all. And although some perspectives are unique to each thinker, the combination of all the aforementioned thinkers helps us to see a more complete picture of African American life. Furthermore, the uniqueness of each approach supports employing an interdisciplinary approach to understand the cultural identity of African Americans. Each reveals dynamics that the major psychodynamic theorists did not consider, which is further evidence that neither Freud, Jung, nor Erikson gave full consideration to the African American context. In the last chapter, I present a new framework for accessing African Americans, which is my contribution to the liberation effort.

9

Restoring Our Souls

One of the first things we notice about people when we meet them (along with their sex) is their race. We utilize race to provide clues about who a person is. This fact is made painfully obvious when we encounter someone whom we cannot conveniently racially categorize—someone who is, for example, racially "mixed" or of an ethnic/racial group with which we are not familiar. Such an encounter becomes a source of discomfort and momentarily a crisis of racial meaning. Without a racial identity, one is in danger of having no identity.

MICHAEL OMI AND HOWARD WINANT

When we become Afro-Saxon we become Incog-Negro.

ROBERT L. WOODSON SR., FOUNDER AND PRESIDENT OF THE
NATIONAL CENTER FOR NEIGHBORHOOD ENTERPRISE

Randall Bailey has identified four African American academic approaches to biblical texts,[1] each influenced by Africentric concerns. The four approaches to interpreting biblical texts are: arguing for African presence, responses to racist/White supremacist interpretations, cultural-historical interpretation, and ideological criticism. I have actualized each of the four approaches in varying degrees throughout this text. Largely, my task has been to present a rationale for an indigenous African American pastoral psychology that evaluates African American identity both theoretically and functionally. This chapter presents my theoretical model for understanding the identity formation of African Americans.

The Grounds for a New Theory

An individual identity develops in relationship to other individuals. No personal past can be extracted independent of a cultural history because personality and identity develop within a context. Therefore, if anyone would choose to claim a universal theory of identity, given worldwide cultural diversity, the driving critique would have to be, "How can such a claim be validated?" Even though we are not talking about differences in humanity, we must acknowledge the diversity of the human experience.

My intellectual development has not been very different from most African Americans. When it came time to select a topic for advanced degree studies, I was encouraged to study traditional European and European American theorists along with some topic unrelated to the African American community. One of the statements supporting this encouraged rationale was: "If your graduate studies focus upon Black folks, then people will think all you can do is Black stuff." So I initially directed my graduate studies to examine issues only remotely related to African American life. Not being settled on the matter, I continued to raise the question to other African American scholars. After considerable reflection on my passion and where I felt my career path leading me, it became clear that as an African American man, no matter what body of knowledge I mastered, I would still be seen as an African American man who only knows "Black stuff." With that conclusion, I allowed my heart to be my guide and began researching the identity question within African American life.[2]

Pastoral psychological theorists concentrating on the identity formation of African Americans are few and far between. The bulk of the research from pastoral psychologists focuses upon faith development, conversion, Black family therapy, and religious experience. Of course, implicit in those foci is a concern for identity, but a psychological framework that coordinates psychology and theology with attentiveness to spirituality for an understanding of the African American identity represents a different endeavor.[3]

African American culture is a distinctive cultural group, and assessing the culture requires an indigenous approach. According to the psychodynamic personality theories reviewed in chapter 6, the individual self develops in the context of other individuals and derives meaning from the collective of individuals. Yet even as psychodynamic psychology lifts up both the individual and the collective identities, its work remains focused on the individual in relationship. Within this understanding, "the one" remains more important than "the many." In some contexts, community is defined as a coalition of individuals who bond together to accomplish a particular task. This is particularly true of collectives that emphasize community over personal fulfillment. In those cases, individuality is not lost as much as it is recognized that the individual participates in a larger system.

We can, however, understand community in another way, a way that has been central to the African American way of life. This way regards the community as being what is most important. Identity is formed with community as the main focus. This way stands opposed to one that sees the person formed by the community to be an individualistic being.

Breaking Psychological Chains

The African American context historically emphasized communal life. Furthermore, a significant portion of communal life has emphasized religious life. As I stated previously, African spirituality and cosmology stress a connectedness of all things without a distinct separation between the sacred and the secular.[4] This worldview was maintained as a legacy within the early African community in American and nurtured both the individual and the collective identities of the displaced Africans. Revealed in African American religiosity through spirituality, African cosmology encouraged the dialogue between the individual and the community for promoting self-understanding and survival. The profound spirituality of early African Americans constructed our consciousness and self-concept. It shaped our world along with giving meaning to it.

My construction of a new theory of identity combines psychology and theology, with attentiveness to religion, spirituality, and history as the basic resources for exploring African American identity. I have already reviewed my psychological foundations. Here, I also want to lift up my other theoretical and hermeneutical foundations. My work began with the study of religion and ultimately led to a study of African American religious history. I then incorporated "systematic theology" and "philosophical theology." Both systematic theology and philosophical theology reflect upon the human condition and stress the many issues that help to discern religion and faith. They strive to organize the ways that human beings attend to the world. They systematize the beliefs that are developed as human beings understand themselves standing in relation to the Divine and to one another. Those considerations are essential to my contemplation of African America.

> Religion, the dominant element in many cultures, reveals much about a people. Religion forms the core foundation of the African world and is central to understanding the numerous Africanisms that carried over into the New World. Some of the most visible Africanisms are found in such African-American religious practices as the ring shout, the passing of children over a dead person's coffin in the Sea Islands, and the placement of objects on top of graves. Many Africans believe that a Supreme Being, or God, exists and is present in all things, both the inner and outer universes, and that a person's life experiences evolve around a world filled with spirituality.[5]

Religion has been the African and African American's primary educational institution for communicating community values and traditions while encouraging a positive self-concept. This fact is sometimes overlooked as African Americans begin their scholarly journeys. The inclination toward forgetfulness is why Randy Bailey argues that we should value our own interpretive traditions and not just attribute value to other systems. We have well-developed systems for knowing the world. However, we have had a tendency to disregard or discard our interpretive frames when we have moved into the academy. Not only have we had a tendency to invalidate our interpretive traditions, we have also had a tendency to invalidate our "classics" as valuable sources for research. The academy teaches what the literary classics are and subsequently declares the appropriate ways of understanding the texts and the world. African American culture is an oral culture, and so we ask, "How does one declare a 'classic' within an oral tradition?" The medium and mode are themselves what are classic, so that *listening* to the storyteller, whom one might call a lecturer, is as vital and relevant as *reading* a printed manuscript. African American religion and education should both be understood as regarding call-and-response as critical pedagogy in the journey of the self.

Religious experience and religious education have meant more than the routine performance of rituals. The combination of the two has represented the engagement of good and evil with the purposeful hope of overcoming evil. Religious testimonies have represented personal experiences of transcendence and the victorious statements of good's triumph over evil. Individual identification with the community and the articulation of individual hopes became community hopes, just as were those communicated in the spirituals. This expression is not merely an instance of the fluidity between the individual and the collective. It is not seen as a ground that shifts between the individual and the collective so much as it is the stable ground, making a firm foundation beneath the feet of the people. The individual and the community live the same reality simultaneously. Community life, which is spiritual at its core, expresses the functional nature of the African American religious experience as the force of its collective identity. From this point of view, organized religion is a collective process of individuals struggling for wholeness.

Other perspectives on religious experience do not radically differ. As I have already suggested, Freud understood a religious experience as the struggle to find a guiding myth, as one's longing to find the "benevolent one," who is within the individual. For Jung, a religious experience was the relational struggle of the part with the whole–the fractured "named self" seeking integration with the "unnamed Self." Tillich, who was very psychoanalytic and existential at the same time, would probably be in agreement with Jung on this point. He understood the individual and collective experiences to be unified in the worship experience that centers the personality.[6] Each highlights the individual who is discovered within the context of relationship and community.

The work of historians such as Sterling Stuckey and religious studies scholars such as Albert Raboteau and John Mbiti make it clear that the Africans (even before their encounters with Christianity and North America) had a clear sense of themselves in relation to the Divine and one another. The enslaved Africans of the seventeenth and eighteenth centuries had a theological perspective, a systematized worldview based upon religion, faith, and community. The Africanist Cheikh Diop stated that "three factors compete to form the collective personality of a people: a psychic factor susceptible of a literary approach...In addition, there are the historical factor and the linguistic factor, both susceptible of being approached scientifically."[7] To consider the collective identity of African Americans, I have reviewed theories and studies as suggested by Diop:

1. the psychic material of theorists from Black psychology and psychodynamic psychology;
2. historical information interpreted by a variety of disciplinary approaches, including psycho-history and religious history; and
3. the linguistic factor considered in the context of the highly symbolic nature of language communicated through Black, womanist, and African American pastoral theology.

I began by reviewing the construct of race and the influence of color prejudice as foundational formative forces that impact the cultural identity of African Americans. My leading interpretive tools were psychology and history. Due to the dominative categories of Western European society, Africans were subjected to horrendous conditions that established a subordinative status. This led me to review the psychodynamic personality theories of Freud, Jung, and Erikson, with major emphasis on Erikson and his psycho-historical approach. These three, in particular, were selected because they are the psychologists most often referenced as resources by pastoral psychologists in America. The three also represent my introduction to the academic study of psychology. Finding their reflections to be, at times, inconsiderate and often inadequate, my vision was expanded by the work of Black (African) psychologists and other Africanists.

Although each of the three psychodynamic personality theorists expressed a similar emphasis on psychic conflict and development, each theorist had a different major thematic focus that informed and guided his understandings. Freud was concerned with childhood repressions and instincts; Jung was interested in religion as psychic phenomena; and Erikson concentrated on the ever-changing and expanding social relationships. None of them emphasized spirituality as a dominant feature of life in relationship. Psychologically, this contributes to the dichotomization of spirituality and sexuality, a reality extremely problematic for African Americans. Separating spirituality from the daily messiness of living places Africans in the position of being regarded as the source of the mess people encounter every day.

The legacy of the psychodynamic personality tradition has to do with the three theorists' similar emphases on internal processes that influence or create external negotiations, but their themes for explicating those processes and negotiations differ. Freud's Oedipal Complex and Thanatos expressed his position that conflicts and neurotic fears are what constitute the individual's struggles. Jung's individuation process, originating in the collective unconscious, highlights his focus on the transformation of the personality in adulthood. Erikson's work in the area of psycho-history illustrates his focus on the centrality of identity and the crises that assault identity. Because each theorist focused on Western Europeans, it would be unfruitful to seek African American wholeness by a strict adherence to their categories. As I suggested earlier, such an attempt would result in the identity of "Slave American." This perspective has been the grounding point for many Black (African) psychologists.[8]

I have sometimes been asked if I still see any benefit to retaining the psychodynamic psychologists in my work. My answer usually is that because I have the responsibility of teaching different racial ethnics, I will continue to reference their work in the classroom. But the work that I do with African Americans necessitates a departure from those traditions. The human body regularly requires a change of diet for healthier functioning. This often means giving up different types of foods. The theories of Freud, Jung, and Erikson (and their neo-constructionists) may be good for some, but African Americans may be healthier without their influence.

Revisiting these concerns from an Africentric understanding of phenomena yields results that differ from those obtained through traditional psychodynamic psychological approaches. Asante states that the "Afrocentric study of phenomena asks questions about location, place, orientation, and perspective that allows Africans to be subjects of historical experiences rather than objects in the fringes of Europe."[9] According to Asante, human experiences can be interpreted in more than one way, and the traditional method has been from the perspective of Europe. African American approaches to freedom and justice have always considered African Americans to be self-determined subjects rather than the nonhuman, unfree objects of America.

After exploring a conceptual understanding of the synoptic psychodynamic personality theories, I revisited the foundational experiences of the African American community through a discussion on the relationship between the psychological and the religious. From there, I explored the concepts of spirituality and survival. I concluded that survival became one of the important dimensions of the African American culture, continually expressed by a collective spirituality. Although survival is often perceived as a negative trait, survival has been our decisive strength to live life in the face of death.

Historically, most European American thinkers have not accurately regarded the strength of African spirituality or African American survival.

Because religion is an essential component of culture, I explored the dynamic relationship between personality and culture. These dynamics have resulted in the cultural container of America as both informing and deforming African American life. Thus, if African Americans are going to be seen as who we truly are, and aspire to be whom we ought to become, it is imperative to construct a theoretical framework representative of the lifeblood of African Americans and revealing an affirming reciprocity between identity and culture. Neither the most prominent European American psychologists nor mainstream European American theologies have tended to consider the history of physical and psychological oppression that Africans have experienced the world over. Placing our affects and experiences into a universal container does not just misinterpret, but it also fails to interpret our story and our psychological accommodations.

Take Erikson's first stage, for example. Survival as a driving force of the African American consciousness is not implicit in his framework unless one considers *Trust vs. Mistrust* to be a survival issue. While basic trust very well may be a survival issue, that has not been the traditional emphasis. Erikson did, however, acknowledge its functionality for the African American community as he responded to a question regarding the educational "instinctive senses" of an African American mother. Erikson "suggested that, given American Negro history, the equivalent 'instinctive sense' may have told the majority of Negro mothers to keep their children, and especially the gifted and the questioning ones, *away* from futile and dangerous competition—that is, for survival's sake to keep them in their place as defined by an indifferent and hateful 'compact majority.'"[10] Yet even here, we find an interpretation that supports and maintains the injustice of the system, and, thereby, misrepresents Black survival.

If we follow Erikson's interpretation, "the gifted and the questioning ones" are not taught how to conceal their giftedness, but are taught to deny their giftedness and "stay in their defined place" in the name of survival. Contrary to the ways most understand African survival, a part of African survival is having the profound gifts of African American life boldly presented while having the viewer see nothing.

After long debates scholars have largely agreed that neither Freud's, Jung's, nor Erikson's theories were gender inclusive; that is, none of them emphasized the true equity of humanity. While Freud's position on women has tended not to be argued, some have contended that Jung was much more inclusive. For instance, Jung's work does explore the anima and animus—the feminine and masculine personifications contained within a man and a woman as inferior functions. Still, he maintained a hierarchical description of the functions in which the anima represents lust and emotionality and the animus represents reason and intellect. Erikson does give attention to the differences between men and women in "Womanhood and the Inner Space,"[11] but no one denies that his theories were primarily based upon male socialization.

My position is that these theories were also not racially inclusive. That necessitates reimagining the psyches and souls of Black folks and developing new theories. Traditional approaches to pastoral psychology have not been considerate of the social-psychological adjustments regularly made by African Americans. Furthermore, a blind spot remains regarding the racist ideology that prevails when applying traditional pastoral psychological theories to African Americans.

These men did not grow up within contexts of racial diversity. The ethnic diversity of their contexts, which were sometimes racialized, could be overcome by name changes. Racial issues, largely expressed by color issues, were either not considered, or they were simply regarded as the byproducts of a dualistic, superiority/inferiority context. In any case, their interpretive skills were shaped and directed by anti-Blackness ideologies.[12] Freud acknowledged that a person is born with phylogenetic material that linked him or her to the experiences of his or her ancestors. But this for him did not reshape the context for understanding sexual repression, which by and large was a Western European cultural phenomenon. According to Basil Davidson (the British historian of African life), Africans' sexual morality appeared to be nonexistent in the estimation of most outsiders' eyes, so why would sexual repression be a diagnosis? Or why should a Victorian ideology be applied to a non-Victorian context?

> [Morality] appeared most absent to many Europeans, as we have seen. Catching a glimpse of what was allowed or disallowed, they found it ludicrous to apply any such term as 'moral order' to people who seemed quite without a European sense of shame. Travellers from afar found much to shock them. The Venda of the Transvaal are only one among many peoples, for example, who have considered that premarital sexual experience was morally, because socially, valuable and even necessary, provided always that it not lead to pregnancy. Premarital pregnancy was severely discouraged because the children of unmarried parents represented an immediate problem for the community, posing the question: to whom should they belong?; so that, at least among the Southern Bantu, the stigma of illegitimacy attached to the parents and not to the offspring. Otherwise, the Venda saw to it that youths and maidens after the age of puberty should be carefully instructed in the 'facts of life,' so as to have a limited form of sexual outlet before marriage...Krige records a ceremony where girls who had clothed themselves were even criticized with the implication that they had led a loose sexual life. Nudity could thus be the reverse of obscene.[13]

Jung, on the other hand, was not even as considerate as Freud in his views of non-Whites. He gave all races the benefit of humanity, but he did not consider all humanity equal. He thought Africans were developmentally inferior to Europeans:

> You cannot live in Africa or any such country without having that country under your skin. If you live with the yellow man, you get yellow under the skin. You cannot prevent it, because somewhere you are the same as the Negro or the Chinese or whomever you live with, you are all just human beings. In the collective unconscious you are the same as a man of another race, you have the same archetypes, just as you have, like him, eyes, a heart, a liver, and so on. It does not matter that his skin is black. It matters to a certain extent, sure enough–he has probably a whole historical layer less than you. The different strata of the mind correspond to the history of the races.[14]

In his attempt to explain the sexual repression of Americans, he concluded the problem was due to living with "Negroes":

> Jung also explained the "energetic sexual repressions" of Americans as a defensive maneuver against blacks. "The causes for the repression," Jung explained at the Second Psychoanalytic Congress in 1910, "can be found in the specific American Complex, namely to the living together with lower races, especially Negroes. Living together with barbaric races exerts a suggestive effect on the laboriously tamed instinct of the white race and tends to pull it down. Hence, the need for strongly developed defensive measures, which precisely show themselves in those specific features of American culture."[15]

Erikson was the most open of the three. In a conversation with Huey Newton, he acknowledged his limitations for studying and interpreting African American affects. During this conversation he said that as an immigrant to the United States, he was unaware of the depths of its racism. He told Newton:

> Only much later, and only when young people put their lives on the line, could we [immigrants], too, fully *perceive* [*emphasis mine*] the fact that we had largely overlooked the fate of the black citizenry who were kept in their place so as to constitute what slaves always meant besides cheap labor–the inferior identity to be superior to.[16]

Consequently, he did not have the resources for fully apprehending the psychosocial adjustments of African Americans.

I approach the subject of identity with the understanding that the interaction between the human internal striving and external realities create religion and faith, and are expressed through spirituality. Therefore spirituality is both a conscious and an unconscious process. I, however, am not in full agreement with Marx's well-known critique of religion. I agree that "humanity makes religion," and religion is *one* response of the oppressed. I disagree that "religion does not make human beings," and also that it is an "opium" for the people. The Marxist critique has been popularized to misinterpret African American religion. The popularized view of African American religion holds that religion made Africans docile and content with enslavement in America. Religion, however, is one of humanity's progenitors. Not only does humanity make religion, religion also participates in shaping humanity. Religion can soothe the suffering soul; but, more importantly, religion promotes a systematic structuring of the world by providing humanity with the integrity to survive and thrive. We are not the black objects being described and castigated. Rather, we are the subjects whose religion becomes the wind and the lenses for ourselves as Black beauties. Through the tumultuous veil of sorrow wrought by racism and genderism, we see that we have been wondrously and miraculously made as fully human in our blackness.

The Transition to a New Theory

A departure from degrading theologies and theories is necessary for African Americans to be liberated and have our souls restored to live a life of joy. African American pastoral psychology, as an interdisciplinary field, is an appropriate approach for coordinating the issues and concerns that affect and influence African American culture and personality. Gathering the voices of Black and womanist theologies, African American history and religious studies, African (Black) psychology, and African American biblical hermeneutics, the African American pastoral psychologist struggles with therapeutic sensitivity to restore the African soul. To help everyone to see the true nature of the African American identity, I have developed the "Theory of African American Communal Identity Formation."

A New Paradigm

First, the "Theory of African American Communal Identity Formation" (TAACIF) is not dualistic, nor is it another stage theory coordinated with age. The Theory of African American Communal Identity Formation is an issue-oriented paradigm. Dividing the fulfilled life into two halves, the TAACIF says that the developing individual will confront particular issues during the first "half" or formative years of life. During the second "half" or constructive years of life, the adult will confront a variation of those same issues. This means that the issues and formative experiences of childhood are the "blueprints" for interpreting and constructing adult life. Rather than a simple cycle, the paralleled issues are understood to relate to each other like the infinity symbol—two distinct halves that loop back into one another. This looping image represents the internal and external negotiations that go on at the various phases of personality development. The loop also represents the continuous struggles of confronting the issues of life for the rest of one's life.

The TAACIF is a developmental theory that purports a healthier way to understand African American identity formation, relationships, and worldview. It stresses the importance of cultural sensitivity and psycho-spiritual legacy. Because of my psychodynamic, developmental orientation, the theory has been influenced by two developmental personality stage theories (Freud's and Erikson's) and by one personality theory of adulthood (Jung's). More important than the influence of psychodynamic personality theories, the TAACIF has been informed by my first teacher: the African American Christian religious heritage. Most developmental stage theories emphasize childhood experiences and their effects on adult life. Some developmental stage theories emphasize the collective's and the Divine's effect on the individual. Almost all developmental stage theories stratified humanity in an effort to understand and explain the human condition. Freud and Erikson stratified humanity with their stage theories; and, to some extent, Jung did the same with his interpretation of the various levels of psychic processes. To the extent that they stratified human life, their perspectives are hierarchical. Stage theories develop due to the consistencies within the context; yet, I have been stressing that few universals exist and that consistencies vary according to cultural expectations. The TAACIF suggests that the African American psyche, which moves according to its roots in African spirituality, makes accommodations according to the circumstances of a given moment. The African American psyche does not respond according to the expectations of the context. It cannot be predicted by the stage descriptions. The African American psyche moves according to the psyche's understanding of the issues and self-concept. If the expectations of the context were always in charge, Africans would never have become African Americans. Why? Because in the American context, Africans are always expected to be animalistic, hedonistic, and antisocial.

The TAACIF coordinates and highlights the commonality of psychody-namic psychology without reducing humanity to the "hard determinism" that is indicative of most stage theories. The most common understandings of stage development produce an expectation that a person has to experience the various stages in lock-step fashion. If a person does not experience the prescribed development when the theory determines, the person is considered deficient or maladaptive. The TAACIF first and foremost leaves room for the appropriation that was characteristic of African peoples during antebellum within the North American context. This means that the theory leaves room for something new to emerge in the course of human events.

Although a significant part of the foundation for this theory has grown out of Erikson's theory of human stage development, the TAACIF emphasizes the negotiation and renegotiation of issues. As in a marriage in which a couple will negotiate terms for relating and later renegotiate the terms due to dispositional changes, the TAACIF highly regards the negotiations of life. It emphasizes two periods in life, a *foundational period* and a *constructive period.* The first life period suggests that the learning that takes place early in life and the issues that are confronted during those formative, foundational years remain as a permanent imprint upon the psyche. During the latter period of life, the individual continues to confront the foundational issues at a more profound level of functioning while she or he constructs a life with integrity, consistency, and wholeness.

It is commonly assumed that the developmental stage theories of psychodynamic psychology are, in some sense, "universal" presentations of human development. For the reasons I stated earlier, I make no such assertion regarding the TAACIF. Insofar as the issues of the TAACIF have been informed by psychodynamic psychology, there will be a degree of applicability to other groups of people. Whereas certain life issues may be the same for all humanity, the negotiation of life issues will vary from group to group. Since the TAACIF is the result of direct observation of the African American community, this framework is culturally specific. As a result, the TAACIF has been conceived as a culturally specific approach to African American identity formation.

My basic assumption regarding the cultural specificity of the TAACIF is that culture and personality are developmentally dependent upon one another, and that, in fact, culture and personality inform, influence, and direct the expressions of culture and personality. Consequently, inasmuch as African Americans have predominantly been on the outside of the mainstream cultural context of the United States, resulting from segregation and racist ideologies of inferiority, African Americans have a separate and distinct culture. African American identity, therefore, is the resulting compilation of African retentions, appropriations, and accommodations within the United States of America's social structure.

> Slave artisans and domestic servants, mainly West Africans, worked in close proximity to European-Americans and were forced to give up their cultural identities to reflect their masters' control and capacity to "civilize" the Africans. By contrast, field workers—largely Central Africans—were relatively removed from this controlling, "civilizing" influence. Given the constraints imposed on artisans and domestic servants by plantation owners, one may logically conclude that the cultures of the Congo-Angola region of Central Africa rather than those of West Africa were dominant in North America. West African culture, nevertheless, supplied mainstream southern society with Africanisms through a process of reciprocal acculturation between Africans and European-Americans.[17]

If one considers the African American communal identity from a historical perspective, antebellum through Jim and Jane Crow *could* be considered part of a foundational period. African antecedents must also be reviewed and regarded as an important part of the foundational period. That assumption places post-civil rights/post-human rights era African Americans in the constructive period of negotiating identity issues, negotiations that have us in a state of crisis. A number of Black psychologists have understood this crisis in terms of Post-traumatic Stress Disorder. While this diagnosis attempts to be descriptive and suggestive of an appropriate prescription, identifying our living as a condition of Post-traumatic Stress can suggest a maladaptive way of living. Indeed, we have been traumatized, but our reactions to our circumstances are not entirely dependent on a single event from the distant past. We continue to be traumatized by life-denying forces. We are in crisis as a community. By this I mean we are at a critical turning point in our communal, cultural history. Rather than identifying our living as a social disorder, I prefer to describe the forces that affect our socialization. Instead of saying Post-traumatic Stress, I prefer to say Protracted-traumatic Stress because we continue to be traumatized by life-denying forces that we must survive and overcome.

The Issues of the Paradigm

The particularity of the issues that constitute the TAACIF are accompanied by three distinctive ideas that participate in the mediating process of negotiations and renegotiations. The issues along with the accompanying mediating ideas are what make the TAAFIC culturally specific. The following is the way I chart the paradigm. The left column is the foundational period, and the right column is the constructive period.

Theory of African American Communal Identity Formation

FOUNDATIONAL		CONSTRUCTIVE
Historical Self	RAGE / CREATIVITY------→	**African Spirituality**
Emotional Development	RAGE / CREATIVITY------→	Relational Development
Existential Longing	RAGE / CREATIVITY------→	Existential Search
Learning the Rules	RAGE / CREATIVITY------→	Living the Paradox
Identity and Play	RAGE / CREATIVITY------→	Identity and Work

I begin my description by identifying the three ideas that mediate the formation issues. On the primary issues side is the foundational idea of the *Historical Self*, while the constructive issues side is directed by *African Spirituality*. Both are very much unconscious guides. These paralleled ideas located on the foundational and constructive sides of life are mediated by the energies of *Rage/Creativity*. This African American personality distinctive is one of the results of the coping skills that were developed and the worldview that was established by the diasporadic Africans during the Middle Passage transport and after their arrival in America between the seventeenth and eighteenth centuries:

> When did [the American Negro] emerge? Out of what strange incunabula did the peculiar heritage and attitudes of the American Negro arise? I suppose it is technically correct to call any African who was brought here and had no chance of ever leaving, from that very minute when his residence and his life had been changed irrevocably, an American Negro. But it is imperative that we realize that the first slaves did not believe they would be here forever. Or even if they did, they thought of themselves as merely captives. This, America, was a foreign land. These people were foreigners, they spoke in a language that was not colonial American; and the only Western customs or mores of that they had any idea at all were that every morning at a certain time certain work had to be done and that they would probably be asked to do it…The stories, myths, moral examples, etc., given in African were about Africa. When America became important enough to the African to be passed on, in those formal renditions, to the young, those renditions were in some kind of Afro-American language. And finally, when a man looked up in some anonymous field and shouted, "Oh, Ahm tired a dis mess,/Oh, yes, Ahm so tired a diss mess," you can be sure he was an American.[18]

I noted in the preface how identity has often been misrepresented and confused with role. Although "slave" was the eighteenth-century African's vocation (work role) in America, it was not the African's profession (stated identity). The enslavers strove very diligently to force Africans to accept their role/labor as their identity. But labor plays only a small part in the development of the identity.

Although Erikson talked about a confused identity, it is nonetheless an identity. Identity confusion means a person has inappropriate identifications that are guiding self-understanding. In the case of African Americans, the claiming of false identifications would have completely distorted and totally denied our Historical Self. Had the Africans of the eighteenth-century accepted their role as their identity, it would have been an identity without integrity. The eighteenth-century vocational identity of slave was an image developed by the enslavers. But the self-image that Africans adopted was an image that emerged from their soul. That image was nonsectarian, reaching inward to the distant generational past and outward to the Divine. It was an image not revealed by flesh and blood alone but by the relational working of the spirit of God.

Once the Bantu reached America they were able to retain much of their cultural identity. Enforced isolation of these Africans by plantation owners allowed them to retain their religion, philosophy, culture, folklore, folkways, folk beliefs, folk tales, storytelling, naming practices, home economics, arts, kinship, and music. These Africanisms were shared and adopted by the various African ethnic groups of the field slave community, and they gradually developed into African-American cooking (soul food), music (jazz, blues, spirituals, gospels), language, religion, philosophy, customs, and arts.[19]

Those foundational traits remain as a legacy within today's African American identity. The Historical Self directs the emerging African American self while African Spirituality guides the communal aspects of African American cultural life. The Historical Self and African Spirituality participate in a collective past that precedes the African presence in America. It is this dialectic legacy that allows Blacks in America to express an "*African* American identity." The Historical Self is analogous to a recessive trait that lies dormant until African Spirituality suddenly awakens it. Therefore, Blacks of America become diasporatic Africans in America with a past (heretofore unknown), and a future (not before recognized), and a new present identity of *African American*:

> Race in the modern world is defined by land of origin: Japanese-American, Mexican-American, Chinese-American. But there is no land mass called Negro, Black, or Afro. These terms are hybrids, with no real reference to the African continent. The term African-American defines black people on the basis of identification with their historic place of origin...Thus this debate has come full circle, from *African* through *brown, colored, Afro-American, Negro,* and *black* back to *African,* the term originally used by blacks in America to define themselves. The changes in terminology reflect many changes in attitude, from strong African identification to nationalism, integration, and attempts at assimilation back to cultural identification. This struggle to reshape and define blackness in both the concrete and the abstract also reflects the renewed pride of black people in shaping a future based on the concept of one African people living in the African diaspora.[20]

The line that divides the Historical Self from African Spirituality is the Rage/Creativity that is present within every African American. We are not just angry about our experiences with oppression in America. Our feelings run deeper than that. We live with a constant rage that is so deep that to even point to it frightens the onlookers. Whereas this rage could have become a primary destructive force within African American consciousness, its energy was transformed into a creative force, and a new way of living in the world emerged. African spirituality energized African American creativity, making creativity a powerful adversary against the forces of hate and degradation.

The cry for justice is sometimes connected to a spirituality of violence, not unlike what is found in Psalm 137:

By the rivers of Babylon we sat and wept
when we remembered Zion.
There on the poplars we hung our harps,
for there our captors asked us for songs,
 our tormentors demanded songs of joy;
they said, "Sing us one of the songs of Zion!"
How can we sing the songs of the LORD
while in a foreign land?
If I forget you, O Jerusalem,
may my right hand forget [its skill].
May my tongue cling to the roof of my mouth
 if I do not remember you,
 if I do not consider Jerusalem
 my highest joy.
Remember, O LORD, what the Edomites did
 on the day Jerusalem fell. "Tear it down," they cried,
 "tear it down to its foundations!"
O Daughter of Babylon, doomed to destruction,
happy is he who repays you
for what you have done to us—
he who seizes your infants
 and dashes them against the rocks. (Ps. 137: 1–9, NIV)

Often only a thinly veiled line exists between a cry for justice and expressions of hate. Although a statement like that found in Psalm 137 tends not to be religiously acceptable (that is why people tend only to read half the text in worship), the mood, feelings, and movement of the text from sadness to anger to rage are no less true. Rage has a way of being uncontrollable and unstoppable. Unless its energy is redirected, rage will not only consume the enemy; it will also consume the innocent and, eventually, the self.

While the human spirit has the capacity to rise above devastation—to move from victim to survivor—something about victimization always reminds the survivor of the atrocity that has been committed. As victim, one's wounds are still susceptible. Even as survivor, amnesia regarding what has happened does not define a survivor's existence. When the survivor is reminded of his or her victimization, that reminder releases the rage that has been held within. People tend to do everything within their power to suppress the expression of deep emotional content, believing that emotions make one vulnerable to attack. Because rage is usually considered to be deep anger completely out of control, people tend to go to great lengths to deny its validity.

Rage develops when my humanity is denied and my existence is controlled by a force that seeks to diminish my identity. At such times my feelings remain controlled by a whimsical, uncaring person who has no interest in relational wholeness. The future, then, is out of my own hands. Rage becomes the destructive expression that could delight in infants being dashed upon rocks. Massacres, riots, community-wide addictions, and moral bankruptcy are all results of the devastating effects of rage. The task, however, is not to deny the rage, but to transform its energy into a creative force. The creative transformation of rage conquers the enemy and restores the soul to living a life with joy. That's why the scriptures say, "Love your enemies and pray for those who persecute you" (Mt. 5:44). This point is not about "redemptive suffering" but about redirecting the source of one's life.

One of the virtuous strengths of enslaved diasporadic Africans in America was their adaptability. The ability to make adjustments in living without losing their sense of self is what provided them with the impetus to outlive their tormentors. Earlier I spoke of spirituality as an unconscious energy that organizes the personality. In addition, it is the activity and maintenance of a spiritual life, a stirring within the soul, as one responds to the inner call of God. This understanding of spirituality was particularly true within African village life. When the enslavers stole Africans and put them aboard ships, a new process of identity formation was initiated. What the enslavers thought was a process to create a lost and docile soul actually resulted in the development of a courageously resilient human being. By confining Africans in a perilous and desperate situation, they set the stage for tribal groups who formerly had no relationship to develop kinship bonds in the wake of harsh realities.[21] Thus, African American culture was founded and established upon the interaction of the Historical African Self, African Spirituality, and the Creativity to maintain an identity of courage and integrity, rather than being overtaken and destroyed by Rage.

> From the eighteenth century through the first third of the nineteenth century, black religious and educational organizations used the prefix *African* in their names, providing a sense of cultural integrity and a link to their African heritage. The first black religious organization established in Savannah in 1787 was the First African Baptist Church. The second oldest black denomination in North America, founded in 1787, was the African Methodist Episcopal. In 1806 blacks constructed the first African Meeting House in Boston. This pattern also is seen in such names as African Free School, African Clarkson Society, African Dorcas Society, Children

of Africa, and Sons of Africa. The first mutual beneficial societies that had direct roots in African secret societies called themselves African as late as 1841. One such society was the New York African Society for Mutual Relief.[22]

In addition to the fulcrum of the Historical Self and African Spirituality, I suggest that four pairs of issues interact with one another toward the development of African American identity. The Historical Self is present at every issue level on the foundational side; likewise, African Spirituality is present at every issue level on the constructive side. Rage/Creativity is always the negotiating force present at every level of the TAACIF. I have not attempted to correlate these issues to any age framework. This is primarily due to the fact I am not attempting to introduce another personality theory based upon life-cycle stages. Rather than posit life-cycle stages tied to certain ages, I suggest that the more accurate understanding of human development can be capsulated as learning to live and struggling to live in the wake of what has been learned from life.

The Theoretical Issues

Emotional Development

The first issue on the foundational side is Emotional Development. Very early in life, we are taught to distinguish, express, control, and deny our emotional impulses. The expression of our feelings is encouraged and inhibited, bought and bargained with, adored and belittled. Everything we learn in life is experienced and filtered through the emotions. Our emotions cause us to scream out of fear. We kick and scream out of frustration. We laugh and cry from one moment to the next. Emotions are very sensitive to the experience of the body. As a collective preferential style, African Americans tend to be more inclined to being emotionally expressive. We are passionately committed to bodily expressions. At the same time, we have a tendency to fervently seek to escape our black bodies. Recognizing our issues with the black body, our emotionality can be as dramatic as our discomfort of living in our own skin. A dependence on the cognitive functions, which might be thought of as denying emotions, tends to be less appealing because it is less embodied. This, of course, has nothing to do with intellectual ability. It is simply a statement of preferential styles of negotiating with the world—we tend not to deny our emotions even as we engage in behaviors that promote escaping our bodies. Learning to accept our emotions and our bodies completely will bring about a miraculous change.

Relational Development

The issue on the constructive side is Relational Development. The manner in which we have been taught to express ourselves is tested as we encounter others in social settings, romantic interludes, as friends and acquaintances, and in the search for ecstasy in another. If one learns that emotions are valued and ought to be expressed, then the person tends to be more comfortable and confident with what can be signified with the body. If, on the other hand, one has learned that the repression of feelings, whether joyous or hostile, is valued more highly than expressing one's true sentiments, then the body becomes a hiding place governed by deceptive expression. This repression results in spirituality and sexuality being separated, causing relationships to become disembodied encounters governed by a confusing set of mixed feelings. An unresolved emotional life will lead to a complicated relational life.

Adults who are inclined to being emotional "ponds of still waters running deep" are often full of rage and resentment. With America having been so intent on degrading emotionality–defining it as immature and at the same time abusive of our bodies–it should be no surprise that our deep rage sometimes "spills" over into acts of aggression and violence. Anytime an environment forces one to "swallow" one's pride–one's true feelings–for the sake of survival, at some point one will gag and heave in a violent eruption. This is evidenced in escalating urban violence, domestic violence, and sexual violence, as we experience the resurgence of racial violence. However, the rage can be transformed through a variety of creative social and physical activities. We must encourage creativity by helping African American men and women to move from emotional *self-hate* to relational *self-respect and mutual fulfillment.*

Existential Longing

The second issue on the foundational side is an Existential Longing. The dynamic negotiations of this issue, in effect, become the individual's religious foundation. Very early in life, we embark on our quest for meaning, our search for the Eternal. A longing for the stability and security we experienced in the womb propels us. As it was within the garden called Eden, everything was provided for us; and the divine presence was all around us. The number of children who experience the post-traumatic stress of drugs or poor prenatal care might lead some to challenge this perspective, but evidence shows that even these children long for stability and security. The conflicts confronted and negotiated in this state of longing have a direct impact upon our perception of the world as generally nurturing or hostile. The result is an overall sense of hopefulness or dread. Testing the longing in the context of relationship reveals who is giving, warm, and kind. It also reveals who has a complete disdain for our existence.

Existential Search

The second issue on the constructive side is an Existential Search. Engaging this issue becomes the individual's religious expression. A search in adulthood for ultimate truth, a search for the answers to human finiteness, intensifies the lessons taught and learned through negotiating the longing issue. This is a search for individual and collective deliverance. It is the search to find God, self, and other within and without. It is the search to be embraced and affirmed no matter in what condition we find ourselves. Whether we choose to "shout the devil down" or stand in the breech declaring justice must be done, we believe within the depths of our being that our fate is linked with the fate of others.

Unfortunately, a person who is frustrated by the search for true deliverance might also substitute escapist activities for the journey. Disengaging from the world, however, is never an appropriate substitute for true deliverance. Ultimately, there is no escape from the powers in the world. I am not referencing escapism in the sense of it being an "opiate." This expression of escapism is the rage that is turned inward. It manifests itself as self-destructive behavior or by destroying others that look like the self. People who join churches with a high theology of human depravity and avoidance of the world often have a very high "anti-Blackness quotient." Given our long history of human degradation at the hands of racism and genderism, a high theology of human depravity only supports racist and misogynist claims. When the existential search manifests itself as escapism, it reveals suicide and homicide to be inseparable expressions that result in the genocide of all.

The creative expression of the search can be seen in the movements to reclaim our African heritage and celebrate African American life. One does not have to be nationalistic to be Africentric. The Existential Search is the journey to know one's origins and to declare one's hopes. The creative ventures that declare the search tend to be described as "African genius" or "Black ingenuity." We *feel* our way through the search in the creative impulses that give us spirituals, gospel, the blues, and jazz. We listen to the dynamic elements of the search in the sermon, the novel, the drama of the moment. We find or construct a story that gives us the strength to stand together against the furies. We give assent, testimony, and response to the call with declarations that shout in unison, "My soul says Yes!" and "That's my story!"

Learning the Rules

The third issue on the foundational side is Learning the Rules. These are the issues of socialization. We learn the rules of personal governance and taboo, as well as right and wrong. Here we must learn to distinguish between what is stated and what is observed. We are confronted with the issues of "this is right" and "that is wrong." We hear, "if you do good and strive to be the best, good things will follow and hard work will pay off." Along with those basic rules, as African Americans we are taught that we must live by additional rules that do not apply to non-African Americans.

There are rules like 100 percent is not enough for us, "We must always give 110 percent."

Living the Paradox

On the constructive side of the issue is Living the Paradox. As children, we are taught there is "right and wrong," "good and bad." As adults, we must struggle to make sense of the paradoxes that sometimes say that those things that seem *right* are *wrong*. Although the rules are clearly stated, there is not always a clear delineation between "good and bad." We are taught as children, "honesty is the best policy." As adults, we observe the paradoxical reality, "Don't get caught!" In like manner, we discover that the rules do not always hold true for African Americans. Even when we give 110 percent, we still tend to be regarded as only operating at a 50 percent level and as only "3/5 human." Paradoxes like these have a tendency to lead to rage. We daily run up against the paradox of the impossibility of living into the nation's claim of "freedom and justice for all."

We creatively live with the paradoxes by accentuating the positive and reshaping the negative. Historically, we can see this process at work in the Negro spirituals, such as the song that says, "I got shoes, you got shoes, all God's children got shoes," whereas the very one who "lined" the song (and first sang the song) was probably barefoot. Always operating within African American life is a reconstructive edge to reshape oppressive systems into liberating religious systems for African American people. Creatively living the paradoxes is what produced African American liberation theologies and African (Black) psychology.

Identity and Play

The fourth and final issue on the foundational side of the TAACIF is Identity and Play. Here, the essential issue is to answer the question, "Who are we?" Yet, this issue also makes an impact by directing our perceptions of "what we are." Our identity as social-sexual beings is shaped by the way we play, with whom we play, and the items with which we are permitted to play. The foundation established creates our understandings of our maleness/femaleness, masculinity/femininity, and superiority/inferiority. The rationale for the games we can or cannot play reveals a direct connection to our identities as men and women of color. We learn the difference between winning and losing, but the lesson also includes the importance of how one "plays the game." Engaging in sports and "wargames" has, in some instances, given rise to hope; however, in most urban settings, the war is not much of a game!

Identity and Work

The final issue on the constructive side is Identity and Work. Adult life states emphatically that "who we are" is defined by "what we do."

Then a very subtle shift takes place. The focus is no longer on who we are but on "what we are." Our perceptions of our roles and our jobs, for the most part, are thought to be direct expressions of our identity. As children, we play games that pit good against evil, the beautiful against the unattractive, and the "haves" against the "have nots." When we reach adulthood, we do not want to be judged by the content of our character or the color of our skin. We don't want to be judged, period. We want what every other human being wants: the dignity of personhood with no qualifying strings attached.

To our dismay, disappointing work opportunities and discriminatory social settings tend to swell the rage within us. No matter how friendly the context, we are constantly reminded that we are negatively judged by the color of our skin and/or the attributes of our bodies. We are regularly seen as token contributors no matter how extensive our qualifications. We are often met with a deep sigh of frustration and treated with paternalistic tolerance because the quota mentality says we have to be let in. When we refuse to accept being treated as less than, our resistance is seen as making trouble. Unwilling to endure the disregarding treatment, some of us express our identity and work in a life of crime. Beneath it all is a struggle to avoid reexperiencing the genocide of the Middle Passage and enslavement. Only by transforming the rage to creativity can we separate "who we are" from "what we are."

Encouraging us to creatively maintain a focus on who we are is not to develop some new notion of "doubling"[23] that says that "what one does" should have no influence upon "who one is." My point is this: although what I do may be menial labor, I am a significant person with pride, presence, and purpose. Our true identity as African Americans will only be revealed by transcending the negativities of play and work and by reaffirming our humanity, the essence of our being. Our lives must be guided by spirituality, and we must experience dignity as being something deeper than "getting paid."

The African American Community through the Lenses of TAACIF

In 1959, Stanley Elkins wrote a book entitled *Slavery: A Problem in American Institutional and Intellectual Life*.[24] Coordinating the victimizing experiences of Jews in the Nazi death camps with Africans on antebellum American plantations, he developed what is commonly referred to as the "Sambo Personality Theory." Elkins believed that victimizing experiences of total domination have an infantilizing effect on the personality. He concluded that Africans became the imaginary character of Sambo, not as a personified defense mechanism but as a consequence of the victimizing experience. In other words, any African dignity and integrity that had been known was completely destroyed and replaced by Sambo. So, who was Sambo? Sambo was a fictitious character who came to represent all enslaved

Africans. Elkins identified the characteristics of Sambo as being representative of enslaved Africans' personality type. Elkins describe the Sambo
type in this way:

> Sambo, the typical plantation slave, was docile but irresponsible,
> loyal but lazy, humble but chronically given to lying and stealing;
> his behavior was full of infantile silliness, and his talk inflated with
> childish exaggeration. His relationship with his master was one of
> utter dependence and childlike attachment: it was indeed this
> childlike quality that was the very key to his being.[25]

Although enslaved Africans were described as childlike, Sambo was
more severely regressive than a child. While other enslaved groups around
the globe were traumatized by cruel and unusual punishment, Sambo was
a manifestation thought only to be actualized within Africans. To the White
mind, Sambo was completely devoid of autonomy and industry.

If one were to compare Elkins' psychological analysis with Thomas
Jefferson's social description of enslaved Africans in America, the underlying
attitudes for each thinker would be indistinguishable. Neither man could
see beyond the stereotypical images that defined Africans in America. When
the images and understandings that guide the interpretations of one's
observations are guided by inaccurate and inappropriate categories, the
concluding thoughts will always be inaccurate and inappropriate.
Furthermore, the Sambo personality theory was never intended to be a
helpful theory to be resourced by Africans Americans. We were the objects
of the analysis rather than the subjects to be the beneficiaries.

Although Elkin's effort was intended to be a liberal's supportive analysis,
his guiding images reveal a deep racism that guided his reflections. His
reflection on the Jews did not result in a theory identified with a derogatory
image, as it did with his reflection on the lives of Africans in antebellum
America. The choice of Sambo, however, declares one of the most
popularized images of Africans in the European American mind.

The idea of a theoretical resource specifically intended to benefit the
African American community is an absolute requirement. Most theories,
like the Sambo theory, were intended to address the security needs of
European Americans and not support the developmental needs of African
Americans. Another example of this psychological approach to African
Americans is to look at the larger history of theory development and
psychological diagnostics. Consider the purpose and motivation for the
nineteenth-century clinical diagnosis of Africans in America known as
"drapetomania." In his book *Health as Liberation*, Alastair Campbell briefly
notes that in the May 1851 issue of *The New Orleans Medical and Surgical
Journal* arguments were made to declare the anatomical, physiological, and
psychological inferiority of Africans in America. Africans were identified
as having diseases like "drapetomania," that is, the disease of running away

from slavery. The report he quoted from concluded that "there is a radical internal, or physical difference between the two races, so great in kind, as liberty, republican or free institutions, etc., [are] not only unsuitable to the negro race, but actually poisonous to its happiness."[26] Black psychology was developed, specifically and uniquely, to be an opposing, liberating voice in the face of this kind of analysis. While the TAACIF is not a diagnostic tool, it is a theoretical framework that can support diagnostic assessments. The purpose of this theory is to nurture the souls of African Americans at the deepest levels. Self-knowledge opens the doors of change and reveals the resources for growth and a sustaining hope. The liberation of our dignity means that we declare our self-worth through a proclamation of our humanity. By remembering that the battleground was and is our humanity, we save our souls from the extinction of dehumanization and give voice to the lost and forgotten African ancestors who still long for community.

The TAACIF can be applied to support an individual or a community in the present or the past. For instance, the TAACIF may be a resource for reconsidering the civil rights/human rights movements of the 1960s. A popular culture critique holds that the movement was not as radical as it should have been, especially when viewed through the lenses that measure gains and losses. The most popular critiques suggest that brutality should have been met with brutality and that integration should never have been combined with liberation. And yet the movement in all of its manifestations was true to who we have been as a people both in Africa and America.

If one walks through each of issues presented in the TAACIF, our cultural identity is clear. America called us less than human, yet our Historical Self maintained our clear vision of ourselves as human beings. As human beings in America, we are entitled to a right to life. The declarative expression of our humanity was creative and was guided by African Spirituality. Our work for freedom and justice was not understood as simply being political action, but rather political action was joined with and considered religious work. We were treated as people who feel nothing. If fact, our emotions were only thought to be a conditioning resource for our oppressors. It was believed we could be whipped into total submission and obedience. Had we followed that plan of action, we would have been nonrelational–completely disconnected from life and love. Instead, we banded together, hand-in-hand and arm-in-arm, and sang many songs with deep relational significance. This was done because, at the core of our being, it was clear that God indwells our humanity. We would not stop until we experienced justice through having the bonds of our existence broken. Learning the Rules and Living the Paradox might lead one to assume that no one should challenge the system. But to the contrary, Living the Paradox means that one is fully aware, totally conscious of the abuses one experiences in life. This, indeed, motivated us to challenge the system.

Furthermore, recognizing the paradox also meant that the absurdity of the relationships were clearly seen and understood. This vision helped us to creatively engage in the work of transformation. The final set of issues spoke most clearly to declare the relationship between who we are and what we do. Knowing the difference between the two, we didn't have to rage. We, in fact, transformed our rage into a divine courage to stand against the destructive force of the enemy and declare we are entitled to the same promises of the nation: of life, liberty, property, and the pursuit of happiness.

The Theory of African American Communal Identity Formation is a distinctive approach to what it means to be an African American. It is a theoretical framework that attempts to describe the circumstances in which we find ourselves as African Americans. The way to thwart the forces of genocide that are directed at us is to reinforce our identity—our system of survival—through our unity as a people under the Creator.

Notes

Preface

[1]Chapters 6 and 8 review the names and texts that I have found most valuable for this reflection. Because pastoral psychological method coordinates the voices of theology and psychology, the names of the thinkers at this point are not as important as the disciplines themselves.

[2]My introduction to contextualization came by way of the late missiologist, Orlando Costas. So I share his understanding here: "[Context] represents a conceptual category. It refers to the time-space boundaries of understanding. The context is the stage where all comprehension takes place. It is the reality that ties together, and therefore shapes, all knowledge. There is no such thing as timeless or nonspatially related knowledge, since knowledge is a fundamental part of life, that is, in turn, a complex, interrelated phenomenon. The Spanish philosopher José Ortega y Gasset used to say, 'I am me and my circumstances.' In other words, I do not exist outside my circumstances. Neither do I know outside historical reality. Everything that I am, everything that I know is intrinsically bound to everything that I do...To contextualize is then not only to ask about the past and present of a text in the light of the past and present of its readers and hearers, but especially to ask about its future, its transforming effect upon those who will come into contact with it." Orlando Costas, *Christ Outside the Gate* (Maryknoll, N.Y.: Orbis Books, 1982), 4–5.

[3]Joseph Bettis notes: "The phenomenological method is a way of describing rather than a way of explaining. The scientific method...[is an] attempt to construct 'models' that are increasingly more adequate organizational structures for the data...Phenomenology is not the development of a position, pushing out the implications as far as possible in every direction, as if one were to begin with a geometrical axiom and deduce theorems and corollaries. Rather, it is the description of elements within one's environment." Joseph D. Bettis, ed., *Phenomenology of Religion* (New York: Harper and Row, 1969), 6–7.

[4]"Phenomenology is the reflective investigation of phenomena—objects to which we have some mode of experiential access precisely as and only as they are given to us in experience. It concerns itself neither with the discovery of empirical facts regarding the objects of our experience nor with the establishment of empirical generalizations embracing broad reaches of such facts, but rather, with the manners in that experienced objects are presented to us, with their modes of givenness." Steven William Laycock, *Foundations for a Phenomenological Theology* (Lewiston, N. Y.: The Edwin Mellen Press, 1988), 11–12.

[5]Molefi Asante, *The Afrocentric Idea* (Philadelphia: Temple University Press, 1987), 6.

[6]Molefi Asante, "First World People," *The Jubilant Review*, a publication of Lancaster county, Pa. (Sept./Oct. 1992).

[7]See Will Coleman, *Tribal Talk: Black Theology, Hermeneutics, and African/American Ways of "Telling the Story"* (University Park: The Pennsylvania State University Press, 2000).

[8]J. Deotis Roberts, *Africentric Christianity: A Theological Appraisal for Ministry* (Valley Forge, Pa.: Judson Press, 2000), 3.

[9]Ibid., 5.

[10]Ibid.

[11]Asante, *Afrocentric Idea,* 10.

[12]Roberts, *Africentric Christianity,* 7.

[13]William McKinley Runyan, *Life Histories and Psychobiography: Exploration in Theory and Method* (New York: Oxford University Press, 1984), 200.

[14]Joel Kovel, *White Racism: A Psychohistory* (New York: Columbia University Press, 1984), 4.

[15]In 1982, Archie Smith stated this point as a possibility. I believe the "die has been cast," and we have lost our solidarity. He noted, "Black people and oppressed minorities may be in danger of losing a sense of collective solidarity and common struggle for emancipation in an exploitative society that seeks to incorporate them within its existing ideology, structure, and system of values. Black people and other ethnic minorities may pay the higher price for

integration into the mainstream of the dominant society. They pay the higher price when they accept, uncritically, the value orientation of modern bourgeois society." Archie Smith, Jr. *The Relational Self: Ethics and Therapy from a Black Church Perspective* (Nashville: Abingdon Press, 1982), 17.

[16]Archie Smith expressed a similar approach, but he placed a greater emphasis upon social systems and social work than I do. His project emphasized the web that speaks the self rather than pushing for a regeneration of the self. He noted: "My position seeks to establish the social, historical, contextual, and hence, the relational character of the self. The notion of sociality or the underlying relatedness of reality is the web that is the primary constitutive condition out of that social and personal reality emerges, and it thus becomes the basis for critical reflection. The idea is that reality is fundamentally interrelated and social and perspectival or plural in character, and it is ever differentiating and evolving." Smith, *Relational Self,* 57–58.

Chapter 1: The Significance of Race and Gender to African American Identity

[1]C. Eric Lincoln, *Race, Religion, and the Continuing American Dilemma* (New York: Hill and Wang Press, 1984), 26–27.

[2]For a fuller discussion of the English Christian colonists' lack of interest in the liberty of enslaved Africans, see Samuel K. Roberts, *African American Christian Ethics* (Cleveland: Pilgrim Press, 2001), chapter 1.

[3]Albert J. Raboteau, *Canaan Land: A Religious History of African Americans* (New York: Oxford University Press, 2001), 10, 14.

[4]Lincoln, *Race,* 29.

Chapter 2: Who Are African Americans?

[1]See Sterling Stuckey, *Slave Culture* (New York: Oxford University Press, 1987), chapters 1 and 4.

[2]This statement is a critique of popular culture and its transmission more than it is a critique of family structure and the research being done related to family formation in the United States. I understand the focus on the nuclear or extended family system in the United States differs by historical period. The dominant view, however, has been, and continues to be, nuclear by way of the American identity being strongly rooted in individualism. Although one could argue that there are many who today oppose the nuclear system as the most valued American family system, African America has never ascribed to the nuclear system. We African Americans have always lived an extended family system and understood our survival to be a family project supported by blood and nonblood relations. From an African American perspective, American mass and popular cultures have consistently misrepresented our familial ties, and the images have not been corrected by America within our contemporary context. We continue to have the unpopular experience of being devalued even as many are now turning to a more appreciative view of the extended system, the system in which we have always lived.

Chapter 3: Race, Racism, and the African American

[1]See Paul Griffin, *Seeds of Racism in the Soul of America* (Cleveland: Pilgrim Press, 1999). He offers a thorough analysis to show that the Puritans, the oldest of the colonists, were in fact the people who gave America its racist instincts by constructing the theological rationale for racism. In the introduction, p. xv, Griffin says, "*Seeds of Racism in the Soul of America* is the first book to search out and examine critically the specific theological ideas that were used to justify slavery in the past and are still used to support racism. So many white liberals continue to believe not only that slavery and racism began in the South in the search for cheap labor, but also that it has been continued mostly by white southerners as a southern phenomenon. Here I show that the distant roots of racism trace back not to southern plantation owners but to Puritans in the North, who first used theological ideas to justify slavery and racism."

[2]Howard Thurman, "The Search in Identity," in *A Strange Freedom: The Best of Howard Thurman on Religious Experience and Public Life,* ed. Walter Earl Fluker and Catherine Tumber (Boston: Beacon Press, 1998), 279–80.

[3]"Native Americans faced genocide, blacks were subjected to slavery, Mexicans were invaded and colonized, and Asians faced exclusion. These were not incidental elements in the history of [this] country, but go to the very center of its political, cultural and economic relations. These were often quite overt policies. Racist discourse was openly used, and made legitimate in different ways over time by specific religious texts, by economic "necessities," and by "neutral" scientific findings in anthropology, eugenics, and so on." Michael Omi and Howard Winant, *Racial Formation in the United States: From the 1960s to the 1980s* (New York: Routledge and Kegan Paul, 1986), viii. Also see what Thurman has said about the treatment of Native Americans and persons of African descent in America as America has sought to work out its identity issues, Thurman, "The Search in Identity," 280–81.

[4]"The slogan 'white supremacy' betrays the fictitious struggle that the white [person] is engaged in to salvage his[her] relative fall in status, and to restore it by the device of 'keeping the Negro[nonwhite] in his[her] place.'" Abram Kardiner and Lionel Ovesey, *The Mark of Oppression* (Cleveland: Meridian Books, 1951), 379.

[5]See Albert Memmi's discussion on the privileges of the colonial. Albert Memmi, *The Colonizer and the Colonized* (Boston: Beacon Press, 1965).

[6]"The eighteenth century is often called the age of reason. What seemed to be the prevailing belief in Western Europe was confidence in [humanity's] mind. [Humanity], so it was held, had heretofore been bound by ignorance and superstition. Now, by the use of reason, *he* was achieving emancipation and there was nothing that, with this tool, *he* could not hope to accomplish. In view of the advances in the natural sciences and mathematics, this attitude is quite understandable...Religiously it found its chief expression in Deism. Deism held to what was called natural religion. This was said to be universal, discernible by all *men* everywhere through their reason, quite apart from special revelation. It believed in God and revered [God] as the great Architect of the Universe. God was to be worshipped. Virtue was [humanity's] true service. After death virtue was to be rewarded and sin punished. But Deism held that God governed all through immutable law which [God] had created. It left no room for miracle, the incarnation, or the Trinity. In the new age in which they were living, so it was maintained, *men* were being enlightened by the use of their reason and were moving away from superstition." Kenneth S. Latourette, *A History of Christianity,* vol. 2 (New York: Harper and Row, 1975), 1003–4. The italics have been added to indicate gender-specific statements. Men were truly the prominent figures of the Enlightenment; and White men believed themselves to be the only enlightened beings.

[7]Erik Erikson, *Dimensions of a New Identity* (New York: W. W. Norton, 1974), 17.

[8]Sidney E. Mead, *History and Identity* (Atlanta: American Academy of Religion, Scholars Press, 1979), 11.

[9]For further discussion of these points, see Eleazar S. Fernandez and Fernando F. Segovia, eds., *A Dream Unfinished: Theological Reflections on America from the Margins* (Maryknoll, N.Y.: Orbis Books, 2001).

[10]These ideas were presented as a "work-in-progress" at the 2004 annual meeting of the Society for the Study of Black Religion. The current research of Marvin McMickle, Ph.D., takes up this notion in his review of the African American preacher in film from 1920s through the 1980s. He identifies the images of the preacher, overwhelmingly negative, and chronicles the repeated presentation that caricaturizes the role of the African American preacher and the life of the African American church as being largely corrupt and for the uneducated.

[11]Although this point was originally given me by the thoughts of Diop, this is also the methodological point of psycho-history. "Three factors compete to form the collective personality of a people: a psychic factor susceptible of a literary approach...In addition, there are the historical factor and the linguistic factor, both susceptible of being approached scientifically." Cheikh Anta Diop, *The African Origin of Civilization: Myth or Reality* (Chicago: Lawrence Hill Books, 1974), xiii.

[12]See the introduction to Cornel West, *Race Matters* (Boston: Beacon Press, 1993).

[13]Joel Kovel, *White Racism: A Psychohistory* (New York: Columbia University Press, 1984), 14.

[14]A defined norm, a standard of rightness and often righteousness wherein all others are judged in relation to it, must be backed up with institutional power, economic power, and both institutional and individual violence. It is the combination of these three elements that makes complete power and control possible. In the United States, that norm is male, white,

heterosexual, Christian, temporarily able-bodied, youthful, with access to wealth and resources. It is important to remember that an established norm does not necessarily represent a majority in terms of numbers; it represents those who have ability to exert power and control over others." Suzanne Pharr, *Homophobia: A Weapon of Sexism* (Inverness, Calif.: Chardon Press, 1988), 53. Also see George Kelsey, *Racism and the Christian Understanding of Man* (New York: Charles Scribner's Sons, 1965), 149.

[15]See Winthrop Jordan, *The White Man's Burden* (New York: Oxford University Press, 1974).

[16]During my three years of regular visits to South Africa, I heard this statement made, almost word for word, by many White South Africans. There was regularly an effort to share that their efforts to end apartheid was simultaneously the restoration of their souls.

[17]Mead, *History and Identity*, 11.

[18]See William Jones, *Is God a White Racist?: A Preamble to Black Theology* (Boston: Beacon Press, 1998).

[19]Marie Augusta Neal, "Civil Religion, Theology, and Politics in America," in *America in Theological Perspective,* ed. Thomas McFadden (New York: The Seabury Press, 1976), 103.

[20]"In 1966 the term 'civil religion' was applied by Robert Bellah to a type of religion he observed in America, a religion not associated with any specific church but characterizing the behavior of civic leaders on solemn occasions such as inaugurations and holidays. This behavior, he felt, had meaning more capable of binding people in solidarity and of compelling adherence than the simple patriotism associated with citizenship. He defined civil religion as "the subordination of the nation to ethical principles that transcend it and in terms of which it should be judged." He added that he is 'convinced that every nation and every people come to some form of religious self-understanding whether the critics like it or not.'…The qualities of American religion he saw as activist, moralistic, and social rather than contemplative, theological, and innerly spiritual." Neal, "Civil Religion," 100–101.

[21]Although I recognize that Riggins Earl sees the works of Kelsey and Thurman as challengeable because their methodologies and questions represent White concerns of faith, I nevertheless have found important statements made by both thinkers on the issue of racism in America. See Riggins Earl Jr., *Dark Salutations: Ritual, God, and Greetings in the African American Community* (Harrisburg, Pa.: Trinity Press International, 2001), 43.

[22]"At first the slaves were a mixed lot, white and black alike suffering varying degrees of forced servitude. As time went on, however, the inner workings of the new North American culture inexorably forced the concepts of black men and slavery into complete one-to-one identity." Kovel, *White Racism,* 16.

[23]Cornel West, *Prophesy Deliverance* (Philadelphia: Westminster Press, 1982); and James Comer, "White Racism: Its Root, Form, and Function," in *Black Psychology*, 3d ed., ed. Reginald Jones (Berkeley, Calif.: Cobb and Henry, 1991).

[24]Comer, "White Racism," 591–92.

[25]Ibid., 593.

[26]Paul R. Griffin, *Seeds of Racism in the Soul of America* (Cleveland: Pilgrim Press, 1999), 14.

[27]James Oakes, *Slavery and Freedom* (New York: Alfred A. Knopf, 1990), 74.

[28]See Cornel West, *Prophesy Deliverance*, chapter 2.

[29]See Winthrop Hudson and John Corrigan, *Religion in America*, 5th ed. (New York: Macmillan, 1992).

[30]C. G. Jung, "On the Nature of Dreams," in *Dreams,* Bollingen Series (Princeton: Princeton University Press, 1974), 68.

[31]Jung, *Dreams,* 73.

[32]"The 1998 DNA test results identify a chromosomal link between Eston Hemings and the male Jefferson line. Thomas Jefferson is included among the twenty-five possible fathers, but he is eliminated because of the lack of admissible evidence. It is surprising that the sources and the nature of the information that make up the Tom and Sally myth has put the academic community into such a quandary. It is a tale that should return to its status as no more than a footnote to the Jefferson legacy." Richard Dixon (2000). www.angelfire.com/va/TJTruth: "Thomas Jefferson–Sally Hemings, Trial Analysis, Evidence on Paternity, The Case Against Thomas Jefferson," Richard E. Dixon, Attorney at Law, 4122 Leonard Drive, Fairfax, Virginia 22030, April 2000.

[33]Oakes, *Slavery and Freedom,* 29–30.

[34]Biblical scholars such as Cain Hope Felder and Randall Bailey have been significant voices to declare that Oriental studies and Egyptology have been the tools of White supremacy. This has meant that large bodies of research have been directed toward the denial of the African presence in the Bible and the denial of the influence of Egypt as a Black African nation on the developmental history of the world. See Randall C. Bailey, "The Use of Africans in Old Testament Poetry and Narratives," in *Stony the Road We Trod: African American Biblical Interpretation,* ed. Cain Hope Felder (Minneapolis: Fortress, 1991), 165–84; Bailey, "Is That Any Name for a Nice Hebrew Boy? Exodus 2:1–10: The De-Africanization of an Israelite Hero," in *The Recovery of Black Presence,* ed. Randall C. Bailey and Jacqueline Grant (Nashville: Abingdon Press, 1995), 25–36; Bailey, "The Danger of Ignoring One's Own Cultural Bias in Interpreting the Text," in *The Postcolonial Bible,* ed. R. S. Sugirtharajah (Sheffield: Sheffield Academic Press, 1998), 66–90; Cain Hope Felder, *Troubling Biblical Waters: Race, Class, and Family* (Maryknoll: Orbis Books, 1989).

[35]Kelsey, *Racism and Christian Understanding,* 32.

[36]Joseph Barndt, *Dismantling Racism* (Minneapolis: Augsburg, 1991), 39.

[37]See Kelsey, *Racism and the Christian Understanding of Man.* I have been arguing that racism has deep historical roots in the life of the nation. My identification of the expressions of racism's destructive force through the identification of hate group activities are only illustrations of what is resident in the soul of the nation. Also see Griffin's section on "Racism as a Bad Religion of the Soul" located in his introduction. He also suggests that racism is at the soul of the nation and not the domain of a few hate groups. As a soul problem, "neither the antebellum antislavery crusades nor the Civil War nor the Reconstruction nor the civil rights movement nor the most recent federal antidiscrimination and affirmative action laws—none of these has offered a permanent cure for the malady. Each of these efforts failed because, despite laudable sincerity and powerful sanctions, it was grounded in the presumption that racism is fundamentally an economic, legal, or political issue." Griffin, *Seeds of Racism,* 7–8.

[38]This history is clear and today can be reviewed in most American history texts. Winthrop D. Jordan covers this history most thoroughly in his work *White Over Black: American Attitudes Toward the Negro, 1550–1812* (New York: W. W. Norton, 1977 [1968]).

[39]Also see JoAnne M. Terrell's reflections on "The Hermeneutics of Sacrifice in Biblical and Historical Perspective," in chapter 1 of her book *Power in the Blood?: The Cross in the African American Experience* (Maryknoll, N.Y.: Orbis Books, 1998), 17–22.

[40]See Anthony B. Pinn, *Terror and Triumph: The Nature of Black Religion* (Minneapolis: Fortress Press, 2003), chapter 3.

[41]See Christopher Lasch's presentations on primary, secondary, and pathological narcissism in *The Culture of Narcissism* (New York: W. W. Norton, 1979), 78–79. Also see Donald Capps, *Social Phobia: Alleviating Anxiety in an Age of Self-promotion* (St. Louis: Chalice Press, 1999), 131–32.

Chapter 4: The Color of "the Self"

[1]Frank M. Snowden, *Before Color Prejudice* (Cambridge, Mass.: Harvard University Press, 1983), 82–83.

[2]Snowden, *Before Color,* 100.

[3]Barry Silverstein, *Children of the Dark Ghetto* (New York: Praeger, 1975), 5.

[4]Wallace Thurman, *The Blacker the Berry, a Novel of Negro Life* (1929; reprint, New York: Macmillan, 1970), 147.

[5]Michael Omi and Howard Winant, *Racial Formation in the United States: From the 1960s to the 1980s* (New York: Routledge and Kegan Paul, 1986), 63.

[6]Gordon Allport, *The Nature of Prejudice* (Reading, Mass.: Addison-Wesley, 1979), 109.

[7]"Let us endeavor to see why the rabbis made the 'curse' on Ham a black skin. This is certain: Next to the Aryans the Jews were more color conscious than any of the ancients. Why? They had been slaves to the Egyptians and Ethiopians who are described in their legends as Negroes. Again, after they had established themselves in Palestine they were twice invaded by Egyptians and Ethiopians. Shishak, Ethiopian ruler of Egypt, ravaged the land, plundered Solomon's Temple, and took a great number of Jews slaves to Egypt. (2 Chr. 12) Another Ethiopian King, Zerah, who came with 'a host of a thousand and three hundred chariots' was beaten off. (2 Chr. 14)

It could be that the Jews before they left Egypt imbibed some of the color prejudice mentioned by Massey but it could not have been strong among them because they were black at that time, because the passage from the Song of Solomon means, 'I was black in Egypt but comely in Egypt.' There is no doubt that after four centuries in Egypt the Jews had mixed much with Egyptians and Ethiopians, whom their legends describe as 'black' and 'wooly-haired.' Thus the main difference between Hebrew and Egyptian was not racial but religious, the form that economic exploitation then took. Miriam's objection to the Ethiopian wife of Moses, Zipporah, was not on color but on religion and more likely on culture. Talk of Semitic and Hamitic as 'race' is sheerest non-sense and is used only by 'parrot' anthropologists.

"How then was it possible for them to place a 'curse' on a black skin? The answer is that centuries after they had left Egypt and being somewhat whitened by mixing with fairer skinned people to the north and with Europeans, they could now look back on the unchanged color of the Ethiopians and Egyptians in comparison with themselves; and their rabbis, that is their 'scientists,' endeavoring to explain how black people came about tacked on that bit of folk-lore of the 'curse' on Ham. It is very important to remember here that the Masoretic text, regarded as the correct one of the ancient Hebrew writings, says nothing whatever of Ham or Canaan's color. It merely says that a curse was placed on Canaan. That the 'black' skin was a later addition is indisputable." J.A. Rogers, *Nature Knows No Color-Line* (New York: 1952), 11–12.

[8]Balch Institute for Ethnic Studies, *Ethnic Images in Advertising* (Philadelphia: The Balch Institute for Ethnic Studies, 1984), 8.

[9]Martin Bernal, *Black Athena: The Afroasiatic Roots of Classical Civilization,* vol. 1 (New Brunswick, N.J.: Rutgers University Press, 1987), 219.

[10]"For theological reasons, the process of sacralization in the O.T. largely remains racially ambiguous, especially with specific reference to Black people. The distinction the O.T. makes is not racial. Rather, the Hebrew Scripture distinguishes groups on the basis of national identity and ethnic tribes. All who do not meet the criteria for salvation as defined by the ethnic or national 'in-groups' are relegated to an inferior status. It is therefore surprising to many that Black people are not only frequently mentioned in numerous O.T. texts but are mentioned in ways that acknowledge their actual and potential role in the salvation history of Israel. By no means are Black people excluded from Israel's story, as long as they claim it and not proclaim their own story apart from the activity of Israel's God." Cain Hope Felder, *Troubling Biblical Waters: Race, Class, and Family* (Maryknoll, N.Y.: Orbis, 1989), 43.

[11]W. Thurman, *The Blacker the Berry...,* 144.

[12]Randall Bailey has done considerable research that traces the transformation of the color white from the Hebrew Bible to our contemporary Christian understandings. Bailey says that the Hebrew Bible texts that reference white, especially in those cases in which white is a condition of the skin, present whiteness as a negative and curse. Our current identifications of white as symbolizing purity are a departure from the biblical understandings. In his article "Beyond Identification: The Use of Africans in Old Testament Poetry and Narratives," in *Stony the Road We Trod: African American Biblical Interpretation,* ed. Cain Hope Felder (Minneapolis: Fortress Press, 1991), Bailey reinterprets Numbers 12:1–10 and identifies the historical context of white being seen as a curse. He says, "This interpretation appears to be sound on two grounds. First is the fact that the punishment meted out to Miriam as a result of this challenge to the status of Moses is that she is turned 'leprous, white as snow' (v. 10). Thus, the punishment for complaining about Cushites as a means of status makes her the exact opposite of the Cushite, white as snow. This ironic twist could not be accomplished unless verse 1 were part of the unit. Second, this interpretation rests upon the understanding that in the Hebrew Canon to be white as snow is a curse," p. 180. In a more recent article by Bailey entitled, "Academic Biblical Interpretation among African Americans in the United States," in *African Americans and the Bible: Sacred Texts and Social Textures,* ed. Vincent L. Wimbush (New York: Continuum, 2001), he states, "Recently I have argued that white supremacy also functions at the translation level of interpretation. In reviewing the English translation of Isaiah 1:18, "Come let us reason together...though your sins are as scarlet, they shall be made white as snow (RSV)." I argued they have turned an announcement of punishment into a salvation oracle by translating the Hebrew word *'im* as 'though' instead of 'if' as it is translated elsewhere in the unit. In other words, the phrase to be made 'white as snow' in the standard English translation was transformed into a blessing, as opposed to its usage in other passages in the Hebrew Bible, where it appeared as a curse," p. 700.

[13]David G. Benner, ed., *Baker Encyclopedia of Psychology* (Grand Rapids, Mich.: Baker Book House, 1987).

[14]Peter Lambley, *The Psychology of Apartheid* (Athens: University of Georgia Press, 1980), 6.

[15]Ibid., 6.

[16]Joseph E. Holloway, *Africanisms in American Culture* (Indianapolis: Indiana University Press, 1990), xx.

[17]Allport, *Nature of Prejudice*, 37, 42.

[18]Rogers, *Nature Knows No Color-Line*, 25.

Chapter 5: African American Genderism

[1]Randall Bailey, "Academic Biblical Interpretation among African Americans in the United States," in *African Americans and the Bible: Sacred Texts and Social Textures*, ed. Vincent L. Wimbush (New York: Continuum, 2001), 704.

[2]Racist and sexist descriptions of God, self, and other espouse an oppressive theological anthropology that must be denounced as evil. Both racism and sexism make the claim that their descriptions of life and efforts to control the lives of others are just and righteous. It is, therefore, essential that liberation efforts include new definitions of humanity without demonizing the enemy.

[3]See Kelly Brown Douglas, *Sexuality and the Black Church: A Womanist Perspective* (Maryknoll, N.Y.: Orbis, 1999), 25–29.

[4]See Elochukwu E. Uzukwu, *Worship as Body Language* (Collegeville, Minn.: The Liturgical Press, 1997), 6–10.

[5]Randall Bailey, "They're Nothing but Incestuous Bastards: The Polemical Use of Sex and Sexuality in Hebrew Canon Narrative," in *Reading from This Place: Social Location and Biblical Interpretation*, ed. Fernando Segovia and Mary Ann Tolbert (Minneapolis: Fortress Press, 1994).

[6]See Anthony B. Pinn, *Terror and Triumph: The Nature of Black Religion* (Minneapolis: Fortress Press, 2003), 142–46.

[7]References to this text, as well as the retelling of the myth of Lilith, are found far and wide. One of the many places the myth can be found is Howard Schwartz, *Lilith's Cave: Jewish Tales of the Supernatural* (Oxford: Oxford University Press, 1989).

Chapter 6: The Psychodynamics of African American Religiosity

[1]See Sigmund Freud, *Moses and Monotheism* (1939; reprint, New York: Vintage Books, 1967).

[2]See Wade W. Nobles, *African Psychology: Toward Its Reclamation, Reascension and Revitalization* (Oakland, Calif.: The Institute for the Advanced Study of Black Family Life and Culture, 1986), chapter 1.

[3]The works of Freud, Jung, and Erikson that focus this study are: Sigmund Freud, *Moses and Monotheism*; Erik Erikson, *Childhood and Society* (New York: W. W. Norton, 1950); C. G. Jung, *Memories, Dreams, and Reflections* (New York: Vintage Books, 1965); Carl G. Jung, *Collected Works of C. G. Jung*, Bollingen series, vol. 9, part 1 (Princeton: Princeton University Press); Sigmund Freud, *The Future of an Illusion* (New York: W. W. Norton, 1961); Carl G. Jung, *Analytical Psychology* (New York: Random House, 1968); Erik H. Erikson, *Young Man Luther* (New York: W. W. Norton, 1958); Sigmund Freud, *Inhibitions, Symptoms and Anxiety* (New York: W. W. Norton, 1959); Erik Erikson, *Insight and Responsibility* (New York: W. W. Norton, 1964).

[4]"This book originated in the practice of psychoanalysis…In these, as in all situations, the psychoanalytic method detects conflict; for this method was first focused on mental disturbance. Through the work of Freud, neurotic conflict has become the most comprehensively studied aspect of human behavior. However, this book avoids the easy conclusion that our relatively advanced knowledge of neurosis permits us to view mass phenomena–culture, religion, revolution–as analogies of neuroses in order to make them amenable to our concepts. We will pursue a different path." Erik Erikson, *Childhood and Society*, 15.

[5]See C. G. Jung, *Memories, Dreams, and Reflections*.

⁶Carl G. Jung, *Collected Works of C. G. Jung,* 288.

⁷Ibid., 279.

⁸Ibid., 354.

⁹See David Wulff, *Psychology of Religion* (New York: John Wiley and Sons, 1991), 369–70.

¹⁰Jacques de Lorimier, *Identity and Faith in Young Adults,* trans. Matthew J. O'Connell (New York: Paulist Press, 1973), 21.

¹¹Gordon W. Allport, *The Individual and His Religion* (New York: Macmillan, 1950), 7–8.

¹²Ibid.

¹³Jung, *Analytical Psychology,* 75.

¹⁴Cited in Heije Faber, *Psychology of Religion* (Philadelphia: The Westminster Press, 1975), 11.

¹⁵Sigmund Freud, *Future of an Illusion* .

¹⁶Robert J. Lifton, *The Life of the Self* (New York: Basic Books, 1983), 20.

¹⁷Ibid., 20.

¹⁸Ernest Becker, *Escape from Evil* (New York: The Free Press, 1975).

¹⁹Lifton, *Life of the Self,* 114–15.

²⁰Cited in Mary Jo Meadow and Richard Kahoe, *Psychology of Religion: Religion in Individual Lives* (New York: Harper and Row, 1984), 18.

²¹Karl Marx, "Religion, the Opium of the People," in *The World Treasury of Modern Religious Thought,* ed. Jaroslav Pelikan (Boston: Little, Brown and Company, 1990), 79–80. Italics represent a paraphrase.

²²Jung, *Analytical Psychology,* 181–82.

²³Erikson, *Young Man Luther,* 21–22.

²⁴Ibid., 22.

²⁵Ibid.

²⁶ Erikson, *Childhood and Society,* 250–51.

²⁷Michael Goldberg, *Theology and Narrative* (Nashville: Abingdon Press, 1982), 175.

²⁸See Joel Kovel, *White Racism: A Psychohistory* (New York: Columbia University Press, 1970).

²⁹See Martin Bernal, *Black Athena: The Afroasiatic Roots of Classical Civilization,* vol. 1 (New Brunswick, N.J.: Rutgers University Press, 1987).

³⁰In the opening of *The Life Cycle Completed* (New York: W.W. Norton, 1982), Erikson showed his commitment to psychoanalysis through his extensive discussion of psychoanalysis. Here is what Freud wrote about "undoing": "It is, as it were, negative magic, and endeavors, by means of motor symbolism, to 'blow away' not merely the consequences of some event (or experience or impression) but the event itself. I choose the term 'blow away' advisedly, so as to remind the reader of the part played by this technique not only in neuroses but in magical acts, popular customs and religious ceremonies as well," Freud, *Inhibitions, Symptoms and Anxiety,* 45.

³¹"Hope is the enduring belief in the attainability of fervent wishes, in spite of the [negative] urges and rages that mark the beginning of existence. Hope is the ontogenetic basis of faith, and is nourished by the adult faith that pervades patterns of care," Erikson, *Insight and Responsibility,* 118.

³²See Edward Reynolds, *Stand the Storm: A History of the Atlantic Slave Trade* (London: W. H. Allen, 1989), 58–62.

Chapter 7: African American Spirituality as Survival

¹Both C. Eric Lincoln and Archie Smith articulate this perspective. See C. Eric Lincoln, *Race, Religion, and the Continuing American Dilemma* (New York: Hill and Wang Press, 1984), 236–37. Smith locates his perspective as follows: "The basis of my own critical consciousness has been the black family, the black church and community in a white racist and materialistic society. Ideally, the black family, church, and community exist in a mutually supportive relationship and together may articulate alternative values that affirm the material and the spiritual, the social and psychic life of the person in the community. Survival of the human subject in the present society and the possibility of transformation in a new and liberating society, to be achieved, is the issue. Survival as black people in the present society is a formidable challenge in a society that continues to deny them authentic freedom and the material and spiritual basis for dignity and self-conscious selfhood. The survival and welfare

of black people in this society is inseparable from the survival and well-being of all people." Archie Smith Jr., *The Relational Self: Ethics and Therapy from a Black Church Perspective* (Nashville: Abingdon Press, 1982), 25.

[2]This is a modification on the DSM category of Post-traumatic Stress Disorder. Post-traumatic is based on the assumption that the trauma was a one-time event in the past that continues to traumatize the soul in the present. The event could be something that has occurred over an extended period of time like war, but the description assumes the war has ended even as the memories exert influence in the present. To speak of African American life in terms of Protracted-traumatic Stress is to declare that the trauma is not a single event in the past, but it is an ongoing, recurring humiliation that we must defend ourselves against daily. See Lee H. Butler Jr., *A Loving Home: Caring for African American Marriages and Family* (Cleveland: Pilgrim Press, 2000), 16–18.

[3]Terrence Des Pres, *The Survivor* (New York: Oxford University Press, 1980), v.

[4]Ibid., 7.

[5]"Black spirituality is joyful resting in the power of God to protect, to defend, and to save; and this joy animates works of love and compassion, of reconciliation and peace. [It] is communal and expresses itself in social concern and social justice." M. Shawn Copeland, "African American Catholics and Black Theology: An Interpretation," in *African American Religious Studies*, ed. Gayraud Wilmore (Durham, N.C.: Duke University Press, 1989), 241–42.

[6]Butler, *A Loving Home,* 58.

[7]"Phenomenologically the black church in America developed out of the deprivation and oppression experienced by the slaves…The church evolved as a new family for those who were continually being uprooted from their original families." Wallace C. Smith, *The Church in the Life of the Black Family* (Valley Forge, Pa.: Judson Press, 1985), 22.

[8]See Butler, *A Loving Home,* 30–34.

[9]Malcolm Cowley, *Black Cargoes* (New York: Viking Press, 1962), 12.

[10]Ibid., 12–13.

[11]Ibid.

[12]bell hooks, *Ain't I a Woman? Black Women and Feminism* (Boston: South End Press, 1981), 18.

[13]Sterling Stuckey, *Slave Culture* (New York: Oxford University Press, 1987), 3.

[14]"The [African] was shackled in a hostile white world without any power to make the [European] recognize him[her] as a person. He[She] had to devise a means of survival…The black church was the creation of a black people whose daily existence was an encounter with the overwhelming and brutalizing reality of white power." James H. Cone, *Black Theology and Black Power* (New York: The Seabury Press, 1969), 92.

[15]John S. Mbiti, *Introduction to African Religion,* 2d rev. ed. (Oxford, Eng.; Portsmouth, N.H.: Heinemann Educational Books, 1991).

[16]"Religion is part of the cultural heritage…It is by far the richest part of the African heritage. Religion is found in all areas of human life. It has dominated the thinking of African peoples to such an extent that it has shaped their cultures, their social life, their political organizations and economic activities. We can say, therefore, that religion is closely bound up with the traditional way of African life, while at the same time, this way of life has shaped religion as well." Ibid., 10.

[17]Ibid., 17.

[18]Ibid., 32.

[19]A significant voice who argued that there are innumerable Africanisms among African Americans in spite of the horrors of the Middle Passage and the brutality of American slavery was Melville Herskovits. See Melville Herskovits, *The Myth of the Negro Past* (Boston: Beacon Press, 1958 [1990]).

[20]Stuckey, *Slave Culture,* 24.

[21]This point was historically debated by E. Franklin Frazier and Melville Herskovits.

[22]Cone, *Black Theology,* 92.

[23]Stuckey, *Slave Culture,* 35–36.

[24]Ibid., 24.

[25]Albert J. Raboteau, *Slave Religion* (New York: Oxford University Press, 1978), 305.

[26]Ibid., 295.

[27]"An archetype means a typos [imprint], a definite grouping of archaic character containing, in form as well as in meaning, mythological motifs. Mythological motifs appear in pure form in fairytales, myths, legends, and folklore." Carl G. Jung, *Analytical Psychology* (New York: Random House, 1968), 41.

[28]Stuckey, *Slave Culture,* 25.

[29]Smith, *Relational Self,* 23.

[30]Raboteau, *Slave Religion,* 318.

[31]Smith, *Relational Self,* 25.

Chapter 8: Liberating Our Identity

[1]Justo L. Gonzalez and Zaida Maldonado Perez, *An Introduction to Christian Theology* (Nashville: Abingdon Press, 2002), 30.

[2]Dwight N. Hopkins, *Introducing Black Theology of Liberation* (Maryknoll, N.Y.: Orbis Books, 1999), 4–5.

[3]Delores S. Williams, *Sisters in the Wilderness* (Maryknoll, N.Y.: Orbis Books, 1993), xiii–xiv.

[4]"Psychology," *Britannica Concise Encyclopedia.* Retrieved June 27, 2004, from *Encyclopedia Britannica* Premium Service. http://www.britannica.com/ebc/article?eu=401375

[5]"It is peculiar to observe that a substantial number of black psychologists, while accepting the existence of or need for African (Black) psychology, do not conceptualize it as an independent enterprise separate from Western Psychology." Joseph A. Baldwin, "African (Black) Psychology: Issues and Synthesis," in *Black Psychology,* ed. Reginald Jones (Berkeley, Calif.: Cobb and Henry, 1991), 125.

[6]Wade W. Nobles, *African Psychology* (Oakland, Calif.: The Institute for the Advanced Study of Black Family Life and Culture, Inc., 1986), 17–18.

[7]Carroll Watkins Ali, *Survival and Liberation: Pastoral Theology in African American Context* (St. Louis: Chalice Press, 1999), 10. Watkins Ali gathers the presented definitions from Rodney Hunter, ed., *Dictionary of Pastoral Care and Counseling* (Nashville: Abingdon Press, 1990), 867.

[8]Watkins Ali, *Survival and Liberation,* 10. Her Seward Hiltner quote comes from his book, *Preface to Pastoral Theology: Ministry and Theory Shepherding* (New York: Abingdon Press, 1958), 20.

[9]"Like black male liberation theology, womanist theology assumes the necessity of responsible freedom for all human beings. But womanist theology especially concerns itself with the faith, survival and freedom-struggle of African-American women. Thus womanist theology identifies and critiques black male oppression of black females while it also critiques white racism that oppresses all African-Americans, female and male. Like white feminist theology, womanist theology affirms the full humanity of all women. But womanist theology also critiques white feminist participation in the perpetuation of white supremacy, which continues to dehumanize black women. Yet womanist theology is organically related to black male liberation theology and feminist theology in its various expressions (including African women's, mujerista, Jewish and Asian women's theology)." Williams, *Sisters,* xiv.

[10]"Though the present interest in the study of Black religion in the United States within the theological community must be seen within the context of the programmatic theological statements of Professor James Cone, his work does not constitute the beginnings of the study of Black religion in the United States by Black scholars within the theological tradition…If Cone's work does not constitute an absolutely new beginning, it does represent a shift that might form a watershed in the study of Black religion. From the work of Cone one is able to set forth a basis from which we might assess the works prior to his time and to plot new and different trends in the study of Black religion." Charles H. Long, "Assessment and New Departures for a Study of Black Religion in the United States of America," in *African American Religious Studies,* ed. Gayraud Wilmore (Durham, N.C.: Duke University Press, 1989), 34.

[11]James H. Cone, *My Soul Looks Back* (Maryknoll, N.Y.: Orbis Books, 1986).

[12]Ibid., 47.

[13]West is a liberation philosopher who has been esteemed by Charles Long and Cain Hope Felder: "I have found that some of the philosophical positions set forth by Jacques Derrida are quite congruent with DuBois's notion of a double consciousness. Especially in his program of deconstruction do I see meaning of radical critique and creativity. I am pleased to find that younger scholars such as Cornel West…are of the same opinion." Long, "Assessment

and New Departures," 46. "Black writers with increasing sharpness recognize the total inadequacy and racial tendentiousness of the West's intellectual tradition in its endeavors to provide allegedly universal conceptual and religious norms. In this respect, Cornel West's *Prophesy Deliverance!* is an invaluable resource for tracing the implicit racist tendencies of the philosophical 'giants' in Europe since the Enlightenment." Cain Hope Felder, "The Bible, Re-Contextualization, and the Black Religious Experience," in *African American Religious Studies*, ed. Gayraud Wilmore, 158.

[14]Cornel West, *Prophesy Deliverance!: An Afro-American Revolutionary Christianity* (Philadelphia: The Westminster Press, 1982).

[15]Delores Williams, *Sisters in the Wilderness* (Maryknoll, N.Y.: Orbis Books, 1993), quotes from Alice Walker, 243.

[16]See bell hooks, *Ain't I a Woman: Black Women and Feminism* (Boston: South End Press, 1981), and Linda Brent, *Incidents in the Life of a Slave Girl* (1861, reprint, San Diego: Harvest/HBJ Book, 1983).

[17]See Lee H. Butler Jr., *A Loving Home: Caring for African American Marriages and Family* (Cleveland: Pilgrim Press, 2000), 85–88.

[18]Delores S. Williams, "James Cone's Liberation: Twenty Years Later," in James Cone, *A Black Theology of Liberation* (Maryknoll, N.Y.: Orbis Books, 1990), 191.

[19]Williams, *Sisters,* 178.

[20]Ibid., 144–45.

[21]Jacqueline Grant, *White Women's Christ and Black Women's Jesus* (Atlanta: Scholars Press, 1989), 198.

[22]Robert V. Guthrie, "The Psychology of African Americans: An Historical Perspective," in *Black Psychology,* ed. Reginald Jones, 40.

[23]Ibid., 41.

[24]Nobles, *African Psychology,* 18.

[25]Wade W. Nobles, "African Philosophy: Foundations for Black Psychology," in *Black Psychology,* ed. Reginald Jones, 57.

[26]Long underscores Cress Welsing's efforts: "I show how meanings regarding a European discourse on wild men, women, and the insane became the normative language for the discussion of the new geographies and cultures discovered by the Europeans from the fifteenth century to the present. This language still pervades many of our common disciplinary fields and it is one of those forms of cultural language that has defined explicitly and adumbrated a range of meanings and interpretative schema concerning Blacks in the United States. Critical and precise hermeneutical attention must be given to this level of our cultural and disciplinary languages as part of the creativity of Black scholarship if this scholarship is ever to form a new framework of interpretation." Long, "Assessment and New Departures," 46.

[27]Frances Cress Welsing, *The Isis Papers* (Chicago: Third World Press, 1991), 4.

[28]Ibid., 12.

[29]Nobles, *African Psychology,* 94.

[30]Ibid., 105–6.

[31]Na'im Akbar, *Akbar Papers in African Psychology* (Tallahassee: Mind Productions & Assoc., 2004), ix.

[32]Na'im Akbar, *Breaking the Chains of Psychological Slavery* (Tallahassee: Mind Productions & Assoc., 1996), 58.

[33]Edward Wimberly, *Pastoral Care in the Black Church* (Nashville: Abingdon Press, 1979), 37.

[34]Ibid., 54.

[35]Homer U. Ashby Jr., *Our Home Is Over Jordan: A Black Pastoral Theology* (St. Louis: Chalice Press, 2003).

[36]Martin Luther King Jr., "I've Been to the Mountaintop," excerpt from the speech given April 3, 1968, Memphis, Tennessee, available online at http://www.stanford.edu/group/King/publications/speeches/I%27ve_been_to_the_mountaintop.pdf.

Chapter 9: Restoring Our Souls

[1]See Randall Bailey, "Academic Biblical Interpretation Among African Americans in the United States," in *African Americans and the Bible: Sacred Texts and Social Textures,* ed. Vincent L. Wimbush (New York: Continuum, 2001), 696–711.

²This decision was greatly influenced by a mentor, Genna Rae McNeil, Ph.D. As a professor of African American history, she taught me the importance of critical analysis for the lives of African Americans. Her encouragement was supported by Gladys Hillman-Jones, M.Ed., may she rest in peace, who declared, "If you are going to be an expert, be an expert of and for your people."

³"[T]raining in the mental health fields largely ignores the role of spirituality and religious beliefs in the development of the psyche and in its impact on family life. In the treatment of Black families, this oversight is a serious one." Nancy Boyd-Franklin, *Black Families in Therapy* (New York: The Guilford Press, 1989), 78.

⁴"All aspects of Nature, then, including consciousness, are interrelated and interdependent, forming one phenomenal reality–a communal phenomenology." Joseph A. Baldwin, "African (Black) Psychology: Issues and Synthesis," in *Black Psychology*, ed. Reginald Jones (Berkeley, Calif.: Cobb and Henry, 1991), 131. Also see Lee H. Butler Jr., *A Loving Home: Caring for African American Marriages and Family* (Cleveland: Pilgrim Press, 2000).

⁵ Joseph E. Holloway, ed.; *Africanisms in American Culture* (Indianapolis: Indiana University Press, 1990), xiv.

⁶See Paul Tillich, *Dynamics of Faith* (New York: Harper Torchbooks, 1957).

⁷ Cheikh Anta Diop, *The African Origin of Civilization: Myth or Reality* (Chicago: Lawrence Hill Books, 1974), xiii.

⁸See Na'im Akbar's "Introduction" in *Akbar Papers in African Psychology* (Tallahassee, Fla.: Mind Productions, 2004).

⁹Molefi Asante, "First World People," *The Jubilant Review*, a publication of Lancaster County, Pa. (Sept./Oct. 1992).

¹⁰Erik Erikson, *Identity, Youth, and Crisis* (New York: W. W. Norton, 1968), 302.

¹¹Erikson, "Womanhood and the Inner Space," in *Identity*.

¹²See Michael Vannoy Adams, *The Multicultural Imagination: "Race," Color, and the Unconscious* (New York: Routledge, 1996), 218–25.

¹³Basil Davidson, *The African Genius* (Boston: Little, Brown, 1969), 71–72.

¹⁴Carl G. Jung, *Analytical Psychology* (New York: Random House, 1968), 51.

¹⁵Alexander Thomas and Samuel Sillen, *Racism and Psychiatry* (Secaucus, N.J.: Carol Publishing Group, 1991), 14.

¹⁶Erik H. Erikson, *In Search of Common Ground: Conversations with Erik H. Erikson and Huey P. Newton* (New York: W. W. Norton, 1973), 54. This book is a transcript from the recorded conversation.

¹⁷Holloway, *Africanisms*, 16.

¹⁸LeRoi Jones [Imamy Amiri Baraka], *Blues People: Negro Music in White America* (New York: Morrow Quill Paperbacks, 1963), xi–xii.

¹⁹Holloway, *Africanisms*, 17.

²⁰Ibid., xx.

²¹See Sterling Stuckey, *Slave Culture* (New York: Oxford University Press, 1987).

²²Holloway, *Africanisms*, xix.

²³A concept developed by Robert Lifton: "the division of the self into two functioning wholes, so that a part-self acts as an entire self." Robert J. Lifton, *The Future of Immortality* (New York: Basic Books, 1987), 196.

²⁴Stanley Elkins, *Slavery: A Problem in American Institutional and Intellectual Life* (Chicago: University of Chicago, 1959).

²⁵Ibid., 82.

²⁶Alastair V. Campbell, *Health as Liberation: Medicine, Theology, and the Quest for Justice* (Cleveland: Pilgrim Press, 1995), 63.

Selected Bibliography

Adams, Michael Vannoy. *The Multicultural Imagination: "Race," Color, and the Unconscious* (New York: Routledge, 1996).

Akbar, Na'im. *Akbar Papers in African Psychology*. Tallahassee, Fla.: Mind Productions & Assoc., 2004.

____. *Breaking the Chains of Psychological Slavery*. Tallahassee, Fla.: Mind Productions & Assoc., 1996.

Allport, Gordon W. *The Individual and His Religion*. New York: Macmillan, 1950.

____. *The Nature of Prejudice*. Reading, Mass.: Addison-Wesley, 1979.

____. *Personality and Social Encounter: Selected Essays*. Chicago: University of Chicago Press, 1960.

Amy, William O. *Human Nature in the Christian Tradition*. Lanham, Md.: University Press of America, 1982.

Asante, Molefi. *The Afrocentric Idea*. Philadelphia: Temple University Press, 1987.

____. "First World People," *The Jubilant Review*. A community paper published in Lancaster County, Pa: Sept/Oct 1992

Ashby, Homer U., Jr. *Our Home Is Over Jordan: A Black Pastoral Theology*. St. Louis: Chalice Press, 2003.

Bailey, Randall. "Academic Biblical Interpretation among African Americans in the United States." In *African Americans and the Bible: Sacred Texts and Social Textures*. Edited by Vincent L. Wimbush. New York: Continuum, 2001.

____. "Beyond Identification: The Use of Africans in Old Testament Poetry and Narratives." In *Stony the Road We Trod: African American Biblical Interpretation*. Edited by Cain Hope Felder. Minneapolis: Fortress Press, 1991.

____. "They're Nothing but Incestuous Bastards: The Polemical Use of Sex and Sexuality in Hebrew Canon Narrative." In *This Place: Social Location and Biblical Interpretation*. Edited by Fernando Segovia and Mary Ann Tolbert. Minneapolis: Fortress Press, 1994.

Balch Institute for Ethnic Studies. *Ethnic Images in Advertising*. Philadelphia: The Balch Institute for Ethnic Studies, 1984.

Baldwin, Joseph. "African (Black) Psychology: Issues and Synthesis." In *Black Psychology*. Edited by Reginald Jones. Berkeley, Calif.: Cobb and Henry, 1991.

Banton, Michael. *Racial Consciousness*. London: Longman, 1988.

Barndt, Joseph. *Dismantling Racism*. Minneapolis: Augsburg, 1991.

Becker, Ernest. *Escape from Evil*. New York: The Free Press, 1975.

Benner, David G., ed. *Baker Encyclopedia of Psychology*. Grand Rapids, Mich.: Baker Book House, 1985.

Bernal, Martin. *Black Athena: The Afroasiatic Roots of Classical Civilization*. New Brunswick, N.J.: Rutgers University Press, 1987.

Berry, Mary F., and John W. Blassingame. *Long Memory: The Black Experience in America*. New York: Oxford University Press, 1982.

Bettis, Joseph D., ed. *Phenomenology of Religion*. New York: Harper and Row, 1969.

Bowker, John. *Problems of Suffering in Religions of the World*. Cambridge: Cambridge University Press, 1970.

Boyd-Franklin, Nancy. *Black Families in Therapy*. New York: The Guilford Press, 1989.

Brent, Linda. *Incidents in the Life of a Slave Girl*. 1861. Reprint, San Diego: Harvest/HBJ Book, 1983.

Brown Douglas, Kelly. *Sexuality and the Black Church: A Womanist Perspective*. Maryknoll, N.Y.: Orbis Books, 1999.

Butler, Lee H., Jr. *A Loving Home: Caring for African American Marriages and Family*. Cleveland: Pilgrim Press, 2000.

Capps, Donald. *Social Phobia: Alleviating Anxiety in an Age of Self-promotion*. St. Louis: Chalice Press, 1999.

Clark, Kenneth. *Dark Ghetto: Dilemmas of Social Power*. New York: Harper and Row, 1965.

Coleman, Will. *Tribal Talk: Black Theology, Hermeneutics*. State College, Pa.: Pennsylvania State University Press, 2000.

Comer, James P. "White Racism: Its Roots, Form, and Function." In *Black Psychology*. Edited by Reginald L. Jones. New York: Harper and Row, 1972.

Cone, James. *Black Theology and Black Power*. New York: The Seabury Press, 1969.

____. *A Black Theology of Liberation*. Philadelphia: Lippincott, 1970.

____. *A Black Theology of Liberation: Twentieth Anniversary Edition*. Maryknoll, N.Y., Orbis Books, 1990.

____. *My Soul Looks Back*. Maryknoll, N.Y., Orbis Books, 1986.

Copeland, M. Shawn. "African American Catholics and Black Theology: An Interpretation," In *African American Religious Studies: An Interdisciplinary Anthology*. Edited by Gayraud Wilmore. Durham, N.C.: Duke University Press, 1989.

Costas, Orlando. *Christ Outside the Gate*. Maryknoll, N.Y.: Orbis Books, 1982.

Costen, Melva Wilson. *African American Christian Worship*. Nashville: Abingdon Press, 1993.

Cowley, Malcolm. *Black Cargoes*. New York: Viking Press, 1962.

Davidson, Basil. *Africa in History*. New York: Macmillan, 1991.

____. *The African Genius*. Atlantic Monthly Press Book edition. Boston: Little, Brown, 1969.

de Lorimier, Jacques. *Identity and Faith in Young Adults*. Translated by Matthew J. O'Connell. New York: Paulist Press, 1973.

DesPres, Terrence. *The Survivor: An Anatomy of Life in the Death Camps*. Oxford: Oxford University Press, 1976.

Deutsch, Morton, and Robert M. Krauss. *Theories in Social Psychology*. New York: Basic Books, 1965.

Diop, Cheikh A. *The African Origin of Civilization: Myth or Reality.* Translated and edited by Mercer Cook. Chicago: Lawrence Hill Books, 1974.

Dixon, Richard. Found at www. angelfire.com/va/TJTruth: "Thomas Jefferson– Sally Hemings, Trial Analysis, Evidence on Paternity, The Case Against Thomas Jefferson," Richard E. Dixon, Attorney at Law, 4122 Leonard Drive, Fairfax, Virginia 22030, April 2000.

Earl, Riggins, Jr. *Dark Salutations: Ritual, God, and Greetings in the African American Community.* Harrisburg, Pa.: Trinity Press International, 2001.

Elkins, Stanley. *Slavery: A Problem in American Institutional and Intellectual Life.* Chicago: University of Chicago, 1959.

Erikson, Erik. *Childhood and Society.* New York: W.W. Norton, 1950.

_____. *Dimensions of a New Identity.* New York: W.W. Norton, 1974.

_____. *In Search of Common Ground: Conversations with Erik H. Erikson and Huey P. Newton.* New York: W.W. Norton, 1973.

_____. *Insight and Responsibility.* New York: W.W. Norton, 1964.

_____. *The Life Cycle Completed.* New York: W.W. Norton, 1985.

_____. *Young Man Luther.* New York: W.W. Norton, 1958.

Faber, Heije. *Psychology of Religion.* Philadelphia: The Westminster Press, 1975.

Felder, Cain Hope. "The Bible, Re-Contextualization and the Black Religious Experience," In *African American Religious Studies.* Edited by Gayraud S. Wilmore. Durham, N.C.: Duke University Press, 1989.

_____, ed. *Stony the Road We Trod: African American Biblical Interpretation.* Minneapolis: Augsburg Fortress Press, 1991.

_____. *Troubling Biblical Waters: Race, Class, and Family.* Maryknoll, N.Y.: Orbis, 1989.

Fernandez, Eleazar S., and Fernando F. Segovia, eds. *A Dream Unfinished: Theological Reflections on America from the Margins.* Maryknoll, N.Y.: Orbis Books, 2001.

Fredrickson, George M. *The Black Image in the White Mind.* New York: Harper and Row, 1971.

Freud, Sigmund. *The Future of an Illusion.* New York: W.W. Norton, 1961.

_____. *Inhibitions, Symptoms and Anxiety.* New York: W.W. Norton, 1959.

_____. *Moses and Monotheism.* New York: Vintage Books, 1967.

_____. *New Introductory Lectures on Psycho-Analysis.* New York: W.W. Norton, 1965.

_____. *An Outline of Psycho-Analysis.* New York: W.W. Norton, 1949.

Garbarino, James. *Children in Danger.* San Francisco: Jossey Bass, 1992.

Gilligan, Carol. *In a Different Voice: Psychological Theory and Women's Development.* Cambridge: Harvard University Press, 1982.

Goldberg, Michael. *Theology and Narrative.* Nashville: Abingdon Press, 1981.

González, Justo L., and Zaida Maldonado Perez. *An Introduction to Christian Theology.* Nashville: Abingdon Press, 2002.

Grant, Jacquelyn. *White Women's Christ and Black Women's Jesus.* Atlanta: Scholars Press, 1989.

_____. "Womanist Theology: Black Women's Experience as a Source for Doing Theology, with Special Reference to Christology." In *African American Religious Studies: An Interdisciplinary Anthology.* Edited by Gayraud Wilmore. Durham, N.C.: Duke University Press, 1989.

Grier, William H., and Price M. Cobb. *Black Rage*. New York: Banton Book, 1968.

Griffin, Paul R. *Seeds of Racism in the Soul of America*. Cleveland: Pilgrim Press, 1999.

Groeschel, Benedict J. *Spiritual Passages*. New York: Crossroad, 1986.

Guthrie, Robert V. "The Psychology of African Americans: An Historical Perspective." In *Black Psychology*, 3d ed. Edited by Reginald L. Jones. Berkeley, Calif.: Cobb & Henry, 1991.

Herskovits, Melville J. *The Myth of the Negro Past*. Boston: Beacon Press, 1958, 1990.

Hick, John. *An Interpretation of Religion*. New Haven, Conn.: Yale University Press, 1989.

Hiltner, Seward. *Preface to Pastoral Theology: Ministry and Theory Shepherding*. New York: Abingdon Press, 1958.

Holloway, Joseph E., ed. *Africanisms in American Culture*. Indianapolis: Indiana University Press, 1990.

hooks, bell. *Ain't I A Woman? Black Women and Feminism*. Boston: South End Press, 1981.

Hopkins, Dwight N. *Introducing Black Theology of Liberation*. Maryknoll, N.Y.: Orbis Books, 1999.

Hudson, Winthrop S., and John Corrigan. *Religion in America,* 5th ed. New York: Macmillan, 1992.

Hunter, Rodney, ed. *Dictionary of Pastoral Care and Counseling*. Nashville: Abingdon Press, 1990.

James, George G. M. *Stolen Legacy*. New York: Philosophical Library, 1954.

Jones, James M. "Conceptual and Strategic Issues in the Relationship of Black Psychology to American Social Science." In *Research Directions of Black Psychologists*. Edited by A. Wade Bodkin. New York: Russell Sage Foundation, 1979.

Jones, LeRoi [Imamu Amiri Baraka]. *Blues People: Negro Music in White America*. New York: Morrow Quill Paperbacks, 1963.

Jones, William. *Is God a White Racist?: A Preamble to Black Theology*. Boston: Beacon Press, 1998.

Jordan, Winthrop. *The White Man's Burden*. New York: Oxford University Press, 1974.

_____. *White Over Black: American Attitudes Toward the Negro, 1550-1812*. New York: W.W. Norton, 1977 [1968].

Jung, Carl G. *Analytical Psychology*. New York: Random House, 1968.

_____. *Answer to Job, Collected Works,* vol. 11. Princeton: Princeton University Press, 1952.

_____. *Collected Works of C.G. Jung*. Bollingen series, vol. 9, part 1. Princeton: Princeton University Press.

_____. *Conscious, Unconscious, and Individuation, Collected Works Vol. 9, part 1*. Princeton: Princeton University Press, 1939.

_____. *Dreams*. Princeton: Bollingen Series, Princeton University Press, 1974.

_____. *Man and His Symbols*. New York: Dell Publishing Co., 1968.

_____. *Memories, Dreams, and Reflections*. New York: Vintage Books, 1965.

____. *Two Essays on Analytical Psychology.* Princeton: Princeton University Press, 1966.

Kardiner, Abram, and Lionel Ovesey. *The Mark of Oppression.* Cleveland: Meridian Books, 1951.

Kelsey, George. *Racism and the Christian Understanding of Man.* New York: Charles Scribner's Sons, 1965.

Kovel, Joel. *White Racism: A Psychohistory.* New York: Columbia University Press, 1970.

Lambley, Peter. *The Psychology of Apartheid.* Athens: University of Georgia Press, 1980.

Lasch, Christopher. *The Culture of Narcissism.* New York: Wagner Books, 1979.

Latourette, Kenneth S. *A History of Christianity,* vol. 2. New York: Harper and Row, 1975.

Laycock, Steven William. *Foundations for a Phenomenological Theology.* Lampeter: The Edwin Mellen Press, 1988.

LeVine, Robert. *Culture, Behavior, and Personality.* New York: Aldine, 1982.

Lifton, Robert J. *The Broken Connection.* New York: Basic Books, 1983.

____. *The Future of Immortality.* New York: Basic Books, 1987.

____. *The Life of the Self.* New York: Basic Books, 1983.

Lincoln, C. Eric. *Race, Religion, and the Continuing American Dilemma.* New York: Hill and Wang Press, 1984.

Long, Charles H. "Assessment and New Departures for a Study of Black Religion in the United States of America." In *African American Religious Studies.* Edited by Gayraud S. Wilmore. Durham, N.C.: Duke University Press, 1989.

Marx, Karl. "Contribution to the Critique of Hegel's `Philosophy of Right'." In *The World Treasury of Modern Religious Thought.* Edited by Jaroslav Pelikan. Boston: Little, Brown and Company, 1990.

____. "Religion, the Opium of the People." In *The World Treasury of Modern Religious Thought.* Edited by Jaroslav Pelikan. Boston: Little, Brown, 1990.

Maslow, Abraham. *Toward a Psychology of Being.* An Insight Book. New York: D. Van Nostrand Company, 1968.

Mbiti, John. *Introduction to African Religion.* Portsmouth, N.H.: Heinemann Educational Books, 1991.

Mead, Sidney E. *History and Identity.* Atlanta: American Academy of Religion, Scholars Press, 1979.

Meadow, Mary Jo, and Richard Kahoe. *Psychology of Religion: Religion in Individual Lives.* New York: Harper and Row, 1984.

Memmi, Albert. *The Colonizer and the Colonized.* Boston: Beacon Press, 1967.

Miller, Jean Baker. *Toward a New Psychology of Women.* Boston: Beacon Press, 1976.

Neal, Marie Augusta. "Civil Religion, Theology and Politics in America." In *America in Theological Perspective.* Edited by Thomas McFadden. New York: The Seabury Press, 1976.

Nobles, Wade W. "African Philosophy: Foundations for Black Psychology." In *Black Psychology,* 3d ed. Edited by Reginald L. Jones. Berkeley, Calif.: Cobb & Henry, 1991.

____. *African Psychology: Toward Its Reclamation, Reascension and Revitalization.* Oakland, Calif.: The Institute for the Advanced Study of Black Family Life and Culture, 1986.

Oakes, James. *Slavery and Freedom.* New York: Alfred A. Knopf, 1990.

Omi, Michael, and Howard Winant. *Racial Formation in the United States: From the 1960s to the 1980s.* New York: Routledge and Kegan Paul, 1986.

Pharr, Suzanne. *Homophobia: A Weapon of Sexism.* Inverness Calif.: Chardon Press, 1988.

Pinn, Anthony B. *Terror and Triumph: The Nature of Black Religion.* Minneapolis: Fortress Press, 2003.

Pressley, Arthur. "Liberation Theology, Pastoral Care and the Spirituality of Violence: An African-American Perspective." Unpublished paper written in 1992.

"Psychology." In *Britannica Concise Encyclopedia.* Retrieved June 27, 2004 from Encyclopedia Britannica Premium Service. http://www.britannica.com/ebc/article?eu=401375

Raboteau, Albert J. *Canaan Land: A Religious History of African Americans.* New York: Oxford University Press, 2001.

____. *Slave Religion.* New York: Oxford University Press, 1978.

Rank, Otto. *Beyond Psychology.* New York: Dover, 1958.

Rauschenbusch, Walter. "A Theology of Social Gospel." In *Walter Rauschenbusch: Selected Readings.* Mahwah, N.J.: Paulist Press, 1984.

Reynolds, Edward. *Stand the Storm: A History of the Atlantic Slave Trade.* London: W.H. Allen, 1989.

Roberts, J. Deotis. *Africentric Christianity: A Theological Appraisal for Ministry.* Valley Forge, Pa.: Judson Press, 2000.

Roberts, Samuel K. *African American Christian Ethics.* Cleveland: Pilgrim Press, 2001.

Rogers, J. A. *Nature Knows No Color-line.* St. Petersburg, Fla.: Helga M. Rogers, 1952.

Rychlak, Joseph F. *Introduction to Personality and Psychotherapy,* 2d ed. Boston: Houghton Mifflin Company, 1981.

Salley, Columbus, and Ronald Behm. *What Color Is Your God?: Black Consciousness and the Christian Faith.* Secaucus, N.J.: Citadel Press, 1988.

Schwartz, Howard. *Lillith's Cave: Jewish Tales of the Supernatural.* Oxford: Oxford University Press, 1989.

Shweder, Richard. "Cultural Psychology—what is it?" In *Cultural Psychology.* Edited by J. Stigler, R. Shweder, and G. Herdt. New York: Cambridge University Press, 1990.

Silverstein, Barry. *Children of the Dark Ghetto.* New York: Praeger, 1975.

Smith, Archie, Jr. *Relational Self: Ethics and Therapy from a Black Church Perspective.* Nashville: Abingdon Press, 1982.

Smith, Wallace C. *The Church in the Life of the Black Family.* Valley Forge, Pa.: Judson Press, 1985.

Snowden, Frank M. *Before Color Prejudice.* Cambridge: Harvard University Press, 1983.

Stuckey, Sterling. *Slave Culture.* New York: Oxford University Press, 1987.

Terrell, JoAnne M. *Power in the Blood?: The Cross in the African American Experience.* Maryknoll, N.Y.: Orbis Books, 1998.

Thomas, Alexander, and Samuel Sillen. *Racism and Psychiatry.* New York: Carol Publishing Group, 1972.

Thurman, Howard. "The Search in Identity." In *A Strange Freedom: The Best of Howard Thurman on Religious Experience and Public Life.* Edited by Walter Earl Fluker and Catherine Tumber. Boston: Beacon Press, 1998.

Thurman, Wallace. *The Blacker the Berry . . .* 1929. Reprint, New York: Macmillan, 1970.

Tillich, Paul. *Dynamics of Faith.* New York: Harper Torchbooks, 1957.

Uzukwu, Elochukwu E. *Worship as Body Language.* Collegeville, Minn.: The Liturgical Press, 1997.

Washington, Joseph. *Anti-Blackness in English Religion, 1500-1800.* Lewiston, N.Y.: The Edwin Mellen Press, 1985.

Watkins Ali, Carroll. *Survival and Liberation: Pastoral Theology in African American Context.* St. Louis: Chalice Press, 1999.

Weems, Renita J. *Just a Sister Away.* San Diego, Calif.: LuraMedia, 1988.

Welsing, Frances Cress. *The Isis Papers.* Chicago: Third World Press, 1991.

West, Cornel. *Prophesy Deliverance!* Philadelphia: Westminster Press, 1982.

———. *Prophetic Fragments.* Grand Rapids, Mich.: W.B. Eerdmans, 1988.

———. *Race Matters.* Boston: Beacon Press, 1993.

Williams, Delores S. *Sisters in the Wilderness.* Maryknoll, N.Y.: Orbis Books, 1993.

———. "James Cone's Liberation: Twenty Years Later." In James Cone, *A Black Theology of Liberation: Twentieth Anniversary Edition.* Maryknoll, N.Y.: Orbis Books, 1990.

Wilmore, Gayraud, ed. *African American Religious Studies.* Durham, N.C.: Duke University Press, 1989.

Wimberly, Edward P. *African American Pastoral Care.* Nashville: Abingdon Press, 1991.

———. *Pastoral Care in the Black Church.* Nashville: Abingdon Press, 1979.

Wulff, David. *Psychology of Religion* New York: John Wiley and Sons, 1991.